Date Due

11/18/53			
JAN 29 1965			

JOHN TAYLOR

LIFE OF JOHN TAYLOR

The Story of a Brilliant Leader in the
Early Virginia State Rights School

HENRY H. SIMMS, Ph. D.
Assistant Professor of History
Ohio State University
Columbus, Ohio

THE WILLIAM BYRD PRESS, INC.
RICHMOND, VA.
1932

PREFACE

Historians have told over and over the story of those Virginians whose fame is world wide, but they have neglected almost entirely others who are entitled to historical recognition. One who deserves no minor place in our intellectual history is John Taylor. He was original in thought and brilliant in mind. The date of his death, 1824, suggests that his political philosophy antedated the similar philosophy of men like Robert J. Turnbull and John C. Calhoun.

The writer hopes that this biography may be a contribution to American history in that it sets forth a view of the Constitution which, in the author's opinion, has a substantial basis, but has been neglected or minimized by the large majority of American historians.

In the preparation of this work the author was aided greatly by Mr. David J. Mays of Richmond, Virginia, who supplied him with most of the Taylor manuscript. In many detailed ways Mrs. Henry Taylor and Miss Mary Taylor of the same city were of assistance. Dr. Lyon G. Tyler, Mr. E. G. Swem, Librarian of William and Mary College, Dr. H. R. McIlwaine, Virginia State Librarian, and his staff of assistants, and Mr. Calvert Tazewell of Norfolk, Virginia, have, in various ways, helped make the work possible. Professors Homer C. Hockett, Lawrence Hill, E. H. Roseboom and F. P. Weisenburger, colleagues of the author at Ohio State University, have read parts of the manuscript. To each and all of the above the author wishes to express his thanks.

CONTENTS

CONTENTS—Continued

LIFE OF JOHN TAYLOR

CHAPTER I

THE BACKGROUND

THE ancestry of John Taylor goes back to James Taylor of Carlisle, England, generally known as "James the First" in Taylor terminology. He was born in 1635, and was among the English gentry who established homes in Tidewater Virginia in the seventeenth century. The section in which he settled became Caroline County in 1727. He was twice married, and to these unions were born six children, three sons and three daughters. One of the sons, John, married Catherine Pendleton, the daughter of Philip and Isabella Hart Pendleton of New Kent County, Virginia. Their son, James, known as "James the Third", to distinguish him from a son of "James the First" by the same name, married Ann Pollard, and to them were born one daughter and John Taylor, known as John Taylor of Caroline, and the subject of this study.[1]

The place and time of Taylor's birth are not definitely established. The preponderance of evidence, however, indicates "Mill Farm" in Caroline County.[2] Taylor's father died a very young man, having been born in 1729, and having died, perhaps, in 1756. The best authority is to the effect that Taylor was born in 1753 (December 19), and Pendleton tells us that the former's father died when the son was three years old.[3] The rearing of Taylor then devolved upon Pendleton.

---

[1] See Hayden, *Virginia Genealogies*, pp. 671–683, and Wingfield, *History of Caroline County*, p. 471.

[2] See Wingfield, *History of Caroline County*, p. 190. He quotes Scott's *History of Orange County* to the same effect. Taylor's close relatives accept this as the place of his birth. Hayden's *Genealogies* gives Orange County.

[3] A family register, belonging to John Taylor's grandfather, and now in possession of Woodson T. White, of Waco, Texas, gives 1729 as date of James Taylor's birth, and the one suggested for J. Taylor. This is in *William and Mary Quarterly*, Vol. 12, pp. 132–134. Pendleton's Pamphlet on Taylor says latter's father died when son was three.

The latter was related to Taylor by blood and marriage. John Taylor, grandfather of John Taylor of Caroline, married Catherine Pendleton, aunt of Edmund Pendleton, and John Taylor of Caroline's great aunt, Mary Taylor, married Edmund Pendleton's father, Henry Pendleton. Thus the subject of this study was Edmund Pendleton's first cousin once removed. Pendleton was also Taylor's uncle-in-law. The former's second wife was Sarah Pollard, sister to Ann Pollard, who married James Taylor, father of John, of Caroline.[4] The cousin and nephew was left in wise and prudent hands. Born in 1721 in Caroline County, the very year his father died, Pendleton had, by 1741, begun his career as an advocate. For twenty-six years, from 1751 to 1777, he was a judge of the County Court of Caroline, and from 1752 to 1774, a member of the House of Burgesses. Profound in his knowledge of law, he was, during this same period, a famous figure before the general court.[5]

As was the case with many other Virginians in that day, Taylor received his early educational training from private tutors [6] and as the result of attending a private school. This school was located in King and Queen County, and was conducted by an Englishman named Donald Robertson, who had come to this country in 1753. Here Taylor studied and played with James Madison, also enrolled as a student, who later referred to Robertson as "The learned teacher". The course of instruction was mainly in languages—English, Greek, Latin, French and Spanish.[7] Incidentally, the life of Taylor parallels closely the lives of the members of the "Virginia Dynasty", Jefferson having been born in 1742, Madison in 1751, and Monroe in 1758. With

4 See Hayden, *Virginia Genealogies*, pp. 672–673. Also Pendleton's statements in Pollard family Bible, in *William and Mary College Quarterly*, Vol. 15, pp. 65–66.

5 Sketch of Pendleton, Pamphlet by D. J. Mays; also address of J. A. C. Chandler before Alumni Society of William and Mary College, 1905.

6 *Taylor, Prophet of Secession*, Dodd. In *Branch Historical Papers*, Vol. II, p. 214.

7 For a brief account of this school, and the names of students in the account books kept in connection with it, see *Virginia Magazine of History and Biography*, Vol. 33, pp. 194–195, and Vol. 34, p. 142. Also Rives, *Life of Madison*, Vol. I, p. 10.

these men, as we shall see in later chapters, the distinguished son of Caroline, once having launched his ship on the turbulent sea of politics, was to have many interesting relations.

As it happened, 1763, the last year Taylor attended Robertson's school, brought to an end the long contest for supremacy between France and England on the American continent. In the seven year period after 1763, before he became a student at William and Mary College, matters of acute controversy between the colonies and the mother country must have left some impress upon the youthful mind of Taylor. The cession of Canada to England by France helped pave the way for the controversies. For at the very time when England, victorious the world over, felt free to make her commercial policy in regard to the colonies something more than a theory, the latter, since the French menace to the North had been removed, felt that they were in a stronger position than ever to assert the principles of colonial self-government.

In accordance with this policy of closer and more effective control of the colonies, the Grenville ministry secured parliamentary legislation in 1764–65 providing better machinery for the enforcement of the navigation acts, imposing revenue duties on certain articles coming into the colonies, with the intention of collecting them, and providing also for an internal tax—the famous Stamp Act. The American colonies were not, and in the very nature of the case could not be represented to advantage in the English Parliament. It was at this juncture that Patrick Henry brought forward, in the Virginia Legislature, his famous Stamp Act Resolutions, to the effect that the first adventurers brought with them the rights, privileges and immunities of Englishmen, that the first two charters declared that they were entitled to such privileges and immunities, that they could be taxed by persons chosen only by themselves, and that if anyone else did tax them, it would destroy British and American freedom. Taylor's kinsman and guardian, Pendleton, along with Peyton Randolph and George Wythe, opposed these resolutions on the grounds that they were too severe and that England had not yet been given a chance to reply to resolutions previously passed and more conciliatory in tone.[8]

Commercial pressure in both America and England brought about the repeal of the Stamp Act, but Parliament, in so doing, stated that it had a right to bind the colonies in all matters whatsoever. Shortly thereafter Parliament passed the Townshend proposals for additional duties on various articles, such duties, after being collected, to be used to make English officials in the colonies independent of colonial assemblies in respect to salaries. Also the New York assembly was to be suspended until such time as appropriations should be made for the upkeep of British troops there. Non-importation was once more attempted on the part of the colonies, and with a degree of success that was largely responsible for bringing about a repeal of all the duties except the tax on tea which was left to "keep up the principle". Such was the situation when John Taylor entered William and Mary College in 1770.

Available records contain little as to his activities as a student. He is listed as an alumnus in 1770, yet Judge Pendleton was incurring the expenses incident to his attendance in both 1770 and 1771.[9] At approximately this same time, it is indicated that John and Thomas Byrd, sons of Colonel William Byrd of Westover; Nathaniel, Robert and William Nelson, sons of Honorable William Nelson; John Cocke, son of Colonel R. Cocke; and William Page, son of Honorable J. Page; all members of prominent families, were students at William and Mary.[10] The College at this time consisted of a school of divinity, one of philosophy, in which natural philosophy and mathematics were

---

[8] Henry, *Life of Henry*, pp. 79–82; Eckenrode, *The Revolution in Virginia*, pp. 19–20.

[9] Randolph and English, *History of College of William and Mary from its Foundation*. This lists him as alumnus, 1770. *William and Mary Quarterly*, Vol. I, New Series, pp. 40 and 128, deals with students 1753 to 1778, and indicates by whom expenses were paid.

[10] *History of College of William and Mary*, p. 92.

taught, a grammar school for instruction in ancient languages, and an Indian school, in which eight to ten Indians had annually been trained since about 1700. For approximately seventy years previous to the Revolution, the average number of students had been sixty a session, but at the outbreak of that struggle, there were seventy enrolled.[11]

Before Taylor ceased to be a student, and thereafter, the faculty was torn by dissensions arising from the colonial controversy with England. Rev. James Horrocks, who had been President of the college from 1764 to 1771, died in that year, and was succeeded by Rev. John Camm.[12] This gentleman had earlier had a controversy with the Board of Visitors. It was a rule of the institution that each professor was entitled to apartments in the college building, but the President alone had the privileges of a wife and family. This rule was violated several times; thus Camm, in order to avoid its violation, married and removed to town. The Board decreed that this vacated the position also, but Camm was upheld by the Authorities in England.[13] But the main reason for the unpopularity of the new President was his interest in the establishment of a resident Anglican bishop in the colonies. Under his influence, Rev. James Horrocks, the commissary in Virginia, had called a convention of ministers to debate the episcopate, but not many responded, since most of them believed that it was simply a scheme to strengthen English political control of the colonies.[14]

Two other professors with pronounced "Tory" sentiments, during Taylor's student days, were Rev. Samuel Henley, professor of moral and intellectual philosophy, and Rev. Thomas Gwatkin, professor of mathematics. The latter was named for his position by the Bishop of London. He gave instructions in

---

[11] *History of College of William and Mary*, p. 46.
[12] *Ibid.*, p. 80.
[13] See address by Lyon G. Tyler, Dec. 5, 1904, before Phi Beta Kappa Society. In *William and Mary Quarterly*, Vol. 14, pp. 71–83.
[14] Eckenrode, *The Revolution in Virginia*, pp. 30–31; *William and Mary Quarterly*, Vol. 19, pp. 28–30.

languages also. Henley was convinced that his own life was in danger while he was at the college. Both of these men received their appointments in 1769, and both in 1775 sailed for England, disgusted with "rebellious colonists and disorderly collegians". Camm was removed in 1777. It appears that Rev. John Dixon, professor of divinity, and Johnson, professor of moral and intellectual philosophy, were loyal to the colonies during the controversial period. In addition to a veritable host of distinguished alumni, including, of course, Taylor, three professors and thirty students of the college joined the army at the outbreak of the Revolution.[15]

After leaving William and Mary, Taylor undertook the study of law under Pendleton, and commenced the practice of his profession in 1774.[16] In the meantime, other developments had prepared his mind for active participation in the Revolution. In order to bolster up the declining fortunes of the British East India Company, Parliament, in 1773, passed an act relieving the company of the payment of duties when the tea was removed from England, and allowing them to designate their own agents to receive it in the colonies. The result was the well-known "Boston Tea Party". This led to the closing of the Port of Boston by parliamentary legislation, as well as to other legislative acts hostile to the colonies, among which was one changing the Massachusetts charter.

Concerted action on the part of the colonies had slowly, but surely, been making progress since Stamp Act days. The Continental Congress of 1774 was not of one mind, but it represented a further step in the direction of unity of action than had been taken up to that time. Pendleton was appointed by the Virginia Convention a delegate to the Congress, chosen, says the biographer of Henry, "for his consummate prudence,

---

[15] *History of College of William and Mary*, pp. 47 and 80–81. *William and Mary Quarterly*, Vol. 19, pp. 28–30, Vol. 26, 221–231.

[16] Chandler, Address to William and Mary Alumni; Pendleton, *Sketch of Life of Taylor*.

and thorough knowledge of law"[17]. He was on the committee which drafted the statement of the rights of the colonies in general, which showed how they had been infringed, and the means most proper for restoring them.[18] By this time the power which the colonies were willing to concede to Parliament consisted in legislation which was for the *bona fide* regulation of trade; but taking property from them, whether by direct or indirect taxation, was a function which belonged exclusively to their own assemblies, chosen expressly by themselves. This principle they based on an appeal to "natural rights, their charters, and the English constitution".

From Pendleton and others, Taylor must have heard much in the proximate pre-Revolutionary days of the natural right of property, of the plausible theory of external control by Parliament and internal control by the colonies, of the principle of freedom of conscience. At least he was ready to enter the fray at the first sign of battle, and his philosophy of later years was to reflect profoundly the principles of the Revolution.

Taylor's military service, which began in 1775, logically falls into three periods. The first comprises the late months of 1775 and the early months of 1776, when he saw service in Virginia; the second, the period from 1776 to 1779, during which he served on northern battlefields; and the third, 1781 after Virginia was invaded by British forces.

Revolutionary movements shaped themselves rapidly in Virginia in 1775. The House of Burgesses, which had been dissolved by Governor Dunmore May 25, 1774, and had met as a convention in electing delegates to the Continental Congress,[19] again met as a convention in March, 1775, this time in Richmond, where it could deliberate without interference from the Governor, who was in Williamsburg.[20] Because of factional

---

[17] Henry, *Life of Henry*, p. 196.
[18] *Ibid.*, pp. 223–224.
[19] Eckenrode, *Revolution in Virginia*, pp. 33–35.
[20] *Ibid.*, p. 45.

strife between the conservatives and the radicals, Dunmore was, for a time, not interfered with, though the convention took steps in the direction of arming the colony. But on April 20, 1775, a squad of British marines carried a quantity of powder from the colony power-house in Williamsburg, with the result that Patrick Henry marched on Williamsburg at the head of a body of volunteers. The flame of revolution was temporarily checked because of compensation for the powder, and Dunmore even called a meeting of the assembly for June 1, 1775. But with the refusal of this body to reopen the courts or to accept North's proposal of compromise, and with the contemporaneous march of riflemen to Williamsburg, the Governor deemed it wise to flee.[21] The Assembly concluded its work without him, and never met again. Dunmore's headquarters were in Norfolk, where, after several months, he had collected a small force of British regulars, slaves and Scotch clerks. Fighting actually commenced in September, 1775.[22]

Taylor had aspired to a captaincy in one of the companies in the Virginia regiments, but being disappointed in this respect, he went to Norfolk as a cadet, or by appointment in the staff.[23] He became connected with the Quartermaster's department of his regiment soon after hostilities commenced, apparently, as he received one month's pay November 4, 1775.[24] The Auditor's papers indicate that he was especially active in providing horses for the necessary operations of his regiment.[25] He received his final pay for his services as quartermaster, March 3, 1776.[26]

That he served well in this capacity is indicated by the fact that Congress, in 1776, elected him a major in what was called

---

[21] Eckenrode, *Revolution in Virginia*, pp. 58–61.

[22] *Ibid.*, pp. 58–61.

[23] Pendleton, *Sketch of Life of Taylor*, in pamphlet form.

[24] State Auditor's Papers in *Virginia Magazine of History and Biography*, Vol. 26, p. 65.

[25] *Ibid.*, Vol. 26, pp. 68 and 186, Vol. 27, pp. 63–64.

[26] *Ibid.*, Vol. 28, p. 360.

their own regiment. He then sold his patrimony upon credit, went northward, and did not return to his native soil and his childhood friends until 1779.[27]

In the Taylor correspondence which has been preserved, there are fortunately several letters which record his impressions of military morale and activities during the period above mentioned. The picture he gives is anything but inspiring. Writing in 1777, he states that he has arrived at a place called camp, and is commanded by a man called a Major General, "for either of which denominations there appears to be equal reason". Their army consisted of not more than 2000 men, and it was scattered over the whole of the Jerseys at stations immensely distant from each other, in fact, so distant that each little cantonment could be easily crushed. At Price Town, where Taylor was situated, there were 400 men, and not more than 2000 rounds of ammunition. The desertions were alarming, some companies having lost more than thirty men.

He did not believe that conditions would improve, for Congress had deceived the men in regard to their enlistments; they had been promised good and ready clothing, yet one-sixth of the men had practically none, and one-third were without blankets. Moreover, soldiers were "sacrificed for the private emolument of commissaries, quartermasters, surgeons, physicians, barrack masters and captains". But this was not the whole story. "The armies of the northern states are really mercenaries, and being foreigners, have no attachment to the country, except what accrues from the emoluments of the service. The high price of commodities having made these contemptible, the defence of America must revert to its original safeguard, to wit: the yeomanry; and as very many of those of the middle states are tories, and the inhabitants of the extreme states mostly undisciplined, I augur ill of events, at least until injury replete shall have put the match more generally to the hearts of our people. Hope for the best, but at the same time fear the worst; I wish, I wish

---

[27] Pendleton, Pamphlet, *Sketch of Life of Taylor.*

from my soul we had more Virginias than one, but as we have not, the honor of preserving America must be acquired by one alone." [28]

Writing less than a month after the sending of the above letter, Taylor declared that "enlistments are rare in the provinces north of Maryland, especially in New England; all the stories of regiments complete in New York and New Jersey are utterly false; ours is the fullest regiment in the service, and we have only 442 men in the field at this place". Recently he had been field officer of the day, when the enemy came out of Brunswick on a foraging expedition, and since their number did not exceed 1000, he had hoped they would come forward. Misfortune and pleasure had both come to him, for he had been thrown from his horse, causing slight injury, and had established "a very agreeable acquaintance with a number of ladies". Howe's plans seemed to him very vague and uncertain, but he believed the British design was a sudden and powerful attack on Virginia.[29]

By the fall of 1777, Taylor had had the command of his regiment for a long period of time, but was weary of arduous duties. His health had been excellent until recently he had experienced a fever and all the symptoms of a long period of illness. He was convinced that there were many more officers in his regiment and others than were needed, so for all these reasons it was natural that he should inquire of Pendleton the latter's opinion in regard to Taylor's resuming the practice of law.[30]

Taylor, however, did not leave the army at this time. In the spring of 1778 he was lamenting the fact that he had been "accidentally removed from the grand army, at the first period when the term could be used with propriety". But he blamed himself for this, for he had been led on by the prospect of adventure and conquest to join "the chimerical Canadian expedition". He was

[28] Taylor MSS., Taylor to Edmund Pendleton, April 13, 1777. In *William and Mary College Quarterly*, Vol. 4, p. 103.
[29] Taylor MSS., Taylor to Pendleton, May 4, 1777. Original in Archives of New York Historical Society.
[30] *Ibid.*, Nov. 17, 1777. Original in Archives of New York Historical Society.

now situated in New York, and while he believed the enemy forces were strong enough to defeat the Americans in that section, yet the reported evacuation of Philadelphia inspired him with the hope that they might evacuate the continent. In that case he would leave the army, unless Congress should send him "to the great scenes of war, which are likely soon to be displayed". (The reference is apparently to the war in the South. He says he is reading constantly French, in anticipation of such a juncture.) [31]

According to Pendleton, Taylor was in several battles, and was constantly spoken of as a valuable officer. However, the colonel of the regiment was usually absent, and the lieutenant colonel was a captive, so Taylor saw little chance of promotion. Thus, when the continental army was reduced in 1779, and many were discharged or given the opportunity to resign, he did the latter.[32]

He shortly thereafter became a member of the Virginia Legislature, and in this capacity aided in legislation which was designed to enable Virginia better to prosecute the war. A Board of War was created, and a bill was passed for the better regulation and disciplining of the militia.[33] When officers were appointed for the militia, Taylor was made a lieutenant-colonel.[34]

Ominous events moved rapidly in Virginia during the last phase of the Revolution. In October, 1780, a British force landed at Portsmouth, but was checked when it moved inward. Arnold invaded the State in the closing days of 1780, sacked Richmond, the capital, early in January of the next year and

---

[31] Taylor MSS., Taylor to Brigadier General Woodford, May 22, 1778. MS. in possession of D. J. Mays, Richmond, Va. Woodford had been Chief Commander of Virginia forces in opposition to Dunmore, 1775–1776. See Eckenrode, *Revolution in Virginia*, pp. 75–77.

[32] Pendleton, *Sketch of Life of Taylor*.

[33] Journal of House of Delegates, May 11, 1779, May 12, 1780. For the purpose of logical sequence, if not strict time sequence, Taylor's legislative career in the House will be treated in a separate chapter.

[34] See address of J. A. C. Chandler before William and Mary Alumni. In possession of H. Taylor, Jr.

then fell back down the James. Cornwallis approached Petersburg, joined Arnold there, and marched on Richmond during the spring months of the same year. Governor Jefferson and the Legislature fled from Richmond, then from Charlottesville, where they had gone, across the mountains to Staunton.[35]

Taylor and the other officers of the legions received their commissions March 21, 1781. His own title was "Lieutenant-Colonel, commanding First Legion".[36] In order to understand the nature of some of the communications of Taylor to Colonel William Davies, an ex-line officer, who had been made commissioner of war in the State after the war board was abolished,[37] and to Governor Thomas Nelson and others, the following quotation, relative to handling the militia, is enclosed: "The custom was to call out a force of militia on the news of any movement of the British, supply them with arms and equipment, which were actually carried off at the end of the service and never seen again, pay them at the rate of Continental troops in treasury certificates, feed them by requisitioning provisions, and furnish transportation by impressing wagons and horses. When the enemy relapsed into quiescence, the militia went home and the horses and wagons returned to their owners." [38]

Soon after his appointment, Taylor, by command of General Spottswood, who had been a former officer in the Continental line, applied to Governor Nelson respecting the equipment of the legions for state defense. A part of the plan was to make enlistments attractive, and this, it was thought, could be done by providing conical caps with a clip of bearskin, so as to add to the stature of the men, by supplying a plume for each man, so as to give the corps a martial look, and by paying the bounty money to those already enlisted.[39] At another time, he described to Lafayette the expedition of an English sympathizer up the

---

[35] Eckenrode, *The Revolution in Virginia*, 211–224.

[36] Calendar Virginia State Papers, Vol. II, p. 646, Taylor enclosing memorandum to Davies, Dec. 10, 1781.

[37] Eckenrode, *The Revolution in Virginia*, p. 207.

[38] Eckenrode, *Revolution in Virginia*, pp. 219–220.

[39] Calendar of State Papers, Vol. II, p. 175, Taylor to Nelson, June 19, 1781.

York River, which resulted in the stealing of goods and negroes. This man, named Walker, operated under a flag of truce. However, Taylor captured his assistant, and sent him, along with other prisoners dangerous to the State, to the Governor.[40]

Taylor, it appears, had temporarily dismissed his men, for he wrote Davies that his command had 204 men up to September 1, that fifty-six had been enlisted lately, and that he was in need of knapsacks, kettles, and tents for the officers at once, since the legion would assemble September 25.[41] He also made a request for equipment for the command of Spottswood, since the latter, having nothing but forage for his troops, had dismissed them, not to assemble again until October 20.[42] The actual extent of Taylor's military activities is not clear, but it appears that troops under his command, collected from Caroline, Gloucester, Middlesex, New Kent, and other counties, were joined to Lafayette's command, stationed in Gloucester County, and there resisted Hessian raids during the few weeks preceding the surrender at Yorktown.[43]

After the Revolution had ended, Colonel Taylor presented land claims to the Council through Governor Harrison, but he made it clear that he did not wish to mix his own claims with those of his kinsman, Captain Reuben Taylor, for whom he was especially solicitous in this respect. The latter was one of ten brothers who saw military service. Some were killed, some were wounded, and this one, after six years service, was forced to resign his captaincy as a result of ill health.[44] For his services as major in the Continental Army, John Taylor was, in 1799, granted 5333 1/3 acres of land in the Ohio territory.[45]

---

[40] Calendar of State Papers, pp. 393 and 406, Taylor to Lafayette, Sept. 5, 1781, and to Nelson, Sept. 9, 1781.

[41] Ibid., p. 493, Taylor to Davies, Sept. 18, 1781.

[42] Ibid., p. 493, Taylor to Davies, Sept. 26, 1781.

[43] Ibid., p. 393, Taylor to Lafayette, Sept. 5, 1781. Also Chandler address to William and Mary Alumni.

[44] Calendar of State Papers, Vol. III, p. 470, Taylor to Harrison.

[45] Military Certificate Book 2, Warrant No. 4911, Virginia Land Office, Richmond, p. 471.

CHAPTER II

FIRST YEARS IN THE LEGISLATURE

TAYLOR saw two periods of service in the Virginia Legislature. The first of these, with the exception of the year 1782, was from 1779 to 1785. The second was from 1796 to 1800.[1] They are the revolutionary years with which we are now concerned.

It was the day of giants in the State Assembly. Pendleton and Jefferson were both members of that body the first year of Taylor's membership, and he was associated during part of the period with Patrick Henry, Richard Henry Lee, John Marshall, Spencer Roane, Henry Tazewell, William Grayson, John Tyler, Wilson Cary Nicholas, Joseph Jones, an uncle of James Monroe, and John Breckenridge, future attorney general of the United States.[2]

The problems confronting this deliberative body during the period of transition from colony to state were varied, and such as to require the best thought of the Commonwealth. Even before the difficult problem of defending the State against an invading foe had assumed major proportions, Mr. Jefferson had begun his assault on what he regarded as an inequitable social system. His first and foremost aim, after he became a member of the assembly, was to make effective by law the theory of religious freedom. He was ably seconded by Madison and George Mason, but strongly opposed by Robert Carter Nicholas and Edmund Pendleton.[3] The result of this struggle was that, between 1776 and 1779, all religious laws were repealed which restrained freedom of worship by penal enactments, and which

---

[1] See Register of General Assembly of Virginia.

[2] Journal of House of Delegates, May 11, 1779, Oct. 21, 1779; Rives, *Life of Madison*, Vol. I, pp. 536–537.

[3] Randall, *Life of Jefferson*, Vol. I, pp. 197–198.

required dissenters to contribute to the support of the established church.[4]

Though Taylor was seeing army service when this part of the program was accomplished, he lent his aid to the final consummation of the struggle for the principle of religious freedom. Soon after he took his seat in the Assembly, he aided in the preparation of a bill "for dissolving the several vestries in this Commonwealth, and for regulating the time and manner of electing vestries in the future".[5] Some of the vestries were dissolved in 1780 and 1783, and this process was completed the next year.[6] As a member of the influential Committee for Courts of Justice, then composed of nine members, among whom were Tyler and Henry, Taylor recommended the further suspension of the salaries given to the clergy of the Church of England.[7] All acts providing for such salaries were repealed before the end of 1779.[8]

But the struggle was not yet ended. Some of the landed gentry revived repeatedly the idea of a general assessment for the support of religious teachers of various denominations. With some of the churches besides the Episcopalian, this was a popular idea. Jefferson was abroad when a bill to this effect was finally negatived in 1784, but Madison and George Mason had carried on successfully, against the brilliant Henry and others, this phase of the struggle.[9] Taylor is not recorded as voting on the measure,[10] but six days later he opposed a resolution providing for the incorporation of all societies of the Christian religion, which might apply for that privilege.[11] The glebe lands were still possessed by the Episcopal Church, but numerous pe-

---

4 Rives, *Life of Madison*, Vol. I, pp. 173–174; Randall, *Life of Jefferson*, Vol. I, pp. 219–223.
5 Journal of House, May 17, 1779.
6 Lingley, *Transition in Virginia from Colony to Commonwealth*, p. 207.
7 Journal of House, Oct. 16, 1779.
8 Hening, *Statutes at Large*, Vol. V, pp. 197–198.
9 Randall, *Life of Jefferson*, Vol. I, pp. 222–223.
10 Journal of House, Nov. 11, 1784.
11 *Ibid.*, Nov. 17, 1784.

titions, asking that such lands be divorced from ecclesiastical control, were received during the latter years of the eighteenth century.[12] When Taylor was again a member of the Assembly in the late 1790's, he aided in the passing of a resolution to the effect that all laws involving restrictions on religion should be swept away.[13] Pursuant to this resolution, the House, in 1799, enacted an act declaring that the Constitution had dissolved the church government existing before the Revolution, that the Bill of Rights of that instrument prevented the new government from reviving any species of ecclesiastical control, and that all laws regarding churches were repealed. At this same time a determined effort was made to leave the question of the disposition of the glebe lands to the courts, but the proposition was defeated, 86 to 57. Taylor voted in the negative. In 1802, the overseers of the poor were directed to sell this species of church property.[14]

The westward movement brought to the attention of the Virginia Legislature a number of problems during the revolutionary era. It was hoped that the western lands in the Commonwealth would attract settlers, and hence increase population, yet there was no legal enactment which made it clear as to just what constituted a valid claim to lands. It was under these conditions that Taylor aided in the preparation of, and himself presented, a bill for establishing a land office, and for ascertaining the terms and manner of granting waste and unappropriated lands.[15] This act was a landmark in Virginia history.[16] Its stated purposes were to encourage foreigners and others to come in and take up waste lands, and to increase the annual revenue, thus creating a fund for discharging the public debt.

---

[12] Lingley, *Transition in Virginia from Colony to Commonwealth*, p. 209.

[13] Journal of House, Jan. 4, 1798. For the purpose of arranging subject matter logically, it is deemed advisable to refer to the final stages of the religious controversy.

[14] *Ibid.*, Jan. 18, 1779; Lingley, *Transition from Colony to Commonwealth*, pp. 209–211.

[15] Journal of House of Delegates, May 11, 1779, June 5, 1779.

[16] The act passed June 25, 1779. See Journal of House that date.

It states how land bounties were to be obtained, how the land was to be surveyed, and how warrants were to be obtained, located and executed. Reservations of quitrents or any other reservations in the patents or grants of land from the Crown of England, under the former government, were declared to be null and void, because any kind of feudal tenure, it was thought, was dangerous to a free state. The price of land was to be forty pounds for every hundred acres. The courts were to provide for the examination of the land office books at least once a year.[17] In a succeeding chapter this legislation will be referred to in connection with Taylor's legal activities.

Before the end of the same year (1779) in which the State land office was established, Taylor joined in a remonstrance, on the part of the Assembly, to the United States in Congress, in regard to the lands northwest of the Ohio River. The Virginia Legislature had passed a bill to prevent settlements there at that time, because it wished to remove every cause of jealousy between the different states. The grievance against Congress was, that it "had received and countenanced petitions" from certain companies, asserting claims to lands under the authority of Virginia. The remonstrance, in part, is as follows: "The General Assembly of Virginia cannot avoid expressing their surprise and concern upon the information that Congress had received and countenanced petitions from certain persons styling themselves the Vandalia and Indiana Companies, asserting claims to lands in defiance of the civil authority, jurisdiction and laws of this Commonwealth, and offering to erect a separate government within the territory thereof. Should Congress assume a jurisdiction, and arrogate to themselves a right of adjudication, not only unwarranted by, but expressly contrary to the fundamental principles of the confederation, superseding or controlling the internal policy, civil regulations, and municipal laws of this, or any other state, it would be a violation of public faith, introduce a most dangerous precedent, which

---

[17] Hening, *Statutes at Large,* Vol. 10, pp. 50 to 65.

might hereafter be urged to deprive of territory or subvert the sovereignty and government of any one or more of the United States, and establish in Congress a power which, in process of time, must degenerate into an intolerable despotism." [18]

The movement of the population westward gave rise to still another land problem, which was controversial in its nature. Tennessee was at this time a part of North Carolina, and Kentucky a part of Virginia. The extension of western settlements made it necessary, in 1779, to extend the boundary line between Virginia and North Carolina. The commissioners appointed by the respective states for this purpose disagreed, with the result that two lines were suggested, Walker's for Virginia, and Henderson's for North Carolina. In the disputed area, there was no protection from either State for those who claimed lands. Entries for lands were made in the land offices of both States, and grants issued from both States.[19]

The year after the extension of the line, the Virginia House of Delegates referred the matter to a committee of which Taylor was chairman. This committee recommended to the assembly of North Carolina that, in order to secure property to owners, who might not be in the state under which they settled, it pass laws to the effect that an individual must have a patent signed by the Governor to give him a valid claim to land. Thus a patent, and not actual settlement, would be the test of validity.[20] Taylor's interest in this controversy did not consist entirely in the fact that he was chairman of the committee, for he had a personal interest also. In June, 1781, a memorial of Edmund Pendleton and Taylor was presented to the House, setting forth that they had claims to certain lands in North Carolina, which, before the extension of the boundary line, were supposed to be within Virginia; that they had obtained patents and other legal

---

[18] Journal of House of Delegates, Dec. 10, 1779. These lands had not been ceded to the central authority at this time. Virginia had claim to them under the Charter of 1609.

[19] John Haywood, *Civil and Political History of the State of Tennessee*, pp. 20–21.

[20] Journal of House of Delegates, July 4, 1780.

confirmation of their title, but that said lands were about to be granted to settlers who claimed them; and asking the Legislature to interfere in their behalf.[21]

The representation of that body to the assembly of North Carolina, soon after the presentation of the memorial, is so intimately connected with the life of the subject of this biography, and portrays so clearly the character of the dispute, that it is given here almost in its entirety. "The Assembly of Virginia, although no notice hath been taken of two representations heretofore made to the legislature of North Carolina, will not yet entertain an idea that the neglect proceeds from any fixed intention of doing injustice; they do, therefore, once more warmly solicit the legislature of North Carolina, to make a provision for those persons who have obtained titles to lands supposed to be in Virginia, but which are now likely to fall in the State of North Carolina; and must at the same time observe, that they shall be compelled by every motive of public policy, and of the protection due to their citizens, to refuse their assent to the establishment of any boundary line, until this their request, so consonant to the principles of the confederation, the bonds of good neighborhood, and the right of mankind, be complied with. How is it that the State of North Carolina have claimed this territory by charters from the King of England, and yet deny efficacy to patents derived from the same source? If these charters are valid to define the limits of states, are not patents which possess the same foundation valid to prescribe the bounds of private ownership? If the Legislature of North Carolina should explode the authority of these patents, they may draw themselves into a disagreeable predicament with respect to the United States, which needs only to be hinted at, to be understood. But if the Indian title is the only good one, then doth Virginia positively claim the lands in dispute, by virtue of a purchase from the Cherokees in the year 1770, by the express permission of the Crown; the bounds of which purchase, and

---

[21] Journal of House of Delegates, June 1, 1781.

not the late extended line, must be the mark of territory between the two States. Indeed, Virginia built Fort Patrick Henry, for the express defense of this land so purchased of the Cherokees. The Assembly of Virginia do not wish the Legislature of North Carolina, to act in a judicial capacity, by saying that the title of any individual is to be preferred, but they ask them to establish the best Virginia title, in whomsoever it may be placed, and to direct that the laws and usages of Virginia, heretofore made, shall be the rule of determination, leaving the several claimants to prosecute their titles in the usual channels." [22]

The Assembly also decided to authorize the Governor to appoint an agent to present to the State of North Carolina the claims of Virginians to lands once in Virginia, but now in the former State, and Taylor recommended Hardie, a member of the Governor's council, to serve in this capacity.[23] This controversy continued until 1791, at which time North Carolina agreed not only to accept Walker's line, which was favorable to Virginia in regard to the boundary, but also to recognize the contention of the latter State as to the validity of the oldest patents in regard to individual claims. However, this settlement was after the date of the deed of cession of western territory by Carolina, so Tennessee refused to accept the boundary decision. This was modified in her favor in 1802, but the individual titles to land were guaranteed, and the states concerned offered mutual protection to such titles.[24]

It was not only in a military capacity both on distant battlefields and on the soil of his native State that Taylor saw service in the Revolution, but also in a political capacity as a member of the Legislature. Virginia was unprepared for invasion in 1779–80. Her resources in men and revenues had been weakened as a result of aiding the colonies in the North, and since then she had responded to the pressing calls in the South. With

---

[22] Journal of House of Delegates, June 11, 1781.
[23] Calendar of Virginia State Papers, Vol. II, p. 517, Taylor to Hon. David Jameson, Oct. 2, 1781.
[24] Haywood, *Civil and Political History of the State of Tennessee*, pp. 21 to 24.

her regulars out of the State, she was depending upon an undisciplined militia, poorly provided with arms.[25] Under these conditions, Taylor was one of a committee, consisting of Jefferson and Richard Henry Lee among others, who prepared a bill for establishing a Board of War. This became effective in May, 1779.[26] The board consisted of five members, who handled all war problems, subject only to the approval of the Governor and Council.[27] He also aided in the framing of legislation for the better organization of the Virginia militia, for its better discipline, and for more effectually providing against invasion and insurrections.[28]

As a member of the Committee for Courts of Justice, Taylor automatically played a large part in shaping Assembly measures, for this committee was to call attention to laws which were about to expire, and to recommend what laws were to be continued, and what to be discontinued. Pursuant to these functions, it recommended in both 1779 and 1780, the continuation of an act empowering the Governor and Council to lay an embargo, and to supply the armies and navies of the United States with grain and flour.[29] It is fortunate that the General Assembly renewed annually an act of this character, for Jefferson was even then a strict constructionist, and this in regard to a State Constitution which gave the Executive very limited powers at best. However, he exercised as Governor the powers conferred, and did lay an embargo on provisions late in 1779.[30]

In the early summer of 1781, when Virginia's situation was desperate, and the lower counties were being overrun, all the militia acts were brought into one, and the Governor was urged

[25] Eckenrode, *The Revolution in Virginia*, pp. 201–205; Randall, *Life of Jefferson*, Vol. I, pp. 241–245.

[26] Journal of House, May 2, 1779.

[27] Hening, *Statutes at Large*, Vol. 10, p. 17.

[28] Journal of House, May 14, 1779; May 12, 1780. Hening, *Statutes at Large*, Vol. 10, p. 83, gives act last mentioned.

[29] Journal of House, Oct. 13 and 16, 1779; June 10, 1780. See Hening, *Statutes at Large*, Vol. 10, pp. 140–142, for acts of their nature passed.

[30] Eckenrode, *Revolution in Virginia*, pp. 199 and 205.

by the Assembly to bring the militia into service at once, since, the resolution said, an army of regulars sufficient to expel the invaders could not then be assembled.[31] Taylor was partly responsible for this action. Shortly thereafter he introduced a measure to establish martial law within twenty miles of the American army or the enemy's camp.[32]

But the passing of measures for her own defense, such as the creation of a Board of War, the extension of the powers of the executive, the various acts designed to develop an effective militia force, was not the only matter that concerned Virginia in these perilous times. A fundamental question was whether aid would be forthcoming from the Northern States. Though the State had been invaded by Arnold, such aid had not come, with the result that in March, 1781, a committee, consisting of Patrick Henry, John Taylor and John Tyler, Sr., was appointed to draw up a protest to Congress. This remonstrance, said to have been the work of Taylor, is a severe indictment of the North for its indifference to the war in Virginia and the South, after its own soil had been relieved of invasion. The contemplated report of the committee is as follows: " 'Tis not from an impulse of vanity that they would remember past transactions, but it is necessary in order to wrest Virginia from that load of obloquy with which she hath been oppressed by those who rashly judge, from detached facts, and not from a collective view of public transactions. Ere the war began, we heard the cries of our brethren at Boston, and paid the tax due to distress. We accompanied our Northern allies during almost every progressive stride it made, where danger seemed to solicit our ardor. We bled with them at Quebec, at Boston, at Harlem, at White Plains, at Fort Washington, at Brandywine, at Germantown, at Mud Island, at White Marsh, at Saratoga, at Monmouth, and at Stony Point. We almost stood alone at Trenton

---

[31] Journal of House, May 29, 1781.

[32] *Ibid.*, June 8, 1781. The Assembly approved the measure. See Hening, *Statutes at Large,* Vol. 10, p. 411.

and Princeton, and during the winter campaign which followed.

"But when we came to look for our Northern allies, after we had thus exhausted our powers in their defense, when Carolina and Georgia became the theatre of the war, they were not to be found. We felt that they were absent at Stono, at Savannah, at Charleston, at Monk's Corner, at Buford's defeat, at Lanneau's Ferry, at Camden, at King's Mountain, at the Cowpens, and at Georgetown. Whilst we are continuing our utmost exertions to repair the mighty losses sustained in defending almost every state in the Union, we at length find ourselves invaded, and threatened with the whole weight of the American war. When the Northern States were attacked, the sluices of paper credit were not only opened, but the force of all America concentred to the point of danger. Now, Northern and Southern departments are formed, calculated more to starve the only active war, than for the purpose of common defence.

"Let it be remembered that Georgia and South Carolina are lost, that North Carolina, in a state of uncertainty from continual alarms, cannot furnish supplies, and that Maryland hath only sent those of men. Virginia, then, impoverished by defending the Northern department, exhausted by the Southern war, now finds the whole weight of it on her shoulders. Even after these departments were formed, Congress called for, and, by a great exertion on our part, actually received half a million for the Northern army. The war having converted its rage from the Northern to the Southern States, the former, then exonerated from the immediate obligations of the Union, might have seized the opportunity of completing their levies, which would have enabled them to return with accumulated vigor to our assistance. But they were employed in availing themselves of resolutions of Congress, by which they got rid of their state paper at the expense of the Union; whilst Virginia was left struggling under that unwieldy load from which no exertions would disengage her, during the continuation of those enor-

mous expenses she was forced to yield to or leave the Southern
war to expire through famine.

"Thus situated, our only resource is the wretched one of more
paper money, in addition to enormous taxes, which are the more
peculiarly distressing or they must be collected whilst near ten
thousand of our citizens, exclusive of our regular troops, are in
the field. A tax of four and a fourth per cent on a specie valu-
ation of property; a tax of thirty pounds of tobacco and two
bushels of corn on each tithable; a tax of three thousand beeves;
a tax of three thousand suits of clothes; a tax of seventy four
wagons and teams, besides many occasional seizures and other
collateral dues, all paid or to be paid in the present year, do,
when added to the emissions of twenty-one millions of pounds
in three months, prove that Virginia hath not been unmindful
of the extraordinary efforts expected from her.

"Thus exhausted with our former exertions, thus straining
every nerve in present defence—pressed with a great hostile
army, and threatened with a greater—beset with enemies both
savage and disciplined—the Assembly of Virginia do, in behalf
of their State and in behalf of the common cause, in the most
solemn manner summon the other states to their assistance.
They demand aids of men, money, and every warlike muni-
tion. If they are denied, the consequences be on the heads of
those who refuse them. The Assembly of Virginia call the
world and future generations to witness that they have done
their duty, that they have prosecuted the war with earnestness,
and they are still ready so to act, in conjunction with the other
states, as to prosecute it to a happy and glorious period." [33]

A brief time after the remonstrance was drawn, Edmund
Pendleton wrote in the spirit of that paper to James Madison:
"Do Congress mean to leave the weight of this Southern War

---

[33] The Remonstrance may be found in Tyler's *Quarterly Historical and Genealogical Magazine*, Vol. XII, No. 4, pp. 39–41; also in Rives, *Life of Madison*, Vol. I, pp.
275–279. The latter states that it was drawn by Taylor, and is among Madison's
papers.

entirely upon Virginia? or suffer our main army to remain idle
spectators of repeated drafts from New York to recruit the
enemy in this quarter, without any corresponding assistance to
us? Surely not; as it must produce the worst consequences. I
am happy to find our people willing to exert themselves on this
great occasion, but know they are not alone able to support
this burden, nor do I believe they will submit to be duped." [34]
Before the report was adopted, Benjamin Harrison was sent as
a commissioner to Congress, and there received a promise that
a part of the Continental Army would be sent South.[35]

Their association in the Virginia Assembly during the revolutionary years gave rise to an enmity between Taylor and
Patrick Henry, which seems to have lasted with the former
until his death twenty-five years after that of Henry. John
Adams thought Wirt's *Life of Henry* too eulogistic of the latter, and Taylor seems to have concurred with him in these
views. This concurrence is expressed in a letter to Adams in
1819. "Permit me to express my concurrence with your re-
marks in relation to Mr. Wirts' History of Mr. Henry. I was
old enough to serve often in our legislature with this gentleman, to know him and many other patriots of the Revolution
personally, and to take a deep interest in the programs from
beginning to end; and although Mr. Henry possessed very
popular talents as an orator, yet I know that he had but little
celebrity as a statesman, and none as a soldier or a writer. He
had certainly some merit as a revolutionary patriot, but I sin-
cerely believe that its efficiency in promoting that event was
not one tenth part of that of many other gentleman, among
whom I cordially and conscientiously class yourself, as an offering to justice, and in some degree (should this letter reach
future times) to supply your forbearance to vindicate your own
claims." [36]

---

[34] Pendleton to Madison, April 7, 1781. In Rives, *Life of Madison*, Vol. I, p. 279.
[35] *Tyler's Quarterly Magazine*, Vol XII, No. 4, p. 41. Henry, *Life of Henry*,
Vol. I, pp. 116–117.
[36] Adams, *Works of John Adams*, Vol. III, see letter by Taylor, Feb. 20, 1819,
pp. 57–58.

But Taylor's charge of lack of revolutionary zeal on Henry's part finds much more direct expression in a conversation in 1824 with John Quincy Adams, as reported by the latter in his Memoirs. "I called at the beginning of the evening upon Colonel John Taylor, the Senator from Virginia. . . . He related to me the anecdote concerning Patrick Henry, which he had related some weeks since at my house; that in the campaign of 1781, Henry actually proposed in a secret session of the Legislature of Virginia that she should be the first to submit to Great Britain—, in order that she might obtain the most favorable terms. Taylor was himself a member of the legislature, and heard him move to go into secret session, there make the proposition, and support it by an eloquent speech. It met with such immediate, indignant, and universal opposition that when the debate closed, he had changed his side, and was among the most ardent and sanguine for perseverance in the war. Taylor thinks there is great exaggeration in the panegyric upon Henry by Mr. Wirt, and says that Henry had much less efficient agency in the revolution than many others."[37] Another biographer of Henry, William Wirt Henry, attributes Taylor's attitude to prejudice, arising from the fact that the latter was a kinsman of Edmund Pendleton, who was not friendly with Henry; and from the additional fact that Henry openly opposed the Virginia Resolutions in 1798–99, though Taylor introduced them. This biographer further suggests the absence of such a motion in the Journals of the House.[38]

During almost the entire time that Taylor was a member of the Assembly, he was one of the Committee for Courts of Justice. This no doubt accounts for the fact that he aided in the preparation of so many bills, for this committee not only made recommendations in regard to continuing existing laws, or *vice versa,* thus necessitating intimate acquaintance with them, but

---

[37] *Memoirs of John Quincy Adams, comprising portions of his Diary from 1795 to 1848,* Vol. VI, p. 263, Feb. 21. 1824.
[38] William Wirt Henry, *Life of Patrick Henry,* Vol. II, pp. 155–159.

also in regard to new laws. Thus we find Taylor associated with Pendleton in framing a bill for constituting justices of the peace and county courts,[39] and with Richard Henry Lee and Patrick Henry one for the more general diffusion of knowledge.[40] It was he who played an active part in providing for the calling in of the State's quota of Continental money.[41]

A very interesting question which concerned Virginians in the proximate post-revolution days was whether foreign vessels should be restricted to enumerated ports, or allowed to move at will up the navigable streams of the State. Mr. Madison's view was that the British traders, by moving inward and giving individual planters long credits, could buy and sell for what they would. But if restricted to a few ports, these traders would have to compete with the rest of the world. Moreover, this type of restriction would concentrate trade and capital.[42] But convenience, the satisfying of local wants, and long credit were factors that tended to stimulate opposition to the policy proposed. In 1784, a measure restricting vessels to five ports, instead of two, as first proposed, passed the House, but by a close vote. Taylor voted in the negative.[43]

It may be well at this point to remind the reader that Taylor's initial experience in public life came at a time when state jealousies of each other and of the idea of a strong central government were very pronounced. It is doubtful whether Congress, before the Articles of Confederation went into effect, had any sound legal basis. Virginia thought it necessary to ratify the alliance with France, and did this when Taylor was in the Assembly.[44] The remonstrance to Congress in regard to the Northwestern territory has already been noted. Even after the Articles of Confederation went into effect, Virginia was not

---

[39] Journal of House, Oct. 21, 1779.
[40] Ibid., May 19, 1780.
[41] Ibid., Dec. 4 and 5, 1781.
[42] Rives, Life of Madison, Vol. I, pp. 542–544.
[43] Journal of House of Delegates, June 17, 1784. The vote was 64 to 58.
[44] Ibid., June 2, 1779.

enthusiastic in regard to increasing the weak powers of Congress through the process of amendment. It was with great reluctance that she approved, in 1783, the amendment to allow Congress to impose revenue duties.[45] Taylor, it appears, was opposed to this proposition. His idea was that his State should have the surplus of the tax, beyond her quota of the annual demand, if there should be a surplus. Otherwise, by importing heavily, she would pay more than her quota of the debt.[46]

In respect to just one matter did Taylor seem inclined to strengthen the powers of Congress, and that was in regard to the surrender of criminals to foreign jurisdiction by the State, upon the authority of Congress. Here, it might be said, a question pertaining to foreign relations and not to matters of a strictly local nature, was involved. The resolution which passed the House in 1784, in the face of strong opposition, was as follows: "That if any citizen or inhabitant of this Commonwealth shall go beyond the limits of the United States, within the acknowledged jurisdiction of any civilized nation; and shall, within the same, commit any crime, for which, in the judgment of the United States in Congress assembled, the law of nations, or any treaty between the United States and a foreign nation requires him to be surrendered to the offended nation; and shall thereafter flee within the limits of this Commonwealth; and the sovereign of the offended nation shall exhibit to the United States in Congress assembled, due and satisfactory evidence of the crime, with a demand of the offender, to be tried and punished where the same was committed; and the United

---

[45] See letter of Joseph Jones to Madison, May 7, 1783, in which he suggests that legislature feels that Congress "lusts for power". Rives, *Life of Madison*, Vol. I, pp. 435–436.

[46] *Letters of Joseph Jones of Virginia*, Edited by W. C. Ford. Jones to Madison, May 25 and June 8, 1783. Jones, an uncle of Monroe, was born in 1727, represented King George in the House of Burgesses, served in the Virginia Convention of 1776, was Judge of the General Court more than a year, and served in the Continental Congress 1780 to 1783. He was observing the Legislature in Richmond when he wrote these letters to Madison. For further confirmation of Taylor's position, see letter of Jefferson to Madison, May 7, 1783, in Rives, *Life of Madison*, Vol. II, p. 240.

States in Congress assembled, shall thereupon notify such demand to the Executive of this State, and call for the surrender of such offender, the Governor, with the advice of the Council of State, is hereby authorized to cause him to be apprehended, and conveyed and delivered to such person, or persons, as the United States in Congress assembled, may prescribe." Taylor is recorded in the affirmative, in the close vote of 41 to 37.[47]

---

[47] Journal of the House, Nov. 2, 1784.

CHAPTER III

BEFORE THE VIRGINIA BAR

THE year that the Peace Treaty was signed with England (1783) Taylor, then a man thirty years of age, married Lucy Penn, the daughter of John Penn.[1] A sketch of the latter has been left us by John Taylor himself. Penn was born in 1741, in Caroline County, Virginia, and was the only child of Moses Penn and Catherine, who was the sister of John Taylor's father. He used Edmund Pendleton's books in the pursuit of legal studies, and became an able and impassioned lawyer, so impassioned in fact, that he is said to have moved both himself and the jury to tears at times. After moving to North Carolina in 1774, he became a prosperous planter, and this occupation, combined with a lucrative income from his legal profession, enabled him to accumulate considerable wealth. He signed the Declaration of Independence, exercised broad powers in the conduct of the American Revolution in North Carolina, and served for five years in the Continental Congress.[2]

Taylor's marriage to the daughter of a prosperous lawyer and planter had vital consequences for the son-in-law's future, for Penn willed him fifteen slaves, and had before given him numerous other valuable presents. Convinced that he had been generous enough to Taylor, the former revoked an original provision in his will, to the effect that his daughter, Lucy, was to receive 30,000 pounds of tobacco.[3] By 1784, when Taylor was yet a member of the Virginia Assembly, and when he was on

---

[1] Hayden's *Virginia Genealogies* fails to give the date of Taylor's marriage. Miss Mary Taylor, a great-great-granddaughter of John Taylor, is authority for the statement that the family papers give the date of birth of the eldest child as Sept. 7, 1784. It would thus be natural to conclude that the marriage was a year or two before.

[2] *Sketch of Life of John Penn*, by John Taylor. Original in possession of Henry Taylor, Jr., of Richmond, Va.

[3] John Penn's Will, date, March 1, 1784. Revocation and reason for same in later will, April 10, 1786. Paper in possession of Henry Taylor, Jr.

the eve of an active legal career, he had started active plantation operations, as shown by the fact that he had sixteen slaves
over sixteen years of age, and eleven under that age. He was
paying a tax of sixteen pounds and seven shillings.[4]

The Taylor family consisted of six sons, John, Edmund, William, Henry, James and George, and two daughters. The two
latter died early in life, as did the son, James.[5] Of the others,
John attended the University of Virginia (1827–29) and became a doctor, Edmund attended William and Mary College
in 1839, and William was a member of the House of Delegates
from Caroline County in 1829, a member of Congress 1833–
1835, and a presidential elector in 1845.[6] In the early nineteenth
century, George was experiencing financial difficulties as a
student at Edinburgh in Scotland.[7]

Taylor's period of active professional activities, as indicated
by Call's Reports of the cases argued before the Virginia Court
of Appeals, was during the ten years following 1783. Many
were the powerful personalities who in that day made up the
Virginia bar. Edmund Pendleton, richly endowed with that
superb training made possible by the long parliamentary struggle with England, was President of the Virginia Court of Appeals.[8] George Wythe, who had represented William and Mary
College in the House of Burgesses, who had been a distinguished law professor there, who had sat in the Virginia Convention of 1776 and 1788, and the Federal Convention of 1787,
was later a member of the Court of Appeals. His amazing
legal stock no doubt helps to explain his independence in arriv-

---

[4] Personal Property Books of Caroline County, 1784. Some account of Taylor's
plantation methods and social life will be given in the chapter on "The Agricultural
Ideal".

[5] This information, from the family papers, was supplied by Miss Mary Taylor of
Richmond, Virginia.

[6] Hayden, *Virginia Genealogies*, p. 682.

[7] See Monroe-Taylor Correspondence in Chapter 7.

[8] Mays, *Sketch of Life of Edmund Pendleton*. Pamphlet in Virginia State Library.

ing at conclusions.[9] Spencer Roane became a member of the
Court of Appeals in the early 1790's. Born in 1762, he had
attended William and Mary College, where he studied law
under Chancellor Wythe, and had served in both the House
of Delegates and the Senate before he became a member of the
highest court.[10] We shall hear of him later. Then there was
Edmund Randolph, nephew of Peyton, not a member of the
Court, but often before it in a legal capacity. Tall and dignified, he was as impressive in manner, as in intellect. At twenty-
three years of age he was a member of the Convention of 1776,
Governor of Virginia ten years later, and the first Attorney-
General of the United States after the Constitution went into
effect. Of him it is said that "his success at the bar was extraordinary. Clients filled his office, and beset him on his way
from the office to the court-house with their papers in one hand,
and with guineas in the other." [11]

Admitted to the bar in 1780–81 was John Marshall, who was
destined to legal combat with Taylor long before the latter
assailed the decisions of the future Chief Justice of the Supreme Court of the United States. His outstanding abilities,
high character, and family antecedents, all enabled him to rise
rapidly in his profession. Patrick Henry, John Wickham, able
and witty, and Alexander Campbell, famed for his eloquence,
were others who gave prestige to the Virginia bar.[12] We can
get a more impressive idea of those with whom Taylor mixed
and mingled when the sessions of the Court made Richmond
of central interest, by the following quotation, describing the
situation when Callender was the defendant in a sedition trial
in 1800. "There was John Marshall, diplomatist and jurist, and

---

[9] For description of Wythe see H. B. Grigsby, *Address on "The Virginia Convention of 1776"*, before Phi Beta Kappa Society at William and Mary College, July 3,
1855, pp. 120–127. He is said to have taken part of several days in making this
address, which is a good sized book.

[10] *Branch Historical Papers*, Vol. II, pp. 5 to 9.

[11] Grigsby, *Convention of 1776*, pp. 76–78.

[12] Magruder, *Life of Marshall*, pp. 25 and 33.

soon to become the official chief of the hated judge (Chase) whose official program was summoning all the country-side. In another group near Marshall stood a handsome, neatly dressed man about thirty years of age, tall, well-formed, and graceful, with a hearty laugh and a confident manner that seemed to fascinate those about him, particularly one keen, boyish-looking listener who hung upon his every word, for William Wirt was already the beau-ideal of the junior bar, and Philip Nicholas had reason to felicitate himself on being associated with such a rising young advocate. In this same group stood George Hay, soon to become one of the best known lawyers in the country, and beside him stood the distinguished leader of the Virginia bar, Edmund Randolph." [13]

Taylor amassed considerable wealth as a result of his law practice. He is said to have made $10,000 a year, when engaged in active practice. Much of this he invested in land, for which he paid actual cash.[14] Before our attention is centered upon a number of interesting cases argued by Taylor before the Virginia Court of Appeals, it is well to direct it upon the wide range of his legal activities. At one time he was acting as an attorney for a Colonel Oliver Towles,[15] but several years later he refused to handle a case for that gentleman, because the opposing individual had been a Taylor client since the Caroline lawyer started the practice of law.[16] At another time he was employed by Colonel Preston in Montgomery County to institute a suit in regard to lands belonging to a large estate, but claimed by others not connected with the estate. This county was far removed from Caroline, Taylor's home.[17] Though he

---

[13] Hill, *Decisive Battles of the Law*, pp. 2 and 3.

[14] Taylor MSS., Letter of Captain John Taylor, eldest grandchild of Taylor, to Julia Taylor, his first cousin, March 7, 1875. Original in possession of Henry Taylor, Jr. He states that he has seen his grandfather weighing gold and silver to make land payments.

[15] Taylor MSS., Taylor to Oliver Towles, Sept. 13, 1783. Original in New York Public Library.

[16] *Ibid.*, March 23, 1786.

[17] Taylor MS., Taylor to executors of Col. Buchanan's Estate, Feb. 2, 1784. Original in possession of Miss Nita Blinkoe, Ashland, Virginia.

appears to have had little success in that capacity, Taylor acted
as an agent for the State in attempting to collect back taxes
due the State from the far southwestern counties of Russell
and Washington.[18]

An examination of Cranch's and Wheaton's Reports suggests
that Taylor was probably before the Supreme Court of the
United States a number of times during the first quarter of the
nineteenth century. In these Reports, however, the last name
only is given, so when the name "Taylor" appears, it is by no
means certain that John Taylor is referred to. In at least one
case it is clear that Taylor was a defendant, and argued his
own case as attorney, for John Taylor is expressly mentioned.
The case is cited as that of "Bodley and Others v. Taylor". The
latter, in 1780, had made an entry with a county surveyor in
Kentucky for 3000 acres of land. It was claimed that he caused
it to be surveyed contrary to location, but because he had a
patent older than that of other claimants, he would not surrender the improved lands in the section he had caused to be
surveyed. Despite Taylor's argument as to priority of patent
the court ruled that lands not within his entry, but within his
patent as well as that of the contestants, must go to the latter.[19]
Ten years later Taylor was engaged in another law suit over
lands in Kentucky.[20a] Land and boundary disputes he was constantly connected with. In addition to his part in the controversy between North Carolina and Virginia over the boundary
line,[20b] he, with John Marshall, James Breckinridge and others,
comprised a committee to whom were referred the findings of
commissioners appointed to adjust the Virginia and Kentucky
boundary line. The committee approved the findings.[21]

But it was before the Virginia Court of Appeals that Taylor

---

[18] Calendar of Virginia State Papers, Vol. VII, pp. 402–403, Nov. 3, 1794.
[19] Cranch 5, pp. 191–234, 1806–1807.
[20a] Wheaton 1, p. 141, March 6, 1816. The case is cited as Taylor v. Walton and
Hundley.
[20b] See Chapter II of this volume.
[21] Calendar of Virginia State Papers, Vol. VIII, pp. 454–455, Dec. 12, 1797.

appeared often, in outstanding cases, and in large part before he was forty years of age. One of the earliest cases in which he appeared was as counsel for The Loyal and Greenbrier Companies, which were presenting claims to lands granted them before the Revolution under orders of the Governor and Council, but the validity of which claims was doubtful, because the companies had not completely surveyed the lands, nor obtained patents for them, within the time periods prescribed by the terms of the grant.[22] Edmund Pendleton, head of the Supreme Court of Appeals, had written the petition of the Loyal Company in 1779, four years before the case was argued before the Court of which he was head. This petition set forth that the Company was to take up 800,000 acres of land July 12, 1749. Four years were given for the survey, but since it was incomplete at the end of that time, four more were given by the Governor and Council. But the Indian War of 1754 stopped the surveys, and the King's Proclamation of 1763, forbidding further settlements in the West, did likewise. It was claimed, however, that in 1773, when the Governor and the Council were instructed to grant lands to officers and soldiers of the French and Indian War, they recognized the grant as valid. Surveys made in 1774 and 1775 had not been returned to the Secretary's Office because of the flight of Governor Dunmore, and the subsequent change of the government. The petition asked for certificates to entitle them to the grants for surveys. The Greenbrier petition was similar to that of the Loyal Company. The former company claimed 100,000 acres on the Greenbrier River.[23]

Taylor, after summarizing the content of the petitions, claimed that the case came expressly within the meaning of the act passed in 1779 for adjusting and settling the titles of claimants

---

[22] *Reports of Cases argued and adjudged in the Court of Appeals of Virginia,* by Daniel Call, 1779–1818, Vol. IV, p. 639, May, 1783. Call and the volume number will hereafter be cited.

[23] Call, IV, pp. 640–642.

to unpatented lands, for the first section of that act provided that all surveys made before January 1, 1778, upon western waters, "upon any order of council, or entry in the council books, should be carried into grant". Another section provided for the protection of mere settlers, and for the right of preëmption to all settlers. The idea then, he contended, was to help all who had been oppressed by difficulties, and the seventh section expressly stated that as regards purchasers and companies, the former should have their titles confirmed by the companies, upon payment of the original price with interest.[24]

Edmund Randolph, Attorney-General, argued for the State that there had been ample time between the orders of council and the Indian War to have carried them into effect, that rapid settlement of the country was the aim of the grants, but that the claimants had suited their own convenience in consummating their claims. He claimed that the seventh section of the land act referred to companies which had so nearly met conditions of the orders of council as to simply require forms to complete the title. Taylor replied that there was no condition to defeat the right; that substantial performance of the terms of the grant was all that was required; that most of the compensation involved had been made, and that the rest could be made without loss to the State.

The claims of Thomas Walker and Thomas Nelson for the Loyal and Greenbrier Companies, respectively, were allowed. All claims based on surveys made by authorized persons previous to 1776 were confirmed by the issuance of patents.[25]

In another celebrated case, Taylor crossed swords with Marshall. The case is cited as "Hite et al. *v.* Fairfax et al.", and came before the court in May, 1786. Edmund Randolph, along with Taylor, argued against Fairfax. The case involved, so many thought, the claim of the heirs of Fairfax to vast terri-

[24] Call, IV, pp. 642–643.
[25] *Ibid.*, p. 643.

tories in the Northern Neck of Virginia and it specifically involved the obligation of those heirs to the heirs of Hite, to
whom Fairfax had originally made promises.[26a]

Marshall devoted most of his argument to a defense of the
validity of the Fairfax claims in general rather than to a defense
of those against Hite. Long possession, the grant by the Crown,
and the recognition of the grant by various acts of the Assembly
had established beyond dispute the right of the Fairfax heirs to
their vast estates, he contended.[26b]

Taylor doubted the validity of the original grant to Fairfax,
or at least its binding character. Charles II, while a fugitive,
made the grant, and James II, in the fourth year of his reign,
but after he had, in fact, ceased to reign, confirmed it. Fairfax
had promised Hite and others, Taylor claimed, that he would
confirm their land titles, if they would remain, and this they
had done. A plantation affairs committee, in a representation
to the King in 1745, set forth that Fairfax had promised to
recognize those who had claims upon the Crown for lands in
the proprietary. The appellants (Hite et al.) should have what
belonged to them under the orders of council. Even though
they did not have patents, they had valid claims; for a general
caveat shut the door to government patents in 1734, and the
claimants had to depend upon government surveys, while the
Fairfax agents continued to distribute patents. As to the claim
that the claimants under Lord Fairfax were entitled to what
they purchased, Taylor contended that the transactions between
Fairfax and the Crown were notorious, and that said claimants
might also have learned from the council office of Fairfax's
doubtful claim.[27]

The Court decided that the Fairfax estate should make compensation to Hite, or rather to his heirs.[28]

As far as local interest was concerned, there was probably no

[26a] Call, IV, pp. 652–653.
[26b] Beveridge, *Life of Marshall*, Vol. I, pp. 191–195.
[27] Call, IV, pp. 655–656.
[28] *Ibid*, p. 660.

matter of judicial controversy which attracted more attention, during Taylor's period as an active legal practitioner, than the case of Rev. John Bracken against the Visitors of William and Mary College. Under the original charter to the college, the statutes were to be made, or changed, by a board of trustees, nominated and elected by the General Assembly, but at a meeting of the Board of Visitors, December 4, 1779, a statute was passed for reforming the college. Pursuant to this statute the grammar school was discontinued, and Rev. Bracken, as grammar master and professor of humanity, was dismissed. Thus the questions at issue were whether the Visitors of the college had the power to change the schools and put down professorships; and whether a writ of mandamus should be issued to restore the plaintiff to the office of grammar master and professor of humanity in the college.[29]

The judges of the Court at this time were Edmund Pendleton, President, Spencer Roane, Peter Lyons, William Fleming and Paul Carrington.[30] Taylor argued for the plaintiff, and John Marshall for the college. Both of these men were alumni of William and Mary, and, strongly suggestive of their future interpretations of the Constitution of the United States, the former contended for a strict construction of the original college charter, and the latter for a loose construction.

Marshall held that the college was a mere eleemosynary institution, that it was founded on charity, and that the Visitors were appointed for its government and direction. They had not exceeded their authority under the charter, for they could make laws not contrary to it, and there was no requirement nor necessity that the grammar master should form a part of the system.[31]

Taylor claimed that the college was a corporation for purposes of further government, that the authority of the Board

[29] Call, III, pp. 607–610. Case argued Dec. 8, 1790.
[30] Ibid., p. 422.
[31] Ibid., 609–610.

of Visitors was limited by and subordinate to the charter and original statutes, and that the visitorial act exceeded their power. The charter "is the constitution of the college, and like all other constitutions, ought to be preserved inviolate". This charter, he continued, erected three branches of government for the corporate body, whose rights were separate and distinct and in most instances independent of each other: the trustees, the visitors and governors, and the president and masters. Since the masters were thus provided for, though not named, in the fundamental instrument, they could not be annihilated by the Visitors simply because that order could try them. Taylor was destined to write and talk much after 1790 of the necessity of keeping intact the divisions of power among the different departments of our government, so it is not surprising to find him contending here that no creature of a political regulation has a right to destroy another of the same political regulation, that "that which cannot create, cannot destroy".

Taylor reached the climax of his argument by the following comparison and contrast between the old charter and the new one, resulting from the action of the Board of Visitors in 1779.

"The old charter has the support of religion for an object. The modern one deserts it . . .

"The old charter established a grammar school to teach the ancient languages. The modern one barters these for the modern languages and the fine arts.

"Under the old charter, the masters held large estates, a right of representation in the Legislature, fixed salaries, and were a body corporate; nor could any individual lose these rights, except by 'death, resignation, or deprivation'.

"By the new, he holds them at the will and pleasure of the Visitors, and may be dismissed without any reason whatsoever.

"By the old constitution, the trustees only had power to erect schools, or appoint professorships.

"Under the new one, the Visitors assume this power, and exercise it."

Since the master held his office by virtue of the charter, and since the Visitors could make rules, but could not destroy; since Bracken was not dead and had not resigned, and had not been deprived of his position (the latter process, he claimed, involved a personal summons or trial) Taylor thus held the act of the Visitors to be void.[32]

Marshall reiterated his argument that the college was private, because corporations for public government have neither founder nor visitor. He claimed that the Visitors had general powers, and since no special powers were stipulated, they had all incident to their position. He admitted that they could not change the charter, but said that the grammar school was not provided by that instrument.[33]

The Court upheld the action of the Visitors in dismissing the professor.[34]

Another case, very technical in nature, came before the Court in July, 1790. It is cited as that of "Beall v. Cockburn", and involved a contract between these two individuals in regard to the sale of sterling money in Jamaica, by Cockburn to Beall in the United States. The interest in the case consists in the fact that there was brilliant legal talent on both sides, Taylor for Cockburn, and John Wickham and John Marshall for Beall. Taylor centered his whole argument around the nature of the original contract, and his powerful and searching analysis of the contract, and his insistence that it be adhered to in its original form, were no doubt decisive factors in the decision of the court in favor of Cockburn.[35]

In June, 1791, Taylor and Marshall were once more opposing counsel, in a case involving claims to western lands.[36] Only once, in the Reports, did the writer find these two men associated in a case. This involved a debt question, and was entitled:

[32] Call, III, pp. 610–612.
[33] *Ibid*, pp. 613–614.
[34] *Ibid*, p. 615.
[35] Call, IV, pp. 687–693.
[36] *Ibid*, pp. 698–701 (Hamilton *v*. Mays).

"Braxton et al., surviving Executors of Philip W. Claiborne, deceased, *v.* Winslow et al., surviving Justices of Spottsylvania County". The decision was in favor of their clients, though they were opposed by Wickham, Baker and William Nelson.[37]

At the May term, 1795, of the Circuit Court of the United States in Virginia, Taylor delivered an argument regarding the constitutionality of the carriage tax. This tax had been imposed by Congress without regard to apportionment among the states, since it was regarded as an indirect, and not a direct tax. Taylor started his argument with the proposition that, if passive obedience to Legislative majorities were orthodox, the Constitution never could be enforced, because it allowed those designed to be restrained, exclusively to interpret its principles.[38]

He claimed that the carriage tax was a direct tax. Congress had the power "to lay and collect taxes, duties, imports and excises", but they were restrained by the clause to the effect that "no capitation or other direct tax shall be laid, unless in proportion to the census or enumeration herein before directed to be taken". But "if without apportionment among the states, by the rule of the census, Congress can tax the drink, the food, the clothing and all necessaries, raised or kept by individuals for their own ease and subsistence, without limitation, is there any real restriction of their power of taxation?" Carriages, he contended, were for man's own use, and not even an excise could be conceded, in the case of this character of article. He distinguished between indirect and direct taxes in this way: "An indirect is a circulating, a direct, a local tax . . . By an indirect tax we can only be incommoded, by a direct tax annihilated".[39]

Taylor then proceeded to show that the Constitution aimed to preserve the equality of states. He pointed out that direct

[37] Call, IV, pp. 736–739.

[38] *An argument respecting the Constitutionality of the Carriage Tax,* by Taylor, pp. 2–4. In Rare Book Room in Library of Congress.

[39] *Ibid.,* pp. 5–11.

taxes could be apportioned among the states, and hence were, but that indirect, being itinerant, could not, yet that all duties, imports and excises must be uniform, so as to base them, as near as their nature permitted, on the principle of equal representation. The reason that the Constitution prohibited a tax on exports was because they were so dissimilar in different states, and such a tax would have produced inequality of burdens among the states. But if Congress could tax anything at will before exportation, without regard to state population, for which action the carriage tax was a precedent, then the aim of the prohibition was defeated.[40]

Great danger, in his opinion, lurked in any policy of unequal distribution of favors or burdens, for "if oppressed, states will combine—the grand divisions of northern and southern will retaliate as majorities or ministers fluctuate—and a retaliation between nations, invariably ends in a catastrophe".[41]

If the principle that the carriage tax was an indirect tax, and hence did not have to be apportioned among the states according to population, was accepted, Taylor felt that the South was exposed to a peculiar danger, made possible by its "peculiar institution". "Unhappily for the southern states, they possess a species of property, which is peculiarly exposed, and upon which, if this law stands, the whole burden of government may be exclusively laid." He contended that the constitutional stipulations securing slavery were absurd, if emancipation could be forced by taxation.[42]

The argument of Wickham to sustain the constitutionality of the tax, as an indirect one, centered around two main points. He claimed that the accepted distinction from far back in the past between direct and indirect taxes was that a tax upon revenue or income was a direct one, and that upon expense or consumption, an indirect one. In the second place, if Congress

---

[40] *An argument respecting the Constitutionality of the Carriage Tax,* by Taylor, pp. 11–15. Pamphlet in Congressional Library.
[41] *Ibid,* p. 16.
[42] *Ibid,* p. 20.

had imposed this tax according to state populations, it would have worked hardships on some states, and imposed almost no burdens on others. [43]

---

[43] Wickham's Argument may also be found in a rare book in the Rare Book Room, Congressional Library.

CHAPTER IV

IN THE CURRENT OF NATIONAL POLITICS

WE have now seen Taylor as an orphan under the gentle and beneficent care of the wise Pendleton; we have seen him fighting the battles of the Revolution on northern battlefields as well as on the soil of his native State; we have seen him rendering distinguished service in the Assembly of his State during the trying years of transition from colony to state; and we have seen him in a successful role, among brilliant legal lights, before the Virginia bar. We shall now picture him as an inspiring factor in the formation of a great party, deriving its strength from forces which claimed to see in the policies of the opposing party danger to republican institutions.

Taylor was not a member of the Virginia Constitutional Convention of 1788, which, after a long and bitter debate, adopted the Federal Constitution. He is said to have been urged by his cousin, Colonel James Taylor, to seek membership in that body, but he refused to do so.[1] James Taylor, like Pendleton, had for years held most of the gifts in possession of the citizens of Caroline. He had been a member of the Convention of 1776, of the House of Burgesses, and of the House of Delegates.[2] These eminent citizens represented Taylor's county in the convention.

Taylor was opposed to the adoption of the Constitution, unless there were amendments guarding individual and state rights.[3] He was in accord with the arguments presented against

---

[1] See account of conversation at Caroline Court House among Edmund Pendleton, James Taylor and John Taylor. Article by Dr. A. G. Grinnan, in *William and Mary College Quarterly*, Vol. III, pp. 9 to 10, entitled, "President Madison and Colonel John Taylor, of Caroline".

[2] See address by J. A. C. Chandler to William and Mary Alumni. In possession of Henry Taylor, Jr.

[3] Pendleton, Pamphlet, *Sketch of Taylor*.

that instrument by Henry, George Mason, and Richard Henry Lee. These leaders objected to the expression, "We, the people", in the Constitution, as suggesting consolidation, and to the failure, as originally drafted, to provide for trial by jury and freedom of the press. They objected to the power of direct taxation vested in the Federal Government and they were apprehensive that the exercise of the concurrent power of taxation by two governments would result in their clashing.[4] They did not succeed in preventing ratification unless amendments were agreed upon, but the Convention, in ratifying, made it clear that powers not granted were, in its opinion, reserved to the people of the United States, while those granted might be resumed by them, if "perverted to their injury or oppression".[5]

Upon this clause, and upon the tenth amendment to the Constitution, later adopted, Taylor and other Virginia state rights leaders relied to a considerable extent in sustaining their constitutional arguments. In the ratifying clause, the language used does not indicate clearly whether the term "people" is used in a collective sense, or whether it means that Virginia grants the same construction to the other states that she herself placed upon the Constitution. But the tenth amendment, by reserving powers not granted to the Federal Government, nor prohibited to the states, "to the states, respectively, or to the people", seems clearly to suggest that the powers in question belong to individual states. Taylor's early view of the Constitution is well summarized by Pendleton: "He had objec-

---

4 *History of Virginia Federal Convention of 1788,* by H. B. Grigsby. For Henry's arguments, see pp. 80–82, 114–116. For Mason's, pp. 92–93, 189–192. All in Vol. I.

5 *Ibid.,* pp. 347–348. The ratifying clause in question follows: "We, the Delegates of the People of Virginia, . . . do, in the name and in the behalf of the people of Virginia, declare and make known, that the powers granted under the Constitution being derived from the People of the United States, may be resumed by them whensoever the same shall be perverted to their injury or oppression, and that every power not granted thereby remains with them, and at their will; that therefore, no right of any denomination can be cancelled, abridged, restrained, or modified by the Congress, by the Senate or House of Representatives, acting in any capacity, by the President, or any department, or officer of the United States, except in those instances in which power is given by the Constitution for those purposes."

tions to the Federal Constitution, as who had not? But when ratified, he has ever considered it as fixing a rule of conduct to the whole society, governors and governed; and holds it to be a sacred duty in himself and every other citizen to watch over and guard it from violations by their several agents in the administration: being wisely hostile to the project of one general consolidated government for the whole United States, he has been particularly attentive to the strides of the Federal Government, which encroached upon the reserved rights of the state governments, and tended to their annihilation." [6]

One of the first problems confronting the Federal Government, after the Constitution went into effect, was the working out of a financial policy. A foreign debt, and an even larger domestic debt were burdens confronting the Nation. The states had incurred obligations during the period of the Revolution, most of which had been met by the Southern States, but not generally by the Northern States. Hamilton, claiming that it would tend to establish faith in the credit of the Federal Government, proposed to pay the debt at full value, though many of the debt certificates had been bought by speculators at a price far below their par value. He proposed that the Federal Government assume the state debts, which proposition involved unequal burdens upon the South. As a means of paying the debt, and as a means at the same time of making the individual feel the strong hand of the Federal Government, he proposed an excise tax. As a fiscal agency for carrying on the operations of the Government, as well as one for investment possibilities on the part of men of wealth, Hamilton suggested a National Bank. This involved a connection between the Government and private business, since the Government might subscribe one-fifth of the stock of the Bank and also borrow from its funds.

None of these measures, which were passed by Congress, were favored by the agricultural interests of the South. Taylor,

---

[6] Pendleton, Pamphlet, *Sketch of Taylor*. Date of pamphlet not given.

by this time a large planter,[7] became an active foe of all the
Hamiltonian policies. In his correspondence, in lengthy pamphlets, and as a member of the United States Senate, he used
his keen powers of analysis to organize sentiment against the
financial measures. Most of the holders of debt certificates were
in the North, and most of those who had bank stock were
there. A funding interest exacting heavy taxation and a banking interest linked with the funding interest and with the Government also seemed a veritable engine of oppression to the
landed classes. Before Taylor became a member of the Senate,
the Virginia Legislature had drawn up a protest against the
whole debt scheme, in which it was stated that "in an agricultural country like this, . . . to erect, and concentrate, and
perpetuate, a large monied interest in opposition to the landed
interest, is a measure which your memorialists apprehend must,
in the course of human events, produce one or other of two
evils: the prostration of agriculture at the feet of commerce, or
a change in the present form of Federal Government fatal to
the existence of American liberty". On the question of the
assumption of state debts, the memorial condemned that policy
as not only not warranted by the Constitution, but positively
repugnant to its express provisions.[8]

   In 1792, Taylor was elected to the United States Senate to
succeed Richard Henry Lee, who had resigned. He was to
serve the unexpired term as well as a full term after March 4,
1793.[9] Taylor was soon given his first opportunity to give official expression to his anti-bank views. An appropriation bill

---

   7 For account of his plantation operations, see Chapter IX.
   8 Journal of House of Delegates, No. 22, 1790. The argument is as follows:
"That all debts contracted, and engagements entered into, before the adoption of this
constitution, shall be as valid against the United States, as under the Confederation
which amounts to a constitutional ratification of the contracts respecting the state
debts, in the situation in which they exist under the confederation; and resorting to
that standard, there can be no doubt that in the present situation, the rights of states,
as contracting parties with the United States, must be considered as sacred." This
protest, adopted Dec. 16, 1790, also recalled the conditions annexed by Virginia,
when she ratified the Constitution.
   9 Journal of House of Delegates, Oct. 18, 1792.

for governmental expenses for 1793 authorized the President
of the United States to borrow not more than $800,000, at a
rate of interest not exceeding five per cent, to be paid back in
sums of not less than $50,000, at such time as seemed proper.
It was provided that the Bank could legally lend the sum, and
reimbursement was to be through the medium of duties on
imports and tonnage. Both Taylor and Monroe, the other Virginia Senator, voted with a small minority against the bill.[10]

But the recently elected Virginia Senator was planning a
more direct and powerful attack upon the Bank at the next
session of Congress. Since he did not believe that newspapers
were proper channels to impress considerably the public mind,
Taylor wrote a pamphlet, which Pendleton approved, attacking
the funding and banking schemes.[11] When Venable and William B. Giles, a Virginia Congressman who opposed the Bank,[12]
visited Taylor in the summer of 1793, they heartily subscribed
to the idea that this pamphlet should be published and distributed. The author believed that its distribution might effect in
the Virginia Assembly a repeal of the bank laws, and an ex-
pulsion of bank paper, which result would operate against the
banking system in Congress, because it would remove the argument that the State had appropriated the banking system,
and would tend to draw specie from other states to Virginia.[13]
Monroe praised the lengthy pamphlet as one in which he found
"many useful and judicious observations addressed in his (Taylor's) humorous style, concluding in the sentiment that the
banks should be demolished and proprietors of the latter excluded from the public councils".[14]

The nature of the arguments in this and another pamphlet,

---

[10] Annals of Congress, Second Congress, pp. 650–651, Feb. 19, 1793. The vote
was 19 to 9 in the affirmative.
[11] Taylor MSS., Taylor to Madison, May 11, 1793; and June 20, 1793. In
Branch Historical Papers, Vol. II, pp. 253–354.
[12] Anderson, Life of Giles, p. 14.
[13] Ibid., August 5, 1793, Vol. II, p. 258.
[14] Writings of Monroe, Hamilton. Monroe to Madison, May 18, 1793. Vol. I,
p. 254.

written by Taylor, will be examined after an account has been
given of the efforts in Congress, in 1794, to break the power of
the Bank. Among these efforts was a proposition in the Senate
to amend the Constitution so that no person holding any position in connection with the Bank could be a member of either
House, while he held that position.[15] Taylor strongly approved
that proposition, as he did also the motion to repeal that part
of the Bank Bill which allowed the Government to own any
of the Bank's stock. The motion further provided that the
Government should pay its debts to the Bank as soon as possible.[16] Taylor, this time with a small minority, lent his support to a movement to have a committee appointed to ascertain
the principles on which the accounts of the individual states
with the United States were settled, and the credits allowed in
that settlement.[17]

Taylor published two treatises in 1794, one entitled "A Definition of Parties, or the Political effects of the Paper System
Considered", and the second, "An Enquiry into the Principles
and the Tendency of Certain Public Measures". In these works,
Taylor emphasized the idea that a young government must be
rooted in the sound principles of political morality, and that
"usurpation upon constitutional principles, if suffered to acquire
maturity", would yield "to the dreadful remedy of a civil war".[18]
Congress could impose taxes for the common defense and the
general welfare of the United States, but not for the benefit of
individuals, or for their own private emolument. The debt,
he contended, might have been paid on the part of the Union
by imposts, and on the part of the states by direct taxation. The
assumption of state debts still further concentrated a paper
credit, made a direct tax by the Federal Government inevitable,
and was intended to dissolve financial relationships between

---

15 Annals of Third Congress, Jan. 16, 1794, pp. 31–32. The vote was 12 affirmative, 13 negative.
16 Ibid., Jan. 24, 1794, p. 38.
17 Ibid., March 21, 1794. The vote was 6 to 16.
18 Definition of Parties, p. 1; Enquiry into Principles, etc., p. 2.

individuals and separate states, so as to diminish state powers and bring about consolidation.[19]

Taylor pictured a nation divided into two great classes: the stockholders of the Bank, and those who dealt with the Bank. The institution issued a great amount of paper money, and the interest on this was derived from human labor.[20] How this moneyed institution sapped the resources of the Nation, Taylor pointed out in the following way: "The capital of the United States Bank is ten millions, of which the United States own two. The dividend is eight per cent per annum. This alone is an annual income of $800,000, of which $160,000 belong to the Nation. The whole dividend, though but an article of the income, is considerably more than sufficient to defray the whole expense of the civil government. . . . Bank stock is public debt. It is public debt of the worst kind, because it bears an enormous and incomputable interest, as will hereafter be shown. Nothing but a tax can pay this interest, unless it is proved that the interest on the funded debt might have been paid without a tax." [21] He then showed clearly how the banking and funding schemes were connected. Public securities, carrying an interest of six per cent, for three-fourths of the whole amount, were by law receivable as a deposit. They were used as a fund to circulate other paper certificates, and thus were deriving from the public a never ceasing interest. So in addition to the six per cent paid by the government on $7,500,000 of public debt, there was added the ordinary profit made by a bank.[22]

Taylor emphasized the concentration of the funded debt. He claimed that the paper interest numbered 5000, and the rest of the Nation oppressed by it, nearly 5,000,000. "The funding system deprived the 5,000,000, without value received, of 17S. in the pound, upon the whole amount of the national debt—

[19] Definition of Parties, p. 4; Enquiry into Principles, p. 43.
[20] Enquiry into Principles, pp. 8–9, 16.
[21] Ibid, pp. 12 and 14.
[22] Ibid., p. 17.

bestowed it upon the 5000, and doubled the loss upon the 5,000,000, by the remedy of a perpetual tax. . . . Virginia under the paper system of representation, ought to hold 22,000,000 dollars—she holds 1,000,000, and this 1,000,000 is in the hands of 100 individuals. Massachusetts may possibly hold her share of this representative, but it is chiefly, if not entirely, in the hands of 1000 individuals." [23] . . .

A "national debt a national blessing", Taylor considered an artful phrase designed to deceive the poor into perpetual contributions to the wealthy. He claimed that no effort was being made to pay the debt, that the sinking fund did not sink. That fund had been established in 1790, yet less than $1,000,000 of the $1,300,000 in the fund had been applied to the extinguishment of the debt by January, 1793. We had spent nearly that much, he claimed, in periodical purchases of certificates, and moreover had borrowed money in 1790 from Holland and after that date. The Constitution limited "Congress 'to the payment of the debts of the United States', and while the echo of that mandate is yet vibrating in our ears, the funding system declares that they shall *not be paid*".[24] (Italicized by Taylor.) The provision that the Bank could lend to the Government, he considered a vicious principle, one which would inexorably lead the Bank influences to attempt to keep a debt saddled upon the Nation. He pointed out that up to January, 1793, the Bank had loaned the Government $2,400,000, for which the former was receiving interest. The public was paying interest for the credit of the Bank, and that institution none for the money of the people.[25]

And whence would come the funds to meet these lasting debt schemes? They would be derived from land. "A funding system is a conveyance of all the lands of the Nation, subject to a rent charge, payable to a few persons. The deed was made

[23] Definition of Parties, pp. 4–6.
[24] Enquiry into Principles, pp. 21, 45–46.
[25] *Ibid.*, pp. 67–71.

originally by these few persons to themselves. By retaining the direction of the Legislature, they will make the rent perpetual —they will give themselves new mortgages upon the estate, and they will never stop, until they extract from it all the profit it can yield." [26] Taylor believed that a paper system represented a transfer of property by law, hence he was opposed to banks and their legitimate offspring, paper. Specie would equalize itself throughout the commercial world, if banks did not drive it out of existence where they existed. But the banishment of specie creates a necessity for it, and that necessity is met by the only substitute possible, viz., bank paper. When the loss resulting from a circulating medium is greater than the price demanded by the bank for its paper, self-interest leads people to buy it. Thus when circulating specie is banished from a community, that community must pay a tax for its circulating medium. [27] As indicated above, Taylor expressed the hope to Madison that the anti-bank pamphlet would help bring about a repeal of the Virginia bank laws; in one of the pamphlets he suggested that if two or three large states abolished banks, specie would flow to them, the United States would see the advantage and abolish all banks. [28]

In view of Taylor's antipathy to banks, which lasted throughout his career, it is appropriate to suggest here that years later, and sometime after Taylor's death, his anti-bank doctrines were used as potent arguments for a scheme, of debt repudiation in Mississippi, which involved the non-payment of bank bonds. This later influence of the Virginian's teachings, whether their true interpretation or not, may be found in an editorial in the *Richmond Enquirer,* in 1843, on the death of Doctor James Hagan, editor of the Vicksburg (Miss.) *Sentinel,* from which the following extract is given: "He was a monomaniac on the subject of banks, whether well or ill conducted. He once

---

[26] Definition of Parties, p. 7.
[27] Enquiry into Principles, pp. 32–33.
[28] *Ibid,* p. 80.

boasted, that as soon as he put an end to the banks of Mississippi, he should set up a paper in 'bank ridden' Virginia, to overturn her corporations. . . . It was he that first raised the standard of repudiation in the South and carried it through triumphantly in his own State. With great ingenuity, he twisted some expressions of Mr. Jefferson and John Taylor of Caroline, into a justification of the odious doctrines he advocated." [29]

Taylor denied not only the power of Congress to establish a Bank, but its power to create a paper currency. The Constitution gives Congress the power to "coin money", and it restrains the states from "coining money, emitting bills of credit, or making anything but gold and silver a legal tender". The power of creating a paper currency is thus prohibited to the states, and not delegated to Congress. But since Congress had violated the Contitution, it could say nothing to the states that did likewise.[30]

The stalwart Republican leader demanded that the paper interest be excluded from Congress. "If a number of the members of Congress are stockholders, or bank directors, then an illegitimate interest is operating on the national Legislature," for these paper men would be interested in high taxes, since that would mean more money to be deposited, and a greater circulation on the Bank's credit. One of the rules laid down by the Constitution for representatives was "that no representative shall be appointed to any office created, or the emoluments whereof have been increased, during the period for which he was elected; and that no person holding an office shall be a representative". Yet the members of Congress interested in the financial schemes might vote for a *gainful* project, and be the *receiver* of the gain; they might impose a tax on the community, and instead of sharing in the burden, share in the plunder.[31]

[29] *Richmond Enquirer,* June 23, 1843.
[30] Enquiry into Principles, pp. 82–83. Also p. 36.
[31] *Ibid.,* pp. 24–25, 36–38. Also Definition of Parties, pp. 8 and 11.

This financial interest in Congress represented a baneful influence on American politics. They would value their legislative influence more than their funding interest, and they would never consent to a payment of that by which they would lose their political influence. Taylor saw the operation of this evil influence in connection with the treaties signed with the Creeks and Cherokees in 1790. Those treaties, he claimed, had diminished a state, annulled the rights of citizens to landed property and disregarded the veto of the Constitution, all for the purpose of checking the spread of republicanism into frontier regions, since that factor was hostile to the monied interest. The treaty with the Creeks, made August 7, 1790, stipulated "that a boundary should be marked out, *so as to preclude disputes forever*". The treaty with the Cherokees, dated July 2, 1790, established a boundary line, so as "to preclude *forever* all disputes". Yet the Constitution provided that "no new state shall be erected within the jurisdiction of any other state, without the consent of the state". A whole county in Georgia, as well as lands ceded by North Carolina, were surrendered to the Indians. Representation is in proportion to numbers, so Taylor queried whether the power of making treaties could lessen the numbers of a state, whose politics the power disapproved, and thus diminish its representation. Moreover, Congress could dispose of or make needful rules and regulations respecting the territory of the United States, but nothing in the Constitution should be construed to prejudice the claims of any particular state. If the power of disposing of the territory of the Union were limited to Congress, how, asked Taylor, could a part of Congress—the Senate—and the President dispose of the territory of a state, especially when the cessions of the latter were guaranteed by the Constitution against prejudice? [32]

In these pamphlets, Taylor raised finally the question, which was an ever recurring one in his later career, viz., what to do when the Constitution failed, in practice, to limit the power

---

[32] Definition of Parties, pp. 5–7, 12–13.

of Congress. At that time (1794) he did not think a general
convention necessary to meet the situation, but there were two
other remedies which could be applied. The people might
elect members of Congress, whose interests, burdens and habits
were like those of the electors. However, this was a slow process, so the state legislatures, being annual conventions account-
able to the people, and electing senators, might serve as a check.
He did not make clear what he thought the state legislatures
might do, but he declared that they "have at least as good a
right to judge of every infraction of the Constitution, as Congress itself".[33]

Not only did the other leaders of the Republican party heartily endorse the writings of their brilliant co-worker[34] and counsel that he distribute them, but the rank and file of Virginia
voters accepted enthusiastically his political and economic philosophy. Edmund Randolph, Attorney-General of the United
States, took a journey through Virginia in 1793, in accordance
with the suggestion of President Washington. He reported
that many strongly condemned the financial policies, that there
were more enemies of the Administration in Richmond than
friends, and that "Fredericksburg is inflamed by the doctrines
and representations of Colonel Taylor of Caroline, the Senator
of the United States. It would astonish you, sir, to learn the
success which has attended his efforts to rouse the cool and substantial planters. Even Mr. Hoomes of the Bowling-Green,
"who is respectable and intelligent, and has a great deal to lose",
was animated "to a degree which changes his nature essentially".
Randolph visited Pendleton and other prominent leaders on
the same journey.[35] At approximately the same time as these

---

[33] Enquiry into Principles, pp. 54–55.

[34] Attitude of Monroe and Giles noted above. Jefferson wrote Taylor asking for
the bank pamphlet, and expressing regret that his neighbors had not seen it. *Writings
of Jefferson,* Ford Edition, Vol. VI, p. 505, May 1, 1794.

[35] *Omitted Chapters of History Disclosed in the Life and Papers of Edmund
Randolph,* by M. D. Conway. Letter of Randolph to Washington, June 24, 1793,
pp. 151–152.

activities, Taylor was beginning to write his *Inquiry into the Principles and Policy of the Government of the United States,* which work includes among other principles, practically all the arguments included in the pamphlets quoted, and which led to a controversy with John Adams. (See Chapter VIII.)

There were other matters, most of them highly controversial, concerning which Taylor showed his hand while a member of the Senate in the 1790's. In 1793, the Supreme Court in a case entitled "Chisholm *vs.* Georgia", held that a state might be sued by the citizens of another state. The Virginia Legislature promptly passed resolutions, saying that the decision was dangerous to the sovereignty of the states and tended to consolidation, and instructing its senators and requesting its representatives to work to obtain such amendments as would remove or explain any clause of the Constitution which could be construed to mean that a state was compelled to answer in any suit, by individuals, in any court of the United States.[36] Taylor voted to submit to the states the eleventh amendment, whereby the judicial power of the United States was not to extend to suits against one of the United States, by citizens of any state, or by citizens or subjects of any foreign state.[37]

The reader should bear in mind that at this period of our history, the enemies of the Federalists frequently charged that the policies of the latter "smacked of royalty". Addresses to Congress by the pompous and dignified Washington (a stateliness due, his political supporters thought, to military service), the secret sessions of the Senate, the Hamilton-Adams idea that "the rich and well-born" held a preëminent place in American society, these were some of the factors that gave rise to the Republican accusation. Soon after the Federal Government was set in motion, the Virginia Assembly passed resolutions instructing its senators to work for open sessions, when the Sen-

---

[36] Journal of House, Nov. 28, 1793. State Senate agreed Dec. 3, 1793.
[37] Annals of Third Congress, Jan. 14, 1794, pp. 30–31. There were only 2 votes in negative.

ate was sitting in a legislative capacity, and later the instructions embraced open doors when the Senate was sitting in a judicial capacity as well.[38] The fight for this principle waxed warm during Taylor's tenure as a senator. On the plea that the Senate journals were too voluminous and generally defective, those who favored publicity of the proceedings moved that they be published in the newspapers. This motion was defeated by a three to one vote. Taylor and Monroe were among the seven voting in the affirmative.[39] Several motions for open sessions were lost, but finally, a motion to reconsider prevailed, and then it was agreed that, beginning with the next session of Congress, legislative sessions should be public.[40]

Taylor declared in one of his pamphlets that on every question, domestic and foreign, the two parties were far apart.[41] In foreign relations, the Republicans sympathized with France, a sympathy arising in part from the fact that she had aided us in the Revolution, and in part because she had travelled all the way from absolute monarchy to a republic during the three years, 1789 to 1792. The English Government, the Federalists thought, symbolized permanence and stability, and avoided an excess of democracy. One group of controversial matters consisted of the unkept provisions of the Peace Treaty of 1783 between England and the United States. One provision of that treaty was to the effect that the states would put no obstacles in the way of the collection of debts owed by Americans to British creditors, and another, as it was understood, was to the effect that England should make compensation for the slaves she had carried away. How many slaves thus disappeared, it is impossible to say, but an excellent authority on Virginia history has estimated as high as one-fifth of those in the State.[42]

---

[38] Journal of House of Delegates, Nov. 22, 1790, and Nov. 8, 1793.
[39] Annals of Third Congress. Feb. 4, 1793, pp. 637–638. On question of open sessions, the vote was 18 to 10 against.
[40] *Ibid.*, Feb. 19–20.
[41] Definition of Parties, p. 1.
[42] Grigsby, *History of Virginia Federal Convention of 1788*, Vol. I, pp. 13–14.

Once more the Virginia Assembly instructed its Senators this time to use their influence to prevent measures that would facilitate the debt payments until the Executive had guarantees in regard to the return of the negroes.[43]   Pursuant to these instructions, Monroe brought in, and Taylor voted for, a bill to suspend the debt article, until the slave provision was fulfilled.[44]   Taylor registered his protest in another way against Great Britain by voting for non-intercourse with her, the stated reason for this action, in the bill, being, in part, that she had not fulfilled the treaty.[45]

Taylor recorded his sympathy with such motions as evinced a friendly spirit towards France.   He wished to instruct the President to respond to a letter to Congress, from the Committee of Public Safety of the French Republic, in such a way as to show the sincere friendship and good will of the United States for France.   He also favored a motion, which was defeated, congratulating the French Republic on the progress of liberty, and its brilliant successes on the field of battle.[46]

Before Taylor retired from the Senate, he was invited by Rufus King of New York to a committee room, where the latter stated that it was utterly impossible for the Union to survive, that when the two South Carolina Senators were out of the Senate, the Southern interest would prevail, and that the East would never submit to their policies.   King suggested that there should be a peaceable dissolution of the Union, so that it would not be brought about in a less desirable way.   Oliver Ellsworth of Connecticut came into the committee room during the conversation, and concurred in the same sentiments. They wished Taylor to join with them in working out a

[43] Journal of House of Delegates, Dec. 10, 1793.
[44] Annals of Third Congress, May 6, 1794.   Edmund Randolph, in a letter to Jefferson, May 15, 1784, stated that Taylor, on question of British debts, would take the negative within doors.   From the Journals of the House, Taylor does not appear to have voted on the question.   For Randolph's letter see *Omitted Chapters in Life of Randolph,* by Conway.
[45] Annals of Third Congress, April 28, 1799.
[46] Annals of Third Congress, April 24, 1794.

friendly scheme of disunion, but Taylor thought that the Union could be preserved, that the interests of the sections were not incompatible. If he were mistaken, however, he preferred a friendly separation to any other kind. Taylor expressed the opinion that the public debt was the principal cause of difference. One section believed the other meant to use the debt as a great political machine, whereas the latter suspected the other section of an unwillingness to pay it at all. Taylor suggested that the debt be paid promptly, which would dispel both suspicions. He would effect this payment in three ways: by disbanding the Indian army, and substituting special raiding parties to make rapid incursions into the Indian country. Two-thirds of what was spent on the army could thus be used in payment of the debt. Second, by opening a land office for the sale of lands between the Ohio and Illinois, where there were no Indians. Revenue from increased land sales would thus be available. Third, by imposing a new tax based on the principle of equality. But King agreed to none of those propositions, and said that there were other differences besides the one over the debt. Taylor believed that there was a British interest behind the idea suggested.[47]

Taylor resigned from the Senate November 15, 1794.[48] He had contemplated that action after the winter session of 1793, having written to Madison at that time that his hairs were already "becoming white in the service".[49] Before he resigned, he had become disgusted with the proceedings of the majority in Congress. Besides, he was in ill health, and there was illness in his family.[50] After Taylor had decided to resign, he deter-

---

47 This paper was originally in the Madison papers, but was published by Gaillard Hunt in 1905, under the title, "Taylor's Memorandum of a Conversation with King and Ellsworth," May 11, 1794. The pamphlet is in the Library of Congress.

48 Journal of House of Delegates, Nov. 15, 1794. Communication to that effect received that day.

49 Taylor MSS., Taylor to Madison, June 20, 1793. In Branch Historical Papers, Vol. II, p. 254.

50 Taylor MSS., Taylor to Henry Tazewell, Oct. 7, 1794. In Tazewell Collection. Also Pendleton, Pamphlet, Sketch of Taylor.

mined to use all of his influence to have his close friend, Henry
Tazewell, succeed him, and especially to prevent Harry Lee
from winning the senatorship. All the Lee family, he thought,
was averse to republican principles.[51] Tazewell was successful.
The man who succeeded Taylor had had a distinguished career.
At twenty-three, he was in the Virginia Convention of 1776.
He studied law under his uncle, John Tazewell, and served
many years in the Virginia Legislature, after which he became
a member of the General Court, and of the Court of Appeals
in 1793. His physical qualities were said to have been superb,
his eye bright, his lashes long, his forehead high, while his
carriage "blended the freedom of the cavalier with the more
chastened demeanor of the scholar".[52]

To Tazewell, Taylor expressed his bitter opposition to the
Jay Treaty. While in the Senate, the latter had drawn up the
protest of the minority in opposition to Jay's appointment as
minister to England. This he had also published. Taylor
charged that the paper system dictated Jay's Treaty, that it was
meant to provoke a war with France, so that the debt might
be increased. The Treaty gave England commercial privileges, and also had a provision relative to prizes, which provisions seemed at variance with the French Alliance of 1778.
After the Treaty had been ratified (1795), the Republican
House of Representatives attempted to prevent its execution
by refusing appropriations to carry it into execution. Taylor
thought the House should have executed it "with groans and
execrations", on the ground that they could not constitutionally
refuse. Then this compulsory action could have been made the
basis of agitation for amendments to the Constitution, which
would check the whole Federalist system.[53]

Two more acts draw down the curtain on the part that Taylor played in this first drama of national politics. As a presi-

---

[51] Taylor MSS., Taylor to Henry Tazewell, March 24 and July 13, 1794. In Tazewell Collection. Also Pendleton, Pamphlet, *Sketch of Taylor*.
[52] Grigsby, *Virginia Convention of 1776*, pp. 79–82.
[53] Taylor MSS., Taylor to Tazewell, June 15, 1794, and April 13, 1796.

dential elector in 1796, he voted for Jefferson, and was compelled reluctantly to sacrifice Burr, who was a candidate for Vice-President,[54] and as a member of the Virginia Legislature, he refused to endorse Washington's Address, services and administration, until the resolutions of this nature were modified, and had in one place substituted "native state" for "country".[55]

---

[54] Taylor MSS., Taylor to Tazewell, Dec. 8, 1796.
[55] Journal of House of Delegates, Dec. 9, 1796.

CHAPTER V

IN THE LEGISLATURE AGAIN:
THE GREAT DEBATE ON THE NATURE
OF THE UNION

TAYLOR's second period of service in the Virginia Assembly was, in some ways, in marked contrast to his first. The older political leaders of the revolutionary period were either dead or too old for active political service. George Mason died in 1792,[1] Robert Carter Nicholas, of revolutionary fame, had passed the reins on to his son, Wilson Cary, and Patrick Henry was within the shadow of the grave, though he was once more elected to the House in 1799, the year of his death. A younger generation of the sons of the Old Dominion, composed of men such as William B. Giles, James Barbour and George Keith Taylor, was now coming into its own. Then, too, Taylor's active connection with Federal affairs during the early 1790's meant for him a wealth of experience and a pronounced prestige, which he would not otherwise have had. Indicative of this prestige is the fact that he was appointed, in 1797, to all the prominent committees of the House, Courts of Justice, Privileges and Elections, Propositions and Grievances, Religion and Claims.[2]

During these last years of the eighteenth century, Taylor was to be afforded an opportunity, in the Assembly, to show his attitude in regard to a matter which was a fundamental cause of sectionalism in Virginia for many years after 1776. The Constitution of that year held to the principle handed down from colonial times of requiring property qualification for the exercise of the franchise, and it also apportioned representation

[1] Grigsby, *Virginia Convention of 1776*, p. 201.
[2] Journal of House of Delegates, Dec. 8, 1797.

in the House of Delegates in terms of districts, and not population. The Convention that drew up the Constitution passed an ordinance apportioning the Senate, and there was no provision in the Constitution for future apportionments, nor was there any for amending that instrument.[3] Jefferson had favored the calling of a convention soon after 1776 to rectify the evils of the existing frame of government,[4] and in 1784 the House took cognizance of resolutions from the people of Augusta County, asking that that body take steps in the direction of altering the Constitution. The House rejected the resolution on the ground of "such a measure not being within the province of the House of Delegates to assume; but on the contrary, it is the express duty of the representatives of the people at all times, and on all occasions, to preserve the same inviolable, until a majority of all the free people shall direct a reform thereof".[5] The vote is not recorded, but Taylor voted in favor of a rejected amendment to strike out that part of the resolution which declared the House had no such power.

From Patrick and Henry, and the western counties generally, petitions came in great numbers after 1790, praying that a convention be called to remedy an inequitable system, whereby the smaller slave counties of the East had as much representation as the larger and more populous counties of the West.[6] This agitation resulted in the House approving, in 1796, a resolution recommending to the people to instruct the next Legislature to call a convention for revising the Constitution, if it deemed such a step wise. But it did not deem such a step wise, as shown by its rejection of a motion, early in 1798, providing for the calling of said convention.[7] Taylor not only voted in

---

[3] Chandler, *Representation in Virginia,* pp. 18 and 19. In Johns Hopkins University Studies, Vol. XIV.

[4] *Ibid.,* p. 19.

[5] Journal of House, June 21, 1784.

[6] Chandler, *Representation in Virginia,* p. 22.

[7] Journal of House of Delegates, Nov. 28, 1796, and Jan. 9, 1798. Vote in first case was 86 to 56, in second 64 to 84.

favor of both resolutions, but shortly thereafter declared that it was both an unequal and an absurd system, under which a county that had few inhabitants sent the same number of Delegates to the Assembly as the most populous one in the State.[8]

But matters of more ominous import than the reform of Virginia's political system were to concern the members of her General Assembly during the last years of the eighteenth century. The Pro-French and Pro-British attitudes of the American people of that day had received by 1798 added emphasis as the result of our critical relations with France after 1795. The youthful Monroe, ardent in his French sympathies, had, as American minister to France, assured that country that the negotiations of John Jay with England would result in nothing inimical to France. But the Jay Treaty did contain clauses at variance, so France thought, with the Alliance of 1778, and naturally she felt resentment, especially after Monroe's assurances. The latter was recalled on the ground that he had exceeded his instructions, and C. C. Pinckney was sent in his place. Being a Federalist, he was received in a most unwelcome fashion, and left France. Reënforced soon after by John Marshall and Elbridge Gerry, Pinckney returned, but money was demanded of the three by French representatives as a condition prerequisite to treating with them, with the result that our ministerial relations with France were suspended for a time.

Under these conditions, Congress passed the Alien and Sedition Laws. There were two Alien Acts. One provided that the President might order from the country any alien whom he deemed dangerous to the peace and safety of the country, or imprison him, if he did not obey. This act was to last two years. The other Alien Act gave the President wide powers over subjects of any country with which the United States was at war. The Sedition Act declared that unlawful conspiracy and the publication of "any false, scandalous, and malicious

---

[8] See *Richmond Examiner,* Dec. 10, 1799, quoting John Taylor in "Proceedings of Legislature."

writings" against the Government, President, or Congress, with
the attempt to defame them or bring them into disrepute,
would be crimes punishable by the Federal courts. It is obvious
that these acts were the outgrowth of foreign relations, that
they were designed to curb French and other aliens of liberal
tendencies in the United States, yet their chief interest, as far
as this biography is concerned and as far as American history
after that time is concerned, consists in the fact that they gave
rise to a great debate in the Virginia Legislature on the nature
of the Union.

There were still several other factors which prepared the way
for this debate. Following the reception of the three ministers
we had sent to France, we actually came to a state of unofficial
war with that country. Between March 27 and July 16, 1798,
twenty acts were passed for strengthening the national defence.
President Adams had removed the restrictions on the arming
of merchant vessels. They could now defend themselves, and
could take French vessels which interfered with our commerce.[9] The result of this preparation was that the first direct
tax since the Constitution went into effect was laid in 1798. It
was imposed upon lands, houses and slaves, each of the latter
being taxed fifty cents.[10] Coupled with increased taxation was
a decline in tobacco culture, due to duties in England, and
wearing out of the soil at home.[11]

Taylor had been active in his opposition to the policies of the
Adams administration from its beginning. Less than four
months after Adams' inauguration, he accused the latter of trying to appropriate to himself Washington's popularity. He
deplored the lack of energy on the part of the Republicans,
and felt that they aided monarchy and aristocracy in many
ways, citing as examples a book published by Gallatin, excus-
ing, in part, the Hamilton policies, and the approbation by

---

9 Bassett, *The Federalist System*, p. 237.
10 *Manual of Constitution of United States*, Andrews, p. 80.
11 Bassett, *Federalist System*, p. 191.

Gallatin and Madison of the laudatory address on the part of
the House of Representatives to George Washington. The Jefferson followers, he thought, should boldly proclaim that the
threatened war with France was due to the fact that our monarchy hated republican France and was attached to the monarchy of England. He predicted that the "Eastern Generals
of the monarchic order" would favor a land tax as a means of
providing for defense. And "should we get embroiled with
France, the simple question for the states to determine, will be,
whether it will be better to submit to an immovable fixation
of our monarchy for the sake of the Union: or to break the
Union for the sake of destroying our monarchy. In the first
case, the Union will exist, but upon principles which will op-
press human nature—in the other a renovation of it may take
place upon principles which may generate the public good." [12]

In December of this same year (1797), Taylor played an active part in the debate in the Virginia Legislature over petitions
relative to freedom of speech between Representatives and constituents. Some of the Representatives in Congress had sent
circular letters to their constituents criticizing the Government.
In May, a Federal court held at Richmond had received a pre-
sentment from a grand jury, which represents "as a real evil,
the circular letters of several members of the late Congress, and
particularly letters with the signature of Samuel J. Cabell, en-
deavoring at a time of real public danger, to disseminate un-
founded calumnies against the happy government of the United
States, and thereby to separate the people therefrom, and to
increase or produce a foreign influence, ruinous to the peace,
happiness and independence of the United States". Cabell
was from the Albemarle district in Virginia, and the petitions
protesting against the grand jury action were from the counties in this district. The Federals in the Legislature contended

---

12 Taylor MSS., Taylor to Henry Tazewell, June 13, 1797. It would seem from
the latter part of this letter that Taylor was pondering the question as to whether
temporary disunion might not mean reunion on sounder terms. This letter is in
Tazewell collection.

that the matter should be left to the judgment of Congress, but the Republicans, led by Taylor, passed resolutions defending freedom of speech between Representatives and constituents, asserting that the grand jury action was an infringement of the principle of separation of powers between the legislative and judicial departments, which separation was provided for in both the Federal and State Constitutions, and maintaining that the safety of the State and the rights of the people were under the guardianship of the Legislature.[13]

The hurried preparations for war with France, the bitter criticism of those who criticized the Federal Government, and the impending prospect of the passage of the Alien and Sedition Acts, led to a correspondence, in the early summer of 1798, between Jefferson, then Vice-President, and Taylor as to the course which it would be wise for Virginia to follow. Taylor wrote a letter to New, a Congressman from Virginia, in which he is quoted by Jefferson in the following words: "Mr. New showed me your letter on the subject of the patents, which gave me an opportunity of observing what you said as to the effect with you of public proceedings, and that it was not unwise now to estimate the separate mass of Virginia and North Carolina, with a view to their separate existence."[14] It was claimed later, however, that Taylor did not use the term "unwise", but "unusual".[15]

But whatever the term used, Jefferson's letter indicates his own views, and to what extent he was in accord with Taylor. "It is true that we are completely under the saddle of Massachusetts and Connecticut, and that they ride us very hard, cruelly insulting our feelings, as well as exhausting our strength

---

[13] Journal of the House of Delegates, Dec. 28, 1797. The vote was 92 to 53.

[14] Writing of Jefferson, P. L. Ford, Vol. VIII, pp. 263–266, June 1, 1798. Jefferson to Taylor.

[15] Southern Literary Messenger, Vol. IV, May 1838, p. 344. George Tucker, Jefferson's biographer, says that, as result of obscurity of the press-copy, from which the letter was printed, the word had to be deciphered by aid of adjoining words. Original letter, he concludes after examination and correspondence with G. J. Randolph and Mrs. W. P. Taylor, had "unusual" and not "unwise".

and subsistence." Their rule had been made possible by states
with a family feeling, by the cunning of Hamilton, and the
popularity of Washington. But he believed our situation not
a natural one, and that the public avowal of "sentiments hostile
to the leading principles of our Constitution", plus a land tax,
a stamp tax, and an increase of the public debt, would produce
political changes. He concluded that, "in every free and deliberative society, there must be parties, and violent discords,
and no Federal Government could exist, if one is to resort to a
scission of the Union, when the other has a temporary superiority. If we break the rule of Massachusetts and Connecticut,
and cut off New England, then there will be a Pennsylvania
and Virginia party characterized by intense feeling, or even if
we reduce the Union to Virginia and North Carolina, they
will end by breaking into their simple units. . . . If the game
runs against us at home, we must have patience till luck turns,
and then we shall have an opportunity of winning back the
principles we have lost. For this is a game where principles
are the stake." [16]

Taylor replied to the above letter during the actual period of
the passage of the Alien and Sedition Acts. That his views as
to resistance to the measures of the Federal Government were
more pronounced than Jefferson's is indicated by extracts from
his letter. "The party spirit among us is geographical or personal. If geographical, its superiority in either hemisphere, will
beget the insolence of tyranny and the misery of slavery. A
fluctuation of this superiority will enlist revenge as an auxiliary
passion, and annihilate the chance for human happiness.

"If in case of a scission of the Union party spirit would still
be natural, how can it be said that our present situation, the
characteristic of which is party spirit, is unnatural?"

But Taylor had little faith in party principles, and believed
that "a transference of this (present) ascendency to other indi-

---

[16] Writings of Jefferson, Jefferson to Taylor, June 1, 1798, Vol. VII, by P. L. Ford,
pp. 263–266.

viduals will change the tyrant, but not remove the evil. Did the British people ever gain by a change of ministry? Saturated are preferable to hungry flies. A southern aristocracy oppressing the northern states would be as detestable as a northern domineering over the southern states."

"And what is the proper time for opposing this ascendency? Shall it be suffered to run through its natural course? . . . Let England and all personal ascendencies reply. Let the ancient and modern system of villenage illustrate. Let them prove that such usurpation upon the rights of man are more assailable, the more they are matured."

The present measures, he thought ought to lead to an amendment to the Constitution. To check the evils in them he proposed an extension of the right of suffrage, and an abbreviation of the tenure of service. Rotation in office was another excellent remedy. But there should be a new mode of abrogating law, since a change of party or men might not preserve liberty. "The right of the state governments to expound the constitutions might possibly be made the basis of a movement towards its amendment. If this is insufficient, the people in state conventions are incontrovertibly the contracting parties, and possessing the infringing rights, may proceed by orderly steps to attain the objects." Some step was imperative, for "avarice and ambition, entrenched behind perpetual taxation, in a disciplined corps, have become the lords paramount of the creation". Taylor is somewhat vague in regard to the "new mode of abrogating law", but it appears that he wished some method more clearly stated in the Constitution than was there in regard to the checking of oppressive laws, for he says "constitutional paper vetos are nothing, compared with a solid check, so woven into the form of government, as to be incapable of a separation from it".[17]

The policies of the Federal Government constitute the central

---

[17] Taylor MSS., Taylor to Jefferson, June 25, 1798. In John P. Branch Historical Papers, Vol. II, p. 271.

theme of Taylor's correspondence with both Monroe and Tazewell in the spring and summer months of 1798. He informed
Monroe that a book the latter had written, defending his own
attitude in France, was selling so fast, that he, Taylor, had not
been able to secure a copy. He attributed Monroe's recall to
violent party politics, and was convinced that those in control
had laid the foundation of either despotism or civil war at the
expense of the Constitution.[18] The conditions then existing
were the outcome of a political principle which gained with
every new triumph, and war was a secondary matter, designed
to aid this principle.[19]

Once more he urged the Jefferson Republicans to increased
activity. He himself was taking steps to have republished, and
made accessible to the public, Tazewell's argument, which
showed the futility of a constitutional prohibition, if there were
no way of enforcing it. Now was the time to act. "If the republicans fail to lay hold of the approaching juncture, and to
root out that monstrous association, endeavored to be formed
between warring elements, in our constitution, I will bid adieu
to politics, and only endeavor to raise and eat my cabbages and
potatoes, 'whatever king shall reign'." [20]

By the fall of 1798, Jefferson expressed his complete agreement with Taylor as to the necessity for reform and better
security for civil liberty. But they did not see the existing circumstances from exactly the same point of view. Jefferson believed that "the X Y Z delusion, a disease of the imagination",
would soon pass over, "because the doctor, in the guise of a
tax gatherer, is on the way to cure it". The government could
not borrow in Europe, nor one-fourth of what it needed, in
America. Excessive taxation, he thought, would have its effect.
He did not believe that the Federal Government had the power

---

[18] Taylor MSS., Taylor to Monroe, March 27, 1798. John P. Branch Historical
Papers, Vol II, p. 268.
[19] Taylor MSS., Taylor to Henry Tazewell, May 26, 1798. In Tazewell manuscript collection.
[20] *Ibid.*, July 1, 1798.

to make paper money a legal tender, and advocated an amendment to the Constitution, taking from that government the power of borrowing. Such an amendment would reduce wars, and leave the state governments free to lend their credit in borrowing quotas. He would declare the Alien and Sedition Laws "to be against the constitution and merely void, and for addressing the other states to obtain similar declarations". Jury reform was advocated also. Instead of jurors being chosen by lot, select men should be elected, from whom the Federal judge should direct the juries to be taken. If the State Legislature passed such a law, it would force Congress to amend its own in regard to selecting juries, if necessary. This suggestion was the outgrowth of the grand jury action in regard to Cabell, mentioned above.[21]

Taylor, likewise, favored jury reform, but was apprehensive that Congress would stand in the way of such a program. His original idea, when the Assembly met late in December, was to declare the obnoxious laws (Alien and Sedition) unconstitutional and void, thus bring the state and general governments to issue, and then summon the people in convention as the only referee to decide the issue.[22]

Taylor's constituents in Caroline County, led by Edmund Pendleton, Jr., had taken firm ground against the objectionable laws in the summer of 1798. After the usual denunciation of the acts as unconstitutional, the resolutions declare that "symptoms of an alliance with a monarchy, our old foe, and a war with a republic, our old friend; and a cohabitation of tories, refugees and emigrant monarchists with the administration, as monstrous as notorious, are additional solutions of intention. They portend that the American Revolution is to be from monarchy to monarchy . . . Is such the spirit and intention of the Constitution of the United States? What then is to be done?

---

21 Writings of Jefferson, Vol. VII, pp. 309–312. Jefferson to Taylor, Nov. 26, 1798.
22 Taylor MSS., Taylor to Jefferson, 1798, (no specific date). In *Randolph-Macon Historical Papers*, Vol. II, p. 277.

Will the representatives of the people sit quietly, and await the blow, or will they act like men and maintain rights derived from God, and acknowledged by compact?" [23]   They further resolved to support the Legislature in such measures as it shall deem for the public good.

It was under the conditions described above, the country torn by rival sympathies for France and England; party politics at fever heat, partly because the idea of criticism of the party in control of the government was then looked upon by some as a species of disloyalty to country; a direct tax imposed to meet the expenses of the government; Taylor and Jefferson taking counsel together and organizing the Republican forces to resist, in some fashion at least, the supposed violations of the Constitution; it was under such conditions that Taylor, in December, 1798, introduced and opened the debate on the famous resolutions, known to posterity as the Virginia Resolutions.[24]

This debate, as we shall see, involved far more than simply the question as to whether the Alien and Sedition Acts were unconstitutional. It brought into play, in a broad way, the contrasting points of view as to the nature and character of the Constitution and the Union, especially as to the relation between the states and the Federal Government. The Resolutions propose to defend both State and National Constitutions against domestic and foreign aggression, declare a warm attachment to the Union of the states, and claim that it is the duty of the states to oppose every infraction of those principles which constitute the only basis of union. They declare that the Federal Government aims, by a forced construction of the Constitution, to enlarge its powers, to consolidate the states by degrees into one sovereignty, and ultimately to transform our republican system into an absolute or mixed monarchy. They denounce

---

[23] For resolutions, see *Virginia Gazette* and *Richmond Advertiser,* August 8, 1798

[24] Resolutions of Virginia and Kentucky, penned by Madison and Jefferson, in relation to the Alien and Sedition Laws; and Debates in the House of Delegates of Virginia, in December, 1798, on the same, Dec. 13, 1798, p. 3. Hereafter this will be referred to as "Debates".

the Alien and Sedition Laws as unconstitutional, and ask the assistance and coöperation of other states in maintaining the liberties of the states.[25] As originally drawn, the Resolutions stated that the states *alone* were parties to the compact, and that the objectionable acts were "null, void, and of no force or effect".[26] Thus most of the debate took place when the Resolutions were in extreme form.

Taylor opened the debate by stating that if alien friends had any rights, and they were infringed, then the Constitution was broken. He claimed that they did have the common law rights of life, liberty and property, and that the Constitution secured these to them, since it used in all places the term "persons", not "natives". Thus if their rights could be infringed, those of others could also. He regarded the Constitution as a deed of trust made by the people to the government, and the latter went beyond its powers when it deprived any *person* of trial by jury. He commented upon the words "counsel or advise" in the Sedition Act, saying that counsel or advice could be given only in spoken words, and that hence freedom of speech was violated. Licentiousness of speech could be interpreted by judicial construction to mean a difference of opinion. Since religion is a sentiment, Congress, then, could do the same thing with religion.[27]

The Sedition Law, he contended, meant that the government created public opinion through fear, yet "the first born of American rights was the free examination of public servants". The only way to check despotism was through the expression of discontent. Executive power was an enemy to republican principles, yet Congress bestowed upon the President powers not warranted by the Constitution. "A concentration of power in the hands of one individual tends to enslave others; a concentration in the hands of Congress tends to enslave the states.

---

[25] Debates, p. 174, *et sequitur*.
[26] Debates, pp. 164–167.
[27] Debates, pp. 4 to 6.

This oppression and concentration will bring revolution unless the states redress the balance." But the way to preserve the Union was to check these tendencies in the beginning.[28]

Following Taylor in the debate was his namesake, George Keith Taylor, of Prince George County, but, as far as the author could ascertain, not a relative of the former. A Federalist, brilliant, with keen powers of logic, and with that inimitable gift of language which was characteristic of so many political leaders of the old South, he stated in admirable form practically all the arguments that could be brought against the Resolutions. He asked the members to reflect whether, after the laws had been passed by both Houses of Congress, and had been approved by so many state legislatures, they, a part only of the American people, should pass on them. He claimed that the Resolutions encouraged open resistance, that they made it the duty of the people, if they thought the Alien and Sedition Laws unconstitutional, to defend themselves against them. In this, his first speech, he proposed to defend the constitutionality of the Alien Law.[29]

Quoting Vattel on the Law of Nations, he suggested that a nation may prohibit foreigners from coming in, hence it was a favor, not a right, for them to enter. Though entitled to protection while here, they might be sent away, if deemed dangerous. He spoke of the dangers from France, of the possibility of some of the sixteen zealous sovereign states sheltering hostile Frenchmen, when others sent them away, if the Federal Government were not given that power. Whether the amendment reserving powers to the states was in the Constitution or not, it would still follow that Congress had the powers expressly granted it, and such as were necessary and proper for carrying into execution its powers.[30]

The Alien Law, he argued, *necessarily* proceeded from the

---

28 Debates, pp. 6–8.
29 *Ibid.*, pp. 10–11, Dec. 14, 1798.
30 *Ibid.*, pp. 12–14.

following: the Preamble, which stresses domestic tranquility as one of the purposes in forming the Constitution. Among the enumeration of powers is the clause "To define and punish piracies and felonies committed on the high seas, and against the Law of Nations". For an alien to conspire against the peace of the nation, which permitted him a residence therein, he interpreted as an offense against the Law of Nations.

Then, too, the United States guaranteed to the several states protection against invasion. Protection was a prevention, a guarding against, and sending away aliens was a precautionary law, designed to protect the states. Since Congress could not prohibit the migration or importation of such persons as the states cared to admit before 1808, and hence states might admit aliens, he conceded that a permanent law of the character of the Alien Law then existing would be unconstitutional; but in time of war, or strongly anticipated war, it protected the states.[31]

He claimed that the Alien Law did not affect life, liberty and property, and that as for trial by jury, the Constitution secured rights to citizens; aliens were granted a favor, and were not parties to the compact.[32]

Replying to the argument that the Alien Act blended the three-fold division of governmental powers into one, the President, he claimed that this was necessary, since the sittings of Congress were not permanent, and hence it could not easily effect removal; since the courts transacted business publicly, and yet secrecy was necessary in removing aliens.[33]

Taking cognizance of J. Taylor's statement, that Congress had passed a law, and that a good one, to send away alien enemies, he wished to know if that were not implication from the power to declare war.[34]

He emphasized the fact that while both the Constitution of

---

[31] Debates, pp. 14–16.
[32] Ibid., p. 16.
[33] Ibid., p. 17.
[34] Ibid., p. 18.

the United States and of Virginia held trial by jury to be sacred,
yet in 1792 the Virginia Legislature passed a law which authorized the Governor "to apprehend, and secure, and compel to
depart out of the Commonwealth, all suspicious persons, etc.,
from whom the President of the United States should apprehend hostile designs against the said state".[35]

And, finally, he claimed that the Alien Law was particularly
calculated for the protection of the Southern States, because
French aliens had already attempted to incite the slaves to insurrection. Summoning then his oratorical powers to emotional
heights, he reminded his hearers that "In that common calamity (insurrection) the ranks of society will be confounded: the
ties of nature will be cut asunder: the inexorable and blood-
thirsty negro will be careless of the father's groans, the tears of
the mother, and the lamentations of the children".[36]

William Ruffin, of Brunswick County, replied to several of
the arguments of Taylor, of Prince George, but devoted most
of his speech to a discussion of the evils of broad construction.
Taking Taylor's admission that a permanent law would be unconstitutional, he reminded him that a temporary one might
be constantly renewed. Congress could legislate concerning
alien enemies, he said, for it could make peace and declare war;
but power over alien friends is among the powers reserved to
the states.[37]

The doctrine of broad construction and implication, in Ruffin's opinion, produced the war with England. The reason that
there were a specific delineation of the powers of Congress,
and a formation of state constitutions, was to avoid the evil of
implied powers. The "general welfare" he considered the aim,
to be promoted and effected in the specific ways enumerated
in the eighth section of the first article of the Constitution.[38]

[35] Debates, p. 19.
[36] Ibid., pp. 20–21.
[37] Ibid., p. 22.
[38] Ibid., pp. 22–23.

The third day of the debate, John Mercer, of Spottsylvania, delivered a forceful argument in behalf of state rights. The debate was alarming to him, for opposing gentlemen not only defended existing violations of the Constitution, but any infractions which might hereafter be committed.[39]

The states and the people delegated to the general government all the power it had, for they existed first. What they did not delegate is reserved to them completely, and the power over alien friends is not delegated, and "if the remaining rights are sovereign, the states whose sovereignty is invaded by any act of the general government, have it as fully in their power to defend and protect these, as they would have had to defend any of their rights if attacked by a foreign power, before the general government had a being".[40]

He contended that if the states could communicate together to amend the Constitution, so as to give away their rights, they could also communicate to defend those reserved to them. Force was not thought of by anyone; but the coöperation of several or all of the states might bring about a repeal of these laws. Then he justified his contention by quoting Hamilton in the *Federalist* to the effect that "The State Legislatures, who will always be not only vigilant, but suspicious and zealous guardians of the rights of the citizens against encroachments from the Federal Government, will constantly have their attention awake to the conduct of the national rulers, and will be ready enough, if anything improper appears, to sound the alarm to the people, and not only to be the voice, but if necessary, the arm of their discontent". (*Federalist,* Vol. I, p. 166.)[41] He also cited the ratification of the Constitution by the Virginia Convention, in which not only is every power reserved not delegated, but "no right of any denomination can be cancelled, abridged, restrained or modified by . . . any Department of the

---

[39] Debates, p. 24.
[40] *Ibid.,* p. 27.
[41] *Ibid.,* pp. 27–29.

United States, except in those instances in which power is given by the Constitution for those purposes".[42]

Mercer then summarized all the arguments against the Alien Act usually stated, stressing especially the infringements of it upon states rights in two ways; first, Congress assumed a power over aliens, which is reserved to the states, not being delegated; and second, in preventing the migration of such persons as the states chose to admit until 1808.[43]

James Barbour, of Orange County, destined for a distinguished public career, then a mere youth, made one of the most fluent speeches in the entire list of recorded debates. He was born in 1775, not more than twenty miles from the home of Jefferson. After private instruction in his home, he attended school for a brief time at the home of James Waddell, the "Blind Preacher". He was admitted to the bar at nineteen years of age, and was said to have been the youngest man in the House in 1798.[44]

Barbour vigorously denied that the Resolutions invited the people to insurrection and to arms. If he thought so, he would oppose them. "A resort to arms was the last appeal of an oppressed, an injured nation, and was never made but when public servants converted themselves by usurpation into masters, and destroyed rights once participated; and then, it was justifiable." [45]

He claimed that the states and the people formed the compact, that the states alone could alter it, that the Senators were responsible to the state legislatures, that the President was elected by electors who represent the state, and that, therefore, the argument that the states had nothing to do with the matter under discussion, was not sound.[46]

---

[42] Debates, p. 31.
[43] Ibid., pp. 34–36.
[44] Sketch of James Barbour in John P. Branch Historical Papers, by W. S. Lang, pp. 35–39. James Waddell, "the Blind Preacher", is said to have taught a number of prominent Virginians at his home in Orange County.
[45] Debates, p. 43.
[46] Ibid., pp. 43–44.

As to the clause giving Congress power to pass necessary laws for carrying delegated powers into effect, it created no new powers, but had reference to the powers already granted. The acceptance of the doctrine of implication would mean that "those great and inestimable rights which flow from Nature, and are the gift of Nature's God, will be assassinated by the rude and unfeeling hand of ferocious despotism".[47] Answering G. Taylor's argument that the power to pass laws relative to alien enemies was implied, he said that Congress had the express power to declare war, that as soon as war was declared, by the Law of Nations, alien enemies became prisoners of war, and Congress could say what was to be done with them.[48] And then, after a gloomy picture of all the departments of the government swallowed up in one, he exclaimed: "What, then, are the people to wait till the pressure of the evil principle is felt? No. As an elegant author expresses it, they augur misgovernment at a distance, and snuff the approach of tyranny in every tainted breeze. . . . By the adoption of the Resolutions you raise a rampart against the inroads of usurpation, and your names will be wafted down on the stream of time, crowned with laurels, and as they pass, will be hailed by a grateful posterity with plausive acclamations." [49]

The Republican orators had been numerous when, on the sixth day of the debate (Dec. 18, 1798), Archibald Magill, of the large Valley county of Frederick, rose to speak for the Federalists. In his opinion, the Assembly existed for the ordinary purposes of legislation, it had no judicial powers of the kind claimed, and only the Federal courts could declare whether the law was valid or not.[50]

Magill injected a new and highly controversial element into the debate when he claimed that the Common Law justified

---

47 *Debates*, pp. 47–50.
48 *Ibid.*, p. 52.
49 *Ibid*, pp. 63–64.
50 *Ibid.*, p. 65.

the Sedition Act. Everything that act forbade was an offense at common law, and it was clear and evident, he thought, that the common law was the basis of ours.[51] He strongly criticized that part of the Resolutions which declared that states "alone" are parties to the compact, and said that the language "null and void", used in the Virginia and Kentucky Resolutions, meant that those states were entering into a confederacy, which action was forbidden by the Constitution. The Frederick member then skillfully injected another controversial question into the debate by asking how the Legislature could speak for the people of the State, when two hundred, in some cases, had the same voice in that body as one thousand.[52]

The common law argument was immediately attacked by Delegate William Fouchee, of the city of Richmond. Add to this, he said, the arguments derived from implication and the "general welfare" clause, and there would be no reservations left to the states or the people.[53] He indignantly denied that the aim of the Resolutions was to dissolve the government.[54]

Edmund Brooke, of Prince William County, claimed that the Resolutions tended to produce resistance to the laws of the government. The right of petition, guaranteed by the Constitution, could, in his opinion, be resorted to by the people, if they felt laws were unconstitutional. The people of Virginia could be more effective in petitioning Congress, where every thirty thousand persons were represented, than they could in acting through the State Legislature, where, due to the great inequality in representation then existing, fifteen hundred or two thousand freeholders in a large county had two Representatives, and one hundred and fifty or two hundred in a small county had the same number.[55]

---

[51] Debates, pp. 68–69.
[52] Ibid., p. 71. This, of course, is a reference to the Virginia system of representation, based on districts, not population.
[53] Ibid, p. 72.
[54] Ibid., p. 73.
[55] Ibid, pp. 75–76.

He said further, that "when the people of that part of the country which he had the honor to represent, became so extremely degenerate, so lost to all regard for the great advantages and benefits resulting from a connection between the states under the Federal Constitution, as to give him instructions to vote for the adoption of resolutions, having so dangerous and alarming a tendency as those offered by the gentleman from Caroline, he should go in mourning for them, he should bid adieu to legislation, and seek an asylum in some other region of the globe, among a race of men who had more respect for peace and order, and who set a higher value upon the blessings of good government".[56]

William Daniel, Jr., of Cumberland County, answered the argument of the Federalists to the effect that the clause prohibiting Congress from barring, for twenty years, such importation or migration of persons as the states desired, meant simply slaves. The idea, expressed by Southerners at the time the Constitution was made, was to permit immigration also, so that their back lands might be more speedily settled. This clause allowed the states to admit aliens, no power was delegated to the general government to send them away, hence it was a power reserved to the states.[57]

Daniel felt that, if the Constitution meant what the opponents of the Resolutions said it did, the sage and patriotic men who formed it, puzzled themselves to no purpose in defining, enumerating and limiting powers; they might have done nothing but say there should be an Executive, Judicial and Legislative body; prescribe the mode in which the members of the several departments should be brought into office; and declare that "they should have the power to provide for the general welfare".[58] As to the pleading of the Common Law principle

---

[56] Debates, p. 77.
[57] Ibid, pp. 82–83.
[58] Ibid, p. 85.

in justification of the Sedition Act, he strongly denounced the idea that the Common Law was a part of the Constitution.[59]

The ruling principle of the Resolutions, that this was a compact of states, was false in the opinion of General Henry Lee, staunch Federalist of Westmoreland County. The Confederation, he thought, was such a compact, but the government under the Constitution was precisely the reverse, for its style was "We the people", and its power was derived from or based upon the people.[60]

As for aliens, a treaty was the only thing that could give them rights in this country, and as for the Sedition Act, since it was to prevent falsehood, it was a measure of preservation on the part of the government.[61] If these laws needed correction, the Federal judiciary, the people by elections, and the states by suggesting amendments, could supply it.[62]

For seven days, up to this point, John Taylor had heard wit matched against wit, had heard his Resolutions bitterly assailed, and as strongly defended. The unconstitutional character of the Alien and Sedition Acts had been so much emphasized that Taylor did not devote much of his time to demonstrating that fact in this, his second speech. But since gentlemen had taken their stand upon the broad principle "that every government inherently possesses the powers necessary for its own preservation", he proposed to apply this principle to the state government, because, if it is a sound principle, they are equally entitled to its application along with the general government.[63]

He contended strongly that a state had a right to contest the constitutionality of a law of Congress. The people and the states could only have intended that Congress should legislate

---

[59] Debates, pp. 94–95. The Federalists claimed that, if no *previous restraints* were placed on publications, freedom of press was not infringed. Daniel claimed that restraints *after* could just as effectively mould political opinion.

[60] *Ibid.*, p. 107.

[61] *Ibid.*, p. 109.

[62] *Ibid.*, p. 112.

[63] *Ibid.*, p. 117.

constitutionally, and the Constitution retains to the people and the states all powers not surrendered. But would the Constitution be so defective as to have established limitations and reservations, with no mode of making them effective? He thought not, and claimed that the states and Congress each had a check upon the other. This was through the amending process. By this two-thirds of Congress might call upon the states for an explanation of any such controversy as the one then raging, by way of an amendment; and thus correct an erroneous construction of its own acts by a minority of the states. But the case was stronger in favor of a check upon Congress on the part of the states, for Congress cannot alter or amend the Constitution without the concurrence of three-fourths of the states, and although the whole of Congress should disagree, that concurrence can check the encroachments of Congress.

Thus, the states, he held, do not hold their constitutional rights by the courtesy of Congress. Congress, in fact, was the creature of the states and of the people; but neither the states nor the people were the creatures of Congress. It would be absurd that the creature should exclusively construe the instrument of its own existence; and, therefore, this construction was reserved indiscriminately to one or the other of those powers, of which Congress was the joint work; namely, to the people, whenever two-thirds of the states forced Congress to call a convention, or to the states, whenever the operation should be carried on by three-fourths.[64]

Referring to the claim that the Federal judges should decide upon the constitutionality of laws, he claimed that neither Federal nor state judges had a superiority over the other, when a clashing of adjudication ensued; for such superiority in either would lead either to the destruction of state reserved powers or Federal delegated powers. This type of superiority would be more disastrous than that of Congress over the states or

---

[64] Debates, pp. 118–119.

vice versa, for legislative bodies were subject to popular influence, but judges could not be reached in that way.[65]

As to forcible resistance to the measures of Congress, it was not thought of, for "the Republicans have not fleets and armies; they appeal to public opinion for defense and support".[66] The coöperation of the other states was their aim, sufficient coöperation, if possible, to have Congress call a convention to amend the Constitution.

The Common Law doctrine, brought in defense of the Sedition Act, he assailed bitterly. There was hardly any species of oppression it would not justify. The Constitution did nowhere adopt the Common Law, or refer to it as a rule of construction. Since the state constitutions or laws had done so under various forms, the states must have considered its adoption necessary to give it force, and therefore never dreamed they were creating "a government which could at pleasure dip their hands into the inexhaustible treasures of the Common Law, and thence extract as much power as they please".[67]

Replying to the argument of the Federalists that states had nothing to do with Federal laws at all, he replied that, from the commencement of the Constitution to the ending, the sense of the people respecting it was through some representative State Assembly. The instrument itself recognized states as parties to the compact, reserved powers to the states, as well as to the people, and it is only by the action of state sovereignties that the government of the Union is kept in motion. Yet those (the states) who called the convention that made the Constitution, who ratified it, who execute it in many ways, were told, he said, that they must remain silent when their reserved rights were invaded.[68]

The mover of the Resolutions compared liberty to a country

---

[65] Debates, p. 120.
[66] *Ibid.,* p. 119.
[67] *Ibid.,* p. 121.
[68] *Ibid,* pp. 128–130.

to be defended, the Constitution was the fortress, and the people of the states, the garrison. If they surrender the key into their country (liberty) "the inevitable consequence must be a consolidation of these states into one great sovereignty, which will, from its vast extent, as inevitably settle with rapidity into a monarchy, and like all other great Empires, it must resort to those oppressions to support itself, which make the cup of life bitter to man".[69]

For a second time, George Keith Taylor followed John Taylor in the animated debate. He objected strongly to the statement that the "states alone" were parties to the compact. Since each state appointed delegates to the Philadelphia Convention for the purpose of proposing amendments to the Articles, when the delegates went beyond this, they didn't have the sanction of the states. He emphasized the expression "We the people", in the Constitution, and the fact that it was ratified by conventions in the states, rather than by legislatures.[70]

The Common Law, the unwritten law of nature and reason, "attaches itself to every government which the people may establish. It existed in Great Britain when our ancestors emigrated from that country, and it followed them to this. It prevailed in every state throughout the Union, before their separation from the British Empire, and it regulates the whole American people now." [71]

The action of Virginia, in asking other states for coöperation, he claimed, meant agreements or compacts between states, though forbidden by the Constitution. As for John Taylor's suggested Convention, it would breed only distrust between the North and the South.[72]

Another leader, of prominence later in Federal councils, who participated in this debate, was William B. Giles. Giles attacked the Funding System and the Bank, his claim being that

69 Debates, p. 121.
70 Ibid., pp. 131–135.
71 Ibid., p. 145.
72 Ibid., pp. 155–156.

the Sedition Law was designed to suppress the Republicans, that those financial expedients might be kept intact. He was willing to strike out the word "alone" in regard to the states in the making of the compact.[73]

Due perhaps, in part, to the able speech of G. K. Taylor, J. Taylor at this point moved to strike out "alone", where it was stated in the Resolutions that the states alone were parties to the compact, and also to strike out that part of them declaring the Alien and Sedition Laws null and void.[74]

Like Giles, Wilson Cary Nicholas, son of Robert Carter Nicholas, of Revolutionary fame, attacked the Bank and Assumption Laws. He said the Resolutions were partly inspired by those unconstitutional Acts. Moreover, he said, there was an utter neglect of the militia. It was popular with the government to raise standing armies, to authorize the President to employ any number of volunteers, he thought proper, so that the President could appoint officers for them. Militia was not encouraged, because state governments appointed the officers.[75]

General Lee proposed to strike out the clause saying that the Federal Government aimed at establishing a monarchy, and he, Giles, Nicholas and Samuel Tyler entered into a warm debate over the proposition.[76] The final vote on the Resolutions was 100 to 63 in the House, and 14 to 3 in the Senate.[77]

The jury reform idea conceived by Jefferson and Taylor, whereby grand jurors would be selected from a select list rather than at random, was definitely abandoned after the passing of the Resolutions. Taylor frankly expressed the fear that the proposal would be defeated in the Assembly, in which case the Republicans would have been robbed of the victory they had won.[78]

---

[73] Debates, pp. 159–160.
[74] Ibid., pp. 164–167. As finally adopted, these parts were omitted.
[75] Ibid., pp. 168–169.
[76] Ibid., pp. 167–172.
[77] Ibid., pp. 179–180.
[78] Taylor correspondence, Taylor to Jefferson, Feb. 15, 1799. In Randolph-Macon Historical Papers, Vol. II, p. 278.

It seems to have been somewhat habitual on the part of those opposed to the Resolutions of 1798, strongly to imply, if not actually to say, in later years, that the State of Virginia meant to use force at that time.[79] Yet throughout the debate, the writer has been unable to find statements which implied such. On the other hand, John Taylor, James Barbour and John Mercer, simply to mention some, were prominent Republicans who utterly disclaimed the idea of force. In regard to military preparations, the better organization of the militia, and the creation of an armory, there is evidence to show that these preparations were under way before the Alien and Sedition Laws were considered or passed.[80]

The Virginia Legislature having asked the concurrence of other states in respect to the sentiments expressed in the Resolutions, the Federalist states replied in 1799 in a spirit antagonistic to such sentiments. Mr. Madison had consented to return to the Assembly in that year, and, upon the meeting of that body, drew up a defense of the Resolutions. This is known as Madison's Report.

The Report refers to the Bank law and the carriage tax as examples of "forced construction of the Constitution", in addition to the Alien and Sedition laws.[81] It claims that it is not necessary to say how far "interposition" might go, because the Resolutions do not require that that question be discussed.[82]

It refers to the claim of the Resolutions that indications have appeared of a design to expound certain general phrases so as

---

[79] See Von Holst, *Constitutional and Political History of the United States,* Vol. I, pp. 156–158. He quotes Hamilton to that effect at the time, Randolph later, and refers to the establishment of an armory at Richmond. William Wirt Henry in his *Life of Patrick Henry,* Vol. II, p. 589, says: "The party in Virginia certainly looked to violent opposition, and began to make preparations for it in building, an armory, as was confessed by John Randolph afterward." Patrick Henry opposed the Resolutions.

[80] See Article in *American Historical Review,* Jan., 1931, by P. G. Davidson on "Alien and Sedition Laws".

[81] Virginia Report of 1799–1800, Debate and Proceedings thereon, etc., by J. W. Randolph, pp. 197–198. The carriage tax controversy is explained in Chapter IV.

[82] Report of 1799–1800, p. 193.

to destroy the particular enumeration limiting and explaining their meaning, and gives as examples Hamilton's report on Manufactures in 1791, in which he claims the national legislature can use its discretion as to what promotes the general welfare, and the report of a committee of Congress in 1797, recommending the formation of a society at Washington to promote agriculture.[83] It claims that the growth of Federal powers does tend towards monarchy, for laws would be more numerous, and hence more deficient, these deficiencies would lead to an enlargement of Executive power, and thus enable him to confer more offices, honors and emoluments.[84]

Seven pages of the Report are devoted to a denunciation of the Common Law argument, for "As this law relates to every subject of legislation, and would be paramount to the Constitution and laws of the states, the admission of it would overwhelm the residuary sovereignty of the states, and by one constructive operation, new-model the whole political fabric of the country".[85]

The final act of this legislative drama concerning the Alien and Sedition Acts, consisted in instructions early in 1800 by the Legislature to the Senators, Stephen T. Mason and W. C. Nicholas, to work for the repeal of these laws, for the reduction of taxes, for the modification of commercial non-intercourse with France, and against any law based on the principle that the Common Law was in force. The instructions condemned the neglect of the militia, and the raising of a standing army. The reason, they stated, that the tobacco growers were getting one-third the normal price for their tobacco, was because non-intercourse with France had cost them their best market. This policy, it was said, had also reduced revenues from imports. Thus at the very time when, due to the fall in price of their

---

[83] Report of 1799–1800, pp. 198–201.
[84] *Ibid.*, pp. 201–202.
[85] *Ibid.*, pp. 211–217. This Report was adopted by a vote of 100 to 60, and 15 to 6, in House and Senate, respectively.

staple product, they were less able to pay, military preparations were increasing their taxes.[86]

Taylor of course favored the Report and the instructions. It is in accord especially with the spirit of the latter that he wrote Jefferson in February: "I hope I have mistaken our national character, but it appears to unfold itself by an insensibility to the efforts both of tyranny and despotism, exhibiting in the background sordid avarice and skulking fear. A tax-gatherer, you think, is the doctor which will cure the disease; but as this doctor is now under the protection of an army and navy, he may safely administer what doses he pleases".[87]

---

[86] The Report contains other documents, among them the instructions, pp. 240–242. Vote on the instructions was 102 to 49, pp. 247–248.

[87] Taylor MSS., Taylor to Jefferson, Feb. 15, 1799. In John P. Branch Historical Papers, Vol. II, p. 278.

Chapter VI

A JEFFERSONIAN LEADER

In his correspondence with Taylor during the year the Alien and Sedition Laws were passed, Jefferson expressed the conviction that the forthcoming election might prove to be one method of disposing of the obnoxious laws.[1] Taylor himself, in a confidential letter to his close friend, Henry Tazewell, revealed the policy which the Republicans expected to follow after the Resolutions were passed, provided circumstances then seemed to warrant it. They planned to compile the Declaration of Independence, the State Bill of Rights, the debates over the adoption of the Constitution, the Alien and Sedition Laws, the Kentucky and Virginia Resolutions, the laws relative to *habeas corpus* proceedings, and an address to the people, and to distribute twenty thousand pamphlets containing this material.[2]

The Federalists were by no means inactive during the political struggles in the State in 1798–99. The aged Henry came forth from his retirement as an opponent of the Taylor-Jefferson program, stood for the Legislature in Charlotte County, and was elected.[3] Leven Powell, who is said to have founded the Federal party in the large county of Loudoun, and who was elected to Congress in 1798, bitterly denounced Taylor for dividing the people during our critical relations with France, and felt that it was "a melancholy consideration that Virginia should pursue with such fury her present policy". He was

---

[1] Writings of Jefferson. See letters to Taylor in Vol. VII, of Ford's edition, June 1 and Nov. 26, 1798.

[2] Taylor MSS., Taylor to Tazewell, Dec. 14, 1798. In Tazewell manuscript collection.

[3] Henry, *Life of Patrick Henry*, Vol. II, p. 589.

apprehensive that the Virginia Assembly would pass a law to elect members of Congress by a general ticket.[4]

The Federalists won more than one-third of the congressional seats in the State in 1799. Among the representatives of this political faith were John Marshall and General Henry Lee. So bitter were party politics that Marshall is said to have been insulted in a theatre in the normally quiet little town of Fredericksburg.[5]

Taylor sounded a note of despair in the pre-presidential election year. He apparently felt that the Virginia Resolutions had not gone far enough, for he expressed the belief that the Republican cause was daily declining "on account of its fashionable maxim of moderation in its efforts, and waiting as it is called for the public mind". He would proceed in a bolder and more direct fashion, for "unless the people are instructed and combined by something that they can understand, nothing can save us from an Anglo-Monarchic-aristocratic-military government, but one of those unaccountable movements of the people inspired by some sudden fervor, which are rare in other countries, and would be almost miraculous in this, under its present circumstances".[6]

Probably it was the silence of the other Republican legislatures in various states in response to the request for coöperation as regards the Alien and Sedition Acts, that led Taylor to write Jefferson in October that he gave "up all for lost".[7] Neverthe-

---

4 Powell correspondence, Leven Powell to Major Burr Powell, Dec. 14, 1798, and Dec. 25, 1799. Leven Powell was born in Prince William County in 1737, was named by Washington a Lieutenant-Colonel of Sixteenth Regiment of Virginia Continentals in Jan., 1777, sat in Virginia Convention of 1788, favored the Constitution, and was the only elector in Virginia to vote for Adams over Jefferson in 1796. This sketch is in Branch Historical Papers of Randolph-Macon College, Vol. I, pp. 22–23, letters cited, pp. 233–237.

5 Randall, *Life of Jefferson*, Vol. II, pp. 492–495. See also Address by J. A. C. Chandler to William and Mary Alumni, 1905.

6 Taylor MSS., Taylor to Creed Taylor, April 10, 1799. Letter in possession of Judge Daniel Grinnan of Richmond. Creed Taylor was a member of the House.

7 *Ibid.*, Taylor to Jefferson, Oct. 14, 1799. In Branch Historical Papers of Randolph-Macon College, Vol. II, p. 283.

less, these two leaders had been planning to have the "right" man replace Henry Tazewell, deceased, in the United States Senate, when the Legislature should meet later in the year (1799), and Taylor was to play a prominent part in that body not only in choosing the Senator but in the selection of a Governor as well.[8] Massmeetings held during the year tended to aid the election program planned for the Assembly meeting in December. At these, toasts were drunk to the fundamental principles of the Constitution, to the militia as the bulwark of the nation and the safety of the people, and to peace with all nations, but war, if we must have war at all, with a monarchy, and not with a republic.[9]

When the Legislature met, Taylor once more found himself opposed by his rival of the year before, George Keith Taylor, who was ably seconded by Richard Bland Lee. G. Taylor, in renominating John Stewart, who had been Clerk of the House for four years, strongly praised the latter's federalism. John Taylor replied that Stewart had recently made the Virginia Assembly smart under the lash of his pen, in the *Virginia Federalist;* and that if the Assembly elected him, the public would think them so frightened by his vitriolic assaults that they bought his silence by the gift of office.[10]

It was Taylor who placed in nomination Wilson Carey Nicholas, who became the successor to Tazewell in the Senate. The bitterest fight centered around the candidacy of Monroe for the governorship. The Federalists, G. Taylor and Richard Bland Lee, being foremost, claimed that his election would be a reflection upon the Executive who recalled him when he was American minister to France, and that the political motives of

---

[8] Writings of Jefferson, Vol. VII, pp. 322–323, Jefferson to Taylor, Jan. 24, 1799. Taylor MSS., Taylor to Jefferson, Feb. 15, 1799. In Branch Historical Papers, of Randolph-Macon College, Vol. II, p. 278.

[9] *Richmond Examiner,* Dec. 6, 1799.

[10] See "Proceedings of Assembly" in *Richmond Examiner,* Dec. 3, 1799. Stewart was defeated 90 to 49.

his conduct as minister should be investigated. J. Taylor and Madison claimed that there was nothing to investigate, that Monroe's conduct spoke for itself, and that the book he had written in defense of his attitude made his position even clearer.[11]

The signal service of Taylor in aiding in the election of Jefferson in 1800 consisted in the preparation, in the Virginia Legislature, in conjunction with Madison and others, of an act for a different method of choosing electors.[12] Heretofore the electors had been chosen by districts, but under this act they were to be placed upon a statewide ticket. The stated purpose of the act was to prevent a choice for President being made contrary possibly to the will of the United States as well as to the will of the State. According to other provisions of the act, the Governor was to appoint three commissioners each presidential year to conduct elections in each county. Two days were allowed for voting. The voter was to write his name on one side of the ballot, and that of the twenty-one electors on the other.[13]

Once more warring factions clashed, and clashed sharply, for the Federalists instantly perceived that however logical arguments in its favor, this was a shrewd political move, which precluded the possibility of any Federalist electors from Virginia. However, the Federalists tried to prevent the passage of the act, not so much by denouncing the political motive apparent, but by stressing its impracticability. The people had been accustomed to vote by districts, by the *viva voce* method, and under the direction of sheriffs. Thus G. Taylor, R. B. Lee and Robert B. Taylor contended that there should not be so many alterations until the sentiments of the people were known, and they attempted to have the matter deferred until the next meeting

---

11 See "Proceedings of Assembly" in *Richmond Examiner*, Dec. 6, 1799. Monroe won by a vote of 101 to 66.

12 Journal of House of Delegates, Jan. 13, 1800.

13 Hening, *Statutes at Large*, Vol. II, pp. 197–200.

of the General Assembly.[14]   John Taylor and Madison fought bitterly the motion to defer, with the result that by the very close vote of 78 to 73, the act was passed.

The electoral act was the subject of bitter attack during the presidential campaign.   In practice, said the Federalists, "the unprincipled mode of election will wholly silence, or at least render ineffectual, the sentiments and wishes of a respectable portion of the people of Virginia".[15]   Jefferson's religious views, and the tendencies to civil strife, inherent in Virginia's attitude towards the general government, were other objects of attack during the presidential campaign.[16]

The Jeffersonian leaders frankly avowed that the purpose of the general ticket was to help elect Jefferson, and they defended it on the ground that the will of the whole State, with due regard for its proportional power in the Union, was the fundamental principle sought in the election of a President.[17]   That Hamilton's funding system was an instrument for increasing national debt, rather than for paying it; that a standing army not only endangered liberty, but increased taxation; that the attempt to apply Common Law principles in the United States was an attempt to curb free elections, and to mold political thought; that John Adams believed that the masses were destined by the author of nature to be *hewers of wood and drawers*

---

[14] Journal of the House of Delegates, Jan. 17, 1800.   Robert B. Taylor was a brilliant young Federalist who had been elected to the House from Norfolk in 1799. When a mere youth he attended the courts and criticized lawyer's arguments, and was later expelled from William and Mary College for fighting a duel with John Randolph.   He opposed Madison's Report, claiming that the representation of the state in Congress was on a more democratic basis than that of the state in the Assembly.   For this sketch see Branch Historical Papers, Vol. III, pp. 145–150.

[15] Powell correspondence, Thomas Evans to Colonel Leven Powell, Oct. 30, 1800. In Branch Historical Papers, Vol. I, pp. 54–56.   The *Virginia Federalist* also assailed the "unprincipled" character of the act.   Quoted in *Richmond Examiner,* March 25, 1800.

[16] See *Virginia Argus,* Sept. 9, 1800.   Also Powell Correspondence, Evans to Powell, Oct. 30. 1800, and Leven Powell to Burr Lowell, March 26, 1800.   In Branch Historical Papers, Vol. I.

[17] "Address of Republican Committee of General Correspondence", in *Richmond Examiner,* March 25, 1800.

of water; this was the character of the arguments to which the Republicans appealed.[18]

Taylor was a veritable storm center during the campaign. The opposition presses in the State called him an anarchist, a friend to France, an enemy to America, and an office-seeker.[19] The situation in respect to him was made more tense by his connection with the trial of James Thompson Callender, editor of the *Richmond Examiner,* for seditious libel. This trial was in the circuit court at Richmond. Judge Chase was presiding. George Hay, an able member of the Virginia Bar, and son-in-law of James Monroe, was defending Callender. The latter had written *The Prospect Before Us,* in which he bitterly denounced the Alien and Sedition Laws, and those responsible for them. John Taylor appeared as a witness for the defense, to prove the statements in the book mentioned. Chase would not allow him to testify, unless the questions to be asked were first examined and approved by the court. A long argument followed, and Chase had his way. Callender was convicted, sentenced to nine months in prison, fined $200, and bound over to good behavior for two years.[20] He later became a bitter critic of Jefferson himself.[21]

So bitter were the attacks upon Taylor by the *Virginia Federalist,* under the control of John Stewart, whom he had aided in defeating for Clerk of the House, that the *Richmond Examiner* not only denounced the attacks as low and scurrilous, but defended Taylor in the following language: "As for Mr. John Taylor, we make no scruple of asserting, from an acquaintance with his writings, that he is one of the ablest political disputants either in the new world, or in the old one. His private life is as irreproachable, and useful, as his literary publications are instructive and admirable. As an author, he

---

[18] See *Richmond Examiner,* Dec. 13, 1799, Jan. 7, 17, and Oct. 31, 1800. Also *Virginia Argus,* August 29, Sept. 2 and 5, 1800.
[19] Pendleton, Pamphlet, *Sketch of Taylor.*
[20] *Decisive Battles of the Law,* by Frederick Trevor Hill, pp. 3 and 20–26.
[21] *Ibid.,* p. 26.

ranks with Madison, Jefferson, George Hay and Governor Monroe; and they form altogether a quintumvirate, to whom we believe that no single state in the Union can produce anything like a rivalship. In attacking Mr. Taylor, Billy (Stewart) reminds us of the cur barking at the moon." [22]

Taylor and Jefferson had both made efforts to get Edmund Pendleton to write essays in regard to the Alien and Sedition Laws, but without success.[23] However, he became a Jefferson Elector in 1800,[24] and soon after the election of that year, he proposed a number of amendments to the Constitution under the title "The Danger not Over". The Federalists, he thought, had created useless offices, had unnecessarily increased the debt of the nation, and had manifested too decided a tendency to engage in foreign wars. Under Jefferson, the government was in excellent hands, but it might not always remain so. Peace should be our aim, so if the Executive could indirectly formulate a treaty that would bring war, or the judiciary could determine that a state of war existed, then the Constitution was defective and should be remedied. Union, likewise, was our aim and the basis of our prosperity, but Pendleton believed that it could be preserved only by confining the activities of the general government, with precision, to the exercise of the powers clearly required by the general interest, or foreign affairs. This belief was prompted by the conviction that the states were so different in their character and interests, as never to consent to a consolidated government with great powers. If either manufactures or agriculture needed encouragement, this should be effected by state action, in terms of local interests, and not by the general government through protection and bounties.

The following amendments, practically all designed to keep precisely distinct the powers of the Federal and the state govern-

---

[22] *Richmond Examiner*, March 21, 1800 for quotation, March 26 also for controversy with Stewart.

[23] Taylor MSS., Taylor to Jefferson, Feb. 15, 1799. In Branch Historical Papers, Vol. II, p. 278.

[24] *Richmond Examiner*, March 18, 1800.

ments, and the powers of the Federal departments, and probably the product of the joint thought of Taylor, Jefferson and Pendleton, were suggested by the latter:

The President should be ineligible for the succeeding term. The legislature (Congress) should appoint the judges and stationary foreign ministers; making the stipends of the latter no longer discretionary in the President.

The Senate should be deprived of all executive power; the terms of office should be shortened, or the members subjected to removal by their constituents.

The members of Congress and the judges, while in office, and for a limited time thereafter, should be rendered incapable of taking any office whatsoever (except President or Vice-President); and judges should be subjected to removal by concurring vote of both houses of Congress.

The abuse of *public credit* should be checked by amendment.

The fair mode of impaneling juries should be instituted.

No treaty with a foreign nation, so far as it related to peace or war, the expenditure of public money, or to commercial regulations, should be law until ratified by Congress.

Prohibited powers should be more explicitly defined, so as to defy the wiles of construction.

There should be made out with more precision, the distinct powers of the general and state governments.

Pendleton concludes with this sentiment: "Men advanced to power are more inclined to destroy liberty than to defend it; if there is a continual effort for its destruction, it should be met by corresponding efforts for its preservation." [25]

The advent of Jefferson to the presidency meant that the Republicans were no longer to play the role of negative critics, but that they must evolve policies of their own. The President's message, emphasizing peace, economy, dependence upon the militia rather than upon a standing army, and a government

---

[25] See above discussion and proposals in *Richmond Examiner*, Oct. 20, 1801.

very limited in its activities, received warm praise from Taylor. However, he expressed the hope that some suggested amendments (probably Pendleton's) would be passed, so that the nature of our government would not depend upon the President, but upon the principles of the Constitution.[26]

Before Taylor entered the Senate again, one of the matters to which the Republican Congress turned its attention was the repeal of the Judiciary Act of 1801, an eleventh hour enactment of the Federalists. This act had created five new district courts in addition to those created in 1789, had doubled the number of circuit courts then created, and had assigned to the latter courts special judges in place of the Supreme Court and district judges who had performed these functions. Whatever the motives of the Federalists in creating the new courts, the Republicans claimed that they meant increased patronage and useless expense, and hence proposed to abolish them. Moreover, they probably felt that an expansion of the Federal Judiciary represented an increased menace to the State courts.

The matter upon which the debate over repeal turned, in large part, was not practicability, however, but constitutionality. John Breckenridge of Kentucky, who was leading the fight for repeal in the Senate, wrote Taylor, asking the latter's views on the constitutionality of repeal. To understand Taylor's reply, it is necessary first to state the arguments of the Federalists. Senator J. Mason of Massachusetts claimed that judges had a life tenure, that Congress had no authority to abolish their offices, once created, and that, therefore, even if the repeal act passed, the judges were still entitled to compensation, because the act was unconstitutional. He relied upon the clause in the Constitution which says: "The judges, both of the Supreme and inferior courts, shall hold their offices during good behavior, and shall, at stated times, receive for their services, a compensation, which shall not be diminished during their con-

---

[26] Taylor MSS., Taylor to John Breckinridge, Dec. 22, 1801. In Branch Historical Papers, Vol. II, p. 284.

tinuance in office." [27]   Gouverneur Morris of New York emphasized the word "may" in regard to establishing courts, but
"shall" in regard to judges holding office during good behavior.[28] Therefore there was no discretion in the second case.

Taylor supposes in his reply to Breckenridge that Congress
and a President should erect five times as many courts and
judges as were provided under the last act, and then wishes
to know if there would be any remedy. There were, he said,
two questions concerned in repeal of the act; first, whether the
office thus established was to continue, and second, whether
the officer was to continue, after the office was abolished.

In regard to the first question, he pointed out that the constitutional authority for creation of courts was in the clause
"Congress may from time to time ordain and establish inferior
courts". The legislative construction put upon that clause when
the Federalists passed the act was that Congress might *abolish*
as well as create judicial offices; for the act did expressly abolish
the then existing inferior courts, for the purpose of making
way for the ones created.[29] "It is probable", he says, "that this
construction is correct, but is equally pertinent to our object
whether it is or not. If it is, then the present inferior courts
may be abolished, as constitutionally as the last; if it is not,
then the law for abolishing the former courts, and establishing
the present, was unconstitutional, and being so, is undoubtedly
repealable".

As to the second question, whether the officer was to continue, after the office was abolished, Taylor contended that there
could not be "good behavior" in an office that did not exist, and
that the proper construction was "that the officer should hold

---

[27] Annals of Seventh Congress, First Session, Jan. 8, 1802.
[28] *Ibid.*
[29] The act did abolish the existing circuit courts, and in the sixth circuit it abolished two district courts and made the judges of those courts circuit judges. These
special district courts were not regarded as necessary under the new plan. See annals
of Sixth Congress, Appendix, pp. 1536 and 15457.

that which he might hold, namely, an existing office, so long as he did that which he might do, namely, his duty in that office; and not that he should hold an office, which did not exist, or perform duties not sanctioned by law". Moreover, if they had a right to abolish the office, the salary ceased, for the Constitution explicitly stated that they were to be paid "during their continuance in office".[30]

It is not necessary to give the arguments of Breckinridge in Congress, for they are almost precisely the ones stated by Taylor in the letter quoted above.[31] The Republicans were more successful here than in their later assaults on the Federal Judiciary, since they effected a repeal of the Act of 1801.

Taylor had not long ceased to be a member of the Assembly before there was a demand that this "rarely gifted" leader seek a seat in Congress.[32] Aaron Burr, in writing Taylor in regard to the sending of a medal which the latter had won in the Revolution, expressed the wish that he might enter Congress.[33] Taylor declared that he did not seek a seat in the Federal legislature, but that these suggestions to that effect had led to essays in the papers denouncing him in malicious fashion, and claiming that there was a plot to deprive Colonel Anthony New, at that time Representative from the Caroline district, of his seat.[34] Even the urgent requests of his good friend, Nicholas, who had aided him in the fight for the Virginia Resolutions, did not convince Taylor that it was wise to make a canvass for the position.[35] He did, however, accept an appointment on the part

---

[30] Taylor MSS., Taylor to Breckinridge, Dec. 22, 1801. In Branch Historical Papers, Vol. II, p. 284, *et sequitur*.

[31] Annals of Seventh Congress, First Session, Jan. 8, 1802.

[32] See *Richmond Examiner*, Feb. 5, 1803.

[33] Letter of Taylor to Burr, May 25, 1802. In Memoirs of Aaron Burr, Vol. II, p. 198, by Matthew L. Davis.

[34] *Ibid.*, March 25, 1803, p. 235.

[35] Taylor MSS., Taylor to Nicholas, Aug. 26, 1802. Original in Archives of Mass. Historical Society.

of the Governor to the United States Senate, to succeed Stephen T. Mason, deceased,[36] but he indicated soon after that he would decline election by the Assembly when that body convened.[37]

The election of 1800 had demonstrated clearly the necessity of an amendment to the Constitution of the United States. Under the original plan of choosing a President, the man who received the highest number of votes in the electoral college became President, and the one receiving the next highest became Vice-President. Jefferson and Burr had received the same number in 1800, with the result that the election went to the House of Representatives. The Jefferson supporters, knowing that their candidate was intended for President, and having seen the popular will almost thwarted, moved for an amendment during his first term.

Taylor played a conspicuous part in engineering this, the twelfth amendment, through the Senate. The proposed change embraced two principles: electors in voting were to indicate which man was meant for President, and which for Vice-President, and should the choice in the future devolve upon the House, the three highest in the electoral college balloting should be voted upon rather than the five highest, as formerly. Replying to Senator Jonathan Dayton of New Jersey, and others, who had claimed to see in the reduction from five to three an imposition upon the small states, Taylor stated that he did not believe in a classification of states any more than in a classification of men, than in patrician and plebeian orders. He wanted to know if the small states were "prepared to estimate the consequences of violence and the conflict of weakness against strength? Can any gentleman reflect on it without horror? Is it to be presumed that if you set the furious passions in agitation, that the large states will sit patiently and bear unmerited

---

[36] Calendar of Virginia State Papers, Vol. IX, p. 360. Taylor to Governor, June 10, 1803.

[37] Taylor MSS., Taylor to Monroe, Nov. 12, 1803. In Branch Historical Papers, Vol. II, p. 289.

reproach and outrage?"[38] The real purpose of the amendment, the Virginia Senator contended, was to keep the election from the House, for "diets are always exposed to intrigue and corruption". The small numbers of Representatives from the small states would be more easy to corrupt than the larger number from the large states.[39]

Senator Jonathan Dayton of New Jersey accused Taylor of threatening the small states, claimed that it was a question between large and small states, and that five had been allowed by the Constitution to contest in the House so as to benefit the small states.[40]

Taylor then denied that he had threatened the small states and said their Representatives had talked of civil war before his speech. He claimed that three as the maximum number to be voted on in the House would afford a better opportunity for a popular choice than five, and that the purpose of the amendment was to keep the choice from cumulative bodies. He denied that, in referring to the corruption of small states, he had alluded to them in their capacity as states at all but simply to the small number of Representatives.[41]

Adams thought it natural for Dayton to take offense, but reminded him that Taylor was "so ingenious, that like all ingenious men, his sentiments are not at once accessible to plain minds, and to this cause misapprehension ought to be attributed".[42]

Samuel White of Delaware regarded the Constitution as a product of compromise between large and small states, condemned the amendment for making several changes at one time, and believed that the least we tampered with the Constitution, the greater would be our stability. The amendment would lower the dignity of the Vice-President, for now he

---

[38] Annals of Congress, Eighth Congress, First Session, Nov. 24, 1803.
[39] Ibid.
[40] Ibid., Nov. 29, 1803.
[41] Ibid.
[42] Ibid.

would be known, whereas formerly the uncertainty as to who would be President made the people vote for two first-class men. He foresaw the day when the South and West, bound by many ties, would control all elections of both the President and the Vice-President. A separation would be the result, for the East would not countenance this political inequality.[43]

William Plumer of New Hampshire took occasion to denounce the three-fifths ratio, under which he claimed the South had as many electors (18) as there were from four and one-half states. "Will you, by this amendment, lessen the weight and influence of the Eastern states in the election of your first officer, and still retain this unequal article in your Constitution? . . . Will it strengthen the Union?"[44]

Uriah Tracy of Connecticut, in a speech covering twenty pages in the Annals of Congress, claimed that designation opened the way for intrigue among the electors, and that under the plan originally in the Constitution, the two best men were secured, because it was not known which would be President. The amendment would be to the benefit of the agricultural states, for they would grow rapidly, whereas the numerous small states of the East had little possibility of growth for years to come.[45]

Taylor deplored the appeal to "jealousy" on the part of the opposition. "The opposition to this discriminating amendment to the Constitution is condensed into a single stratagem, namely, an effort to excite the passion of jealousy in various forms. Endeavors have been made to excite geographical jealousies; a jealousy of the smaller against the large states; a jealousy in the people against the idea of amending the Constitution; and even a jealousy against individual members of this House."[46]

---

[43] Annals of Congress, Eighth Congress, First Session, Dec. 2, 1803.
[44] Ibid.
[45] Ibid.
[46] Williston, *Eloquence of the United States,* Vol. II, contains Taylor's speech of Dec. 2, 1803. Hereafter this will be referred to as "Eloquence".

The Constitution, he continued, was sustained by two principles: "one, a majority of the people, the other, a majority of the states; the first was necessary to preserve the liberty, or sovereignty of the people; the last, to preserve the liberty, or sovereignty of the states". As an illustration of these principles, he referred to amending the Constitution. "Three-fourths of the states must concur in this object, because a less number, or a majority of states, might not contain a majority of people; therefore, the Constitution is not amendable by a majority of states, but a species of state sovereignty might, under color of amending the Constitution, infringe the right of the people. On the other hand, a majority of the people residing in the large states cannot amend the Constitution, lest they should diminish or destroy the sovereignty of the small states, the federal union, or federalism itself." [47]

Popular choice of the President ought not to be defeated, if it could be avoided by amendment, for such choice was a great check upon executive power; and the choice should be kept from the House, so as to keep the executive and legislative departments independent.

But the most alarming feature of the debate, thought Taylor, was "the attempt to excite a national jealousy against the idea of amending the Constitution". "It is as necessary for the preservation of liberty, that constitutions or political law should be amended from time to time, in order to preserve liberty against the avarice and ambition of men in power, by meeting and controlling their artifices, as it is occasionally to amend municipal law, for the preservation of property against the vicious practices of men not in power.

"A constitution may allegorically be considered as a temple for the preservation of the treasure of liberty. Around it may be posted one, two or three, or more sentinels; but unless these sentinels are themselves watched by the people . . . they may, as

---

[47] Williston, *Eloquence*, Vol. II.

they have done, break into the temple, and convey away the treasure." [48]

Taylor and Tracy engaged in a final tilt over whether the amendment had passed. The vote was twenty-two to ten, but Tracy made the point that twenty-three constituted two-thirds of the whole number. Taylor opposed adjournment until the first of the next week, as he would then be disqualified to sit in the Senate, and wanted an immediate decision as to whether the amendment had passed. The Vice-President decided that it had.[49]

Many of Mr. Jefferson's policies during his first administration were in accord with his central idea of strict construction of the Constitution and hence a Federal Government with limited powers. Economy, the sweeping away of excise taxes and the consequent reduction of executive patronage, the gradual reduction of the national debt with a view to its extinguishment, these might be cited as policies corresponding to his political theory. But the same cannot be said of the purchase of Louisiana. There is no provision in the Constitution for the acquisition of territory. The willingness of France to sell the vast Louisiana country, the possibility that Napoleon might change his mind if we did not purchase promptly, in which case we might have found it necessary to ally ourselves with England, these were the determining factors in taking the momentous step.

Strict construction or faithful adherence on the part of the Federal Government to delegated powers had been the undeviating principle of Taylor since he entered politics. As a Senator, what course would he now pursue? We can better understand Taylor's position by reference, first, to the arguments by Senator Pickering of Massachusetts against the Treaty of acquisition. He objected especially to that provision of the treaty to the effect that "the inhabitants of the ceded territory shall

---

[48] Williston, *Eloquence,* Vol. II.
[49] Annals of Eighth Congress, First Session, Dec. 2, 1803.

be incorporated in the Union of the United States". Neither the President and the Senate, nor the President and Congress had the constitutional power to do this. He believed that it might be acquired and governed as a dependency. He compared the Union to a commercial house, a partnership, in which each member had to consent before an associate could be taken in. Moreover, France had no clear title from Spain, and our action might produce war with the latter.[50]

Uriah Tracy of Connecticut pictured the Union as a voluntary association, entered into by sovereign states, all equal in power, and reserving to themselves all powers not delegated to the general government. The treaty making power, he contended, was restricted by any clause of the Constitution which it violated. The seventh article of the Treaty, he pointed out, violated that clause of the Constitution which forbade a preference of the ports of one part of the country over those of another, since that clause admitted the ships of France and Spain to the ports of the ceded territory free of duty for twelve years. The principles of these people were said to be hostile to our government, and the acquisition, it was claimed, would give the southern and western interest a strength contradictory to the principles of our original Union.[51]

The arguments of Taylor are ingenious, to say the least. He stated that there were two fundamental arguments stated against the Treaty: first, that the United States cannot constitutionally acquire territory, and second, that the Treaty stipulates for the admission of new states into the Union, a stipulation which the treaty making power is unable to comply with. In reference to the first, he claimed that before the Confederation, each state in the Union possessed a right, as attached to sovereignty, of acquiring territory by war, purchase or treaty. That right must still be possessed, or forbidden to each state and the general government, or transferred to the general gov-

---

[50] Annals of Eighth Congress, First Session, Nov. 3, 1803.
[51] Ibid.

ernment. Such a right, in the Union, was not possessed by the states separately, because war and compacts with foreign powers and with each other are forbidden by the Constitution, to a separate state; and no other means of acquiring territory exist. Thus the state is deprived of the right of acquiring territory.

But neither the means nor the right of acquiring territory are forbidden to the United States. On the contrary, the Constitution gives the United States the right "to dispose of and regulate the territory belonging to the United States". This clause was a recognition of the right to hold territory. Since, then, the means of acquiring territory consist of war and compact; and since both are expressly forbidden to the states, and expressly surrendered to Congress; and since Congress has a right of holding territory, it follows that the means plus the right are equivalent to acquiring. He concludes that the right is thus indispensably annexed to the treaty making power, and the power to make war.

As to the second argument, that the Treaty stipulated for the admission of new states into the Union, Taylor conceded that the treaty making power could not erect a new state. But he denied that the words of the Treaty required that the territory be erected into a state. The Constitution recognized and the practice warranted an "incorporation of a territory and its inhabitants into the Union", without admitting either as a state. If the incorporation article meant that Louisiana should become a state in the Union of States, then he saw no reason for another part of the article which stipulated that the inhabitants should be made "citizens as soon as possible, according to the principles of the Federal Constitution". For if the article meant to admit Louisiana as a state, the inhabitants would instantly have been entitled to the privileges of the article in the Constitution declaring that "citizens of each state shall be entitled to all the privileges and immunities of citizens in the several states". "Protection in the meantime for life, liberty and property" meant until the inhabitants could go through some uniform rule of naturalization incident to their becoming citizens of a territory.

Taylor concluded his argument by a comparison of laws and treaties. The former were made "in pursuance of the Constitution", because the objects of legislative power were foreseen and hence could be defined; the latter "under the authority of the United States", because the objects of the treaty making power were not foreseen, and hence could not be defined. That, he thought, was the reason two-thirds of the Senate had to agree to a treaty, viz., it would check the abuse of an undefined power.[52]

Taylor became a Jefferson elector in the election of 1804,[53] and during the same year wrote a series of articles for the *National Intelligencer* under the caption, "A Defence of the Measures of the Administration of Thomas Jefferson". He signed himself "Curtius".[54]

Taylor indicated the approval of the following measures, which he said the President had recommended:

A retrenchment of unnecessary expense.

An abolition of useless offices.

An adherence to specific appropriations.

A reduction of the army.

An impartial selection of jurors.

A revisal of the naturalization laws.

A faithful payment of the interest, and a prompt discharge of the principal of the public debt.

Unceasing efforts to perfect the militia.[55]

He defended the assault of the Administration on the Federal Judiciary and claimed that an absolute control over the laws by that branch of the government was contrary to our theory of government, and opposed to the idea of responsibility to public opinion. The judges, he thought, were more liable to

---

[52] Annals of Eighth Congress, First Session, Nov. 3, 1803.

[53] *Virginia Argus,* Oct. 24, 1804.

[54] These articles are preserved in pamphlet form, under the above title, and will hereafter be referred to as "Defence". "Curtius" is said to have been John Taylor.

[55] Defence, pp. 11–12.

error than the Legislature, for the latter was more amenable to the public will.[56]

The abolition of internal taxes was defended as a highly salutary measure, for "the internal revenues fostered a system of extensive patronage dangerous to a republican government. Five hundred officers were employed in their collection, and two hundred thousand dollars annually expended, amounting to twenty per cent, while the expense of collecting the external duties amounted to only five per cent, without producing any diminution in the aggregate expense by a decrease of duties. Here then is an annual saving of one hundred and fifty thousand dollars." [57]

He claimed that the expenditures of the Navy Department were reduced $200,000, that the military arrangements represented a saving of $522,000, and that the abolition of useless offices brought the total reduction in expense to $1,000,000 a year.[58]

In regard to the payment of the interest, and the gradual discharge of the debt, the Administration, "as true to the principles of justice, as the planetary system to the laws of nature, sacredly respected her eternal mandates. A regard to national good faith obliterated every minor feeling. The regular payment of the interest has not, for a moment, been impeded; while the ultimate discharge of the principal has been hastened beyond all precedent, towards which the annual sum of $7,300,000 has been appropriated." [59]

As to the Louisiana Purchase, he felt that New England need not be apprehensive, for the greater part of the population of the western country would come from that section. Moreover, "the most active rivalries will unquestionably arise between the southern and western states, while there will be no source of

[56] Defence, pp. 36–37.
[57] Ibid., pp. 42–43.
[58] Ibid., p. 49.
[59] Ibid., p. 52.

jealousy between the states of the east and those of the west".[60]

Taylor thus paid a glowing tribute to the Administration of Jefferson; never again would he pen such words of praise in behalf of any political leader.

---

[60] Defence, pp. 135–136.

CHAPTER VII

POLITICAL INDEPENDENCE AND CONTROVERSY

It has been noted in the previous chapter that Pendleton suggested a number of amendments to the Constitution and that Taylor spoke of the imperative necessity of amendments, if liberty itself were to be preserved. Both objected to the large powers wielded by the Federal judges and to the ineffective checks, as they saw it, upon the judicial power. This agitation, and the unsuccessful efforts of the Republicans to impeach Justice Chase, who had assiduously applied the Sedition Act and who had uttered political harangues from the bench, were no doubt factors responsible for the debate which took place in the Virginia Legislature early in 1808 concerning a judicial amendment to the Constitution.

The suggested amendment was to the effect that Federal judges should be removed by a majority of the whole number of Representatives, and a majority of the Senators present. It passed the House of Delegates by a vote of 121 to 55 [1] but was rejected by the Senate, 13 to 6! Both, however, agreed by a large majority to a proposed amendment, whereby a majority of the whole number of members of a state legislature might remove a Senator from office.[2a]

Taylor's strong endorsement of Jefferson's first Administration was at marked variance with his attitude towards his second. Before 1809, he was to become definitely associated in politics with the group known as "Tertium Quids", i. e., those who opposed Mr. Madison's nomination as successor to Jefferson. Taylor had not held any political position since his brief tenure in the Senate in 1803 and 1804. This detached position,

---

[1] For arguments on either side, see *Virginia Argus,* Jan. 12, 1880. For votes, see Journal of House of Delegates, Jan. 13 and Jan. 23, 1808.

[2a] See Journal of House, same dates as above.

of course, contributed to greater freedom of political thought. His relations with Monroe had long been intimate, and this gave added zeal to his attitude during the period of troubled foreign relations, when Monroe, for a time, was a storm center.

We must say a few words concerning this relationship. They were born within a few years of each other (Monroe's birth was in 1758) and lived in the almost contiguous counties of Caroline and Westmoreland. Taylor had warmly defended Monroe when the latter was recalled from France in the 1790's.[2b] Writing to Monroe soon after the recall, he suggested that "a meeting might probably afford a mutual entertainment, because of the contrast in an exhibition, made up in the polite circles of Paris, and the wilds of Virginia. The fine gentlemen and rough farmer might not only be compared with each other by indifferent spectators, but even by the parties themselves, and the result might not strengthen the bond of an old friendship, unless we should mutually struggle against some very common foibles of human nature. Perhaps, therefore, it is fortunate that we have not met, until you have settled down into your old every day habits, which time, and the society of your countrymen, will gradually effect.

"I am here entertained with the society of sundry carpenters and bricklayers—if you can make one of our group—if you can put up with an unfinished house—if you can bear the cry of 'more bricks—mortar here'—and if you can bear the smell of oil and paint—I will do everything in my power to make you happy."[3]

When Monroe was abroad in 1804, Taylor's son, George Taylor, then a student at Edinburgh, implored financial aid from his father's friend. Monroe at first refused such aid, on the ground that a moderately wealthy father might not construe

---

[2b] See Chapter V above.
[3] Taylor MSS., Taylor to Monroe, Mar. 27, 1798. In Branch Historical Papers, Vol. II, p. 268. Written from Taylor's home.

such action as a real favor.[4] He evidently changed his mind upon reflection, for Taylor later thanked him for helping his son tide over the embarrassing debt situation.[5]

There were faint signs of dissensions among the Republicans before 1806. Monroe, as one of the negotiators in the purchase of Louisiana, was criticized by some Virginia Republicans, for not using an appropriation of two million dollars cash to diminish the price of the acquisitions; and he was advised to write his friends a few private letters, without suggesting that any hint had been given, clarifying his position on the point of criticism.[6] Rumor had it in Virginia, early in 1806, that a third party was forming, composed of both Federalists and Republicans, and that this party would be favored by the Administration.[7]

The real break within the Administration party came in the last months of 1806. Ever since the 1790's, the United States had had three outstanding matters of controversy with England: the impressment of American seamen, compensation for cargoes taken on the high seas, when England captured American vessels engaged in what she regarded as illegal trade with French possessions, and concessions in regard to British West Indian trade. The great Napoleonic wars were then raging in Europe, and England had blockaded a part of the coast of Northern Europe, while Napoleon, in November, 1806, had issued the Berlin Decree, cutting off all commerce with the British Isles, and ordering the seizure of vessels coming from England or her colonies to ports under his control. Under these conditions, James Monroe and William Pinkney were negotiating a treaty with England. The tentative treaty had

---

[4] Writings of Monroe-Hamilton, Vol. IV, p. 165. Monroe to George Taylor, April 7, 1804.

[5] Taylor MSS. Taylor to Monroe, Feb. 27, 1806. In Branch Historical Papers, Vol. II, p. 290.

[6] *Ibid.*, Nov. 12, 1803.

[7] *Ibid.*, Feb. 28, 1806.

no provisions in regard to impressments, and compensation for seized cargoes, but did embrace moderate concessions in regard to West Indian trade.   However, England indicated that she would not observe the treaty unless America would give assurances of resistance to the Berlin Decree. Mr. Jefferson did not submit the treaty to the Senate.

Monroe himself felt that the treaty would at least have enabled us to keep peace with foreign nations, by being friendly to one, and Taylor, though conscious of its imperfections, thought that it paved the way for the adjustment of our difficulties with England.[8]   At any rate, the year following its failure, England issued a further order in council, by which ships trading with France and with the countries under Napoleon's control were subject to seizure. Thus by the Berlin Decree and by the Orders in Council, our trade was cut off with Europe. Under these conditions, Jefferson recommended a total prohibition of our trade to foreign nations. This policy of "peaceable coercion" was embraced in the Embargo Act of December, 1807.

After the passage of the Embargo Act, the Monroe movement assumed formidable proportions in Virginia. The turn of events made it less difficult to defend Monroe's negotiations with England, so his friends did not hesitate to charge that the treaty had been rejected by the Administration, so as to aid Mr. Madison's chances for the presidency.[9]   In January, 1808, after 124 members had met in a legislative caucus in Richmond, and had named an electoral ticket favoring Madison,[10] there was held a caucus of fifty-seven members, which endorsed Monroe. Among these were Philip Doddridge, James W. Murdaugh, prominent in the Norfolk district, and Henry St. George Tucker.[11]   A standing corresponding committee was named, which drew up an address, pointing out that there was immi-

---

[8] These sentiments are expressed by Monroe to Taylor, in a letter Jan. 9, 1809. See writings of Monroe, by Hamilton, Vol. V, pp. 87–90.

[9] See *Virginia Argus,* Feb. 16, 1808.

[10] *Ibid.,* Jan. 26, 1808. The caucus was held January 21.

[11] *Ibid.*

nent danger of war, and that Monroe, by reason of his experience abroad, and in terms of his more resolute firmness, was better fitted to meet this crisis, and keep peace, than was Madison. During the early months of the year (1808) seventeen members of Congress issued an address in behalf of Monroe.[12] Among them were four Virginia Congressmen, two of whom were John Randolph and James M. Garnett.[13] They condemned the choice of Madison by a congressional caucus, and claimed that he had more the qualities of a philosopher than those of a statesman.

Taylor was not a radical "Tertium Quid". He even had doubts as to whether it was wise for Monroe to offer as a candidate. He was apprehensive that the movements going on in behalf of the latter would result in personal and lasting enmity with Mr. Madison's friends. Since rumors were afloat that there was to be a union between the Clinton and Monroe forces,[14] he warned especially against that, for, he asked, "is it likely that the nation will give up Jefferson on account of his age, and elect Clinton? Can a man, declared by the Constitution of his own State to have been twenty years unfit for an inferior office from old age, be fit for the presidency of the United States?" Taylor went so far as to advise Monroe to accept the offer of the Orleans government, because the West would soon be asking for a President, and there Monroe would be in a strategic position as a candidate. "On the other hand lies a treasure of fame, wealth and honor, directly leading to the goal I earnestly wish to see you reach. Mr. Jefferson is unquestionably your best friend, and earnestly desirous of advancing your prosperity. The offer of the Orleans government, which I hear he has made and you have refused, is proof of it." But he assured Monroe, that should the latter persevere, "I shall

---

12 See *Virginia Argus*, Mar. 15, 1808.
13 *Richmond Enquirer*, March 11, 1808.
14 *Virginia Argus*, January 15, 1808.

contentedly immolate my little popularity in the funeral pile which will consume yours." [15]

Despite Taylor's caution in regard to Monroe's candidacy, the Monroe corresponding committee formed an electoral ticket early in October with Taylor, Littleton Waller Tazewell, and Henry St. George Tucker among others, included in its personnel. The committee drew up an address which indicated that the possibility of war, and consequently internal taxation, was the fundamental cause of the opposition to Madison. The existing state of national affairs, it was claimed, demanded Monroe, who was highly regarded in both France and England. The address stated that "our foreign commerce is totally suspended, our ships are rotting, our seamen dispersed and gone, and our produce shut up in our warehouses, our public revenue is cut off, and the deficiency resulting from that cause must be supplied by recourse to the expensive system of internal taxation. . . . We ask you, whether it is as probable that they (the present evils) will be removed under the administration of Mr. Madison, who stands committed by his writings and acts on every question between us and foreign nations, as under the administration of a man who is perfectly free from that bias, which regard for consistency of character cannot fail to produce on men even of the purest principles, and most enlightened understanding. We may be mistaken, and shall rejoice if time shall convince us of error; but if Mr. Madison is elected, we see at present no alternative for the United States, but *war,* or an *embargo* of indefinite duration." [16]

Before the election took place, it was apparent that the appeal to the people that Madison was the stronger candidate, that Monroe would split the party, that Clinton might win as a result of the split among the Republicans, would win for Madi-

---

[15] Taylor MSS., Taylor to Monroe, Feb. 22, and Mar. 20, 1808. In Branch Historical Papers, Vol. II, pp. 291–294.
[16] *Virginia Gazette* and *General Advertiser,* Oct. 4, 1808.

son.[17]   One group of Federalists met in Richmond late in October, and endorsed Monroe, because, they said, the general ticket law made it impossible for them to win, and they believed Monroe preferable to Madison.   Another group of Federalists did meet in Staunton and form an electoral ticket, but their idea was simply a protest against the Richmond group.[18]   By the end of October, Monroe was convinced that public support of his candidacy had strengthened the Administration, and that the leaning of the Federals towards him had weakened him even more.[19]   The results verified his spirit of despair.[20]

This presidential campaign gave rise to a controversy between Taylor and Thomas Ritchie, editor of the *Richmond Enquirer,* in which no quarter was given and none asked.   Taylor's letters to Ritchie, only one of which was written before the election contest ended, reveal fully the character of the "Tertium Quid" movement.   In the *Enquirer* of September 20, 1808, Ritchie claimed that the Federalists would support any candidate, Monroe included, to defeat Madison.   He charged that the third party group in Virginia had views similar to the Federalists, and that they were really denouncing the political system of Jefferson.   After pointing out that many Republicans who had supported Monroe were then in the Madison ranks, he added: "Such, however, are not the sentiments of John Taylor of Caroline . . . 'what private griefs *he* has, alas! we know not!' " [21]

Taylor was not the character of man to let his motives be impugned, nor was he unmindful of the fact that Ritchie himself had earlier preferred Monroe.[22]   So he wrote Ritchie that "a charge, that you had transferred an original preference of Mr.

---

[17] For this type of appeal see *Richmond Enquirer,* Mar. 11, 1808, and *Virginia Argus,* Mar. 15, 1808.

[18] See *Richmond Gazette* and *General Advertiser,* Oct. 18 and Nov. 4, 1808.

[19] Writings of Monroe, Vol. V, pp. 66 to 81.   Monroe to Tazewell, Oct. 30, 1808.

[20] As given in *Virginia Argus,* Nov. 25, 1808, the vote was, Madison, 14665, Monroe, 3408, Federals 760.   Monroe's vote came mostly from the tidewater counties.

[21] *Richmond Enquirer,* Sept. 20, 1808.

[22] See statement of Ritchie in *Enquirer,* Mar. 11, 1808.

Monroe to Mr. Madison for a bribe, or from some equivalent motive, would have been more plausible than yours against me, of not having transferred such a preference for want of a bribe or something equivalent. It would have been more plausible also, because you are young and eager, and I am old and indifferent in the pursuits of life; because you have not disclosed an unequivocal indisposition for office; and because there is obviously a better chance for selfish gratification from espousing, than from opposing the election of Mr. Madison." [23] "To soothe and heal, and not to exasperate differences among Republicans" should be their aim, said Taylor. He requested that Ritchie discontinue the paper to him.

He wanted to know of Ritchie if we are "liable to schoolmaster correction, and bound to kiss the rod of a pedagogue editor without murmuring"? [24] Ritchie called the previous letter "by far the most scurrilous piece that ever disgraced the columns of this paper". He claimed that the statement was published without his knowledge, that Taylor put the wrong construction upon "private griefs", that the latter's references to a "pedagogue editor" were not worthy of him, and that there had been excellent pedagogues from Plato on. Ritchie then stated the reasons for his attack upon Taylor. It was his belief that the latter had stated that Mr. Madison was "no republican in principle", and had, when he was in Washington, advised Randolph to attack Madison, but not Jefferson. He further suggested that Taylor was not charmed because Madison's report of 1799 received more praise than Taylor's Resolutions of 1798, and was chagrined because Madison called him a wild and visionary politician. He intimated that Taylor left the Revolutionary War before he had to, and finally expressed the conviction that "we have much more to fear, from the vol-

---

[23] Taylor MSS., Taylor to Ritchie, Sept. 29, 1808. The letters in connection with their controversy are in a pamphlet by E. C. Stanard, Editor of the *Spirit of Seventy-Six,* in which paper letters appeared.

[24] Taylor to Ritchie, Jan. 22, 1809. In *Enquirer* of that date.

lied vultures of John Bull, hovering about our coasts, than from any French flight of crows, which these may arrest in their passage to our country".[25]

Taylor, in his reply, defended in impressive fashion his Revolutionary record. He further informed Ritchie that he was not jealous of the praise accorded Madison's Report, as the former had charged, because Mr. Madison wrote "John Taylor's Resolutions" of 1798 also.[26] Ritchie expressed surprise at this revelation, but added that it detracted from Taylor's reputation. He announced that henceforth the columns of the *Enquirer* were closed to the controversy.[27] " 'Open to all parties, but influenced by none' is the best; and 'open to abuse, but shut against defense,' the most despicable motto, which can define the character of a newspaper." This was Taylor's retort to the closing of the columns.[28]

In a rather voluminous correspondence which followed, Taylor indicated his reasons for opposing Madison and favoring Monroe in 1808. Going back to the origins of opposing schools of thought, he suggested that, in the making of the Union, "the Federal leaders were in favor of a government founded upon the principle of a balance of power between the departments of one government: their opponents, of one founded upon its division between that government and the people, and between two governments. . . . The first party conceived that something like the English system of balancing power, supported by the principle of election, would secure a free government; the second was of the opinion that this experiment had never succeeded; that election could not control power, when it bestowed too much; and that its division was a safer ally of election, than its balance."

---

[25] *Richmond Enquirer,* Feb. 3 and 7, 1809.
[26] Taylor MSS., Taylor to Ritchie, Feb. 10, 1809, but published in *Enquirer,* March 14, 1809.
[27] *Richmond Enquirer,* Mar. 18, 1809.
[28] Taylor MSS., Taylor to Ritchie, Mar. 24, 1809. In Stanard's Pamphlet (referred to above).

The Constitution was founded upon the principle of division of power, but those primarily responsible for the making of that instrument lost its administration, and then started to opposing those in power who favored consolidation, or the destruction of the principle of division. Mr. Madison, he reminded Ritchie, had opposed the latter group, had lent his support to the Resolutions of 1798, and to the instructions to the Virginia Senators, growing out of the resolutions. The Resolutions and instructions had condemned military establishments, had emphasized the sound policy of strengthening the militia instead, had condemned all the centralizing tendencies of the Federalists, and had strongly denounced the policy of commercial non-intercourse with France as tending to reduce the price of products and to cut off needed revenue. Taylor then contended that the same kind of commercial measures against England would bring all the risk Madison and others complained of in 1798–99. "The powers of the general government will be increased by leaving the militia unarmed, and resorting to mercenary troops, as the remedy against invasion and insurrection; by enabling the President to officer a volunteer militia; by unnecessary expenditures of revenue; by an order of public creditors which such expenditures will create; by suspending commerce and resorting to loans, to supply the deficiency of revenue; by sedition laws; by a new order of bankers with a treble capital, and by drawing the state governments under the influence of the general government by shares; by selling charters of credit as kings sell titles and privileges to raise money; and above all, by regulating agriculture and manufactures, which will add a complete internal, to the complete external power already given to the general government." [29]

Not only would the embargo policy, favored by Madison, tend towards consolidation in all the ways mentioned above, but it would, by its prohibitive character, enable manufactures

---

[29] Taylor MSS., Taylor to Ritchie, Mar. 27, 1809.

to thrive at the expense of non-manufacturing elements in American society.[30] Moreover, it sounded ominous to Taylor that Madison had spoken, in his inaugural address, of "authorized encouragements to agriculture, manufactures and education", for "there is no object of the Constitution more clearly expressed, than that all pecuniary impositions by Congress should conform to rules imperatively prescribed, for the exclusion of pecuniary partialities to particular states; by this indirect mode of encouraging manufactures, the cost of a national benefit, supposing it to be one, may be paid by one state, and the profits received by another; and Congress, by the aid of a *retaliating foreign nation,* may render pecuniary burdens excessively unequal".[31]

Taylor and Madison differed not only as to the division of power, but as to the necessity of amendment of the Constitution to preserve that division. Taylor expressed his hearty approval of the amendments suggested by Judge Pendleton (in preceding chapter), claimed that Jefferson had favored all but one, but that Madison had not favored them. The latter believed that election was the remedy for checking the tendency to "monarchy and consolidation", but Taylor claimed that governments and parties were continually "changing their principles, without changing their form or name. And this is done so gently, that although it distinctly appears upon a retrospective view, in a comparison between the old skeleton, and the new body; as a shriveled skin demonstrates the escape of a serpent; yet the process is frequently overlooked, until a government like the snake, comes out, of an increased size and additional malignity." [32]

His belief that Madison favored war with England, and that Monroe did not, was another cause of Taylor's opposition to

---

[30] Manufacturers did receive their first great stimulation as a result of this restrictive policy. See Johnson, *Union and Democracy,* pp. 234–235.

[31] Taylor MSS., Taylor to Ritchie, Mar. 30, 1809. In Stanard's Pamphlet.

[32] *Ibid.,* April 3, 1809.

Madison. And what would we gain by war? We had grievances, he agreed, against both France and England: But "the only certain consequence of war, except when it is undertaken for the purpose of repelling invasion, is that whichever side gains the victory, the people on both sides are vanquished". The taxation incident to a perpetual funding system would be the greatest curse of war, for "the groans of England produced by commercial wars, and loans to carry them on, are audible at this moment across the Atlantic". Funding schemes he called "opiates of present ease and aggravators of future pain". As for the possibility of acquiring Canada by war, he concluded that "the enthusiasm of human nature breaks out in politics, as well as in poetry and religion. What poet ever conceived a more wonderful idea than that of conquering the liberty of the seas, by marching an army near to the North Pole?" [33]

Taylor believed that, if we had to fight either England or France, it was preferable to fight the latter. We had more to lose by fighting England, while the English navy would make a war with France virtually a state of peace. Monroe's treaty would have paved the way for satisfactory negotiations with England, and should have been ratified, in the opinion of Taylor. He would have swept away all restrictions on our commerce, and, wherever feasible, would have retaliated against both England and France, by attaching the property of the citizens belonging to those countries. [34]

The controversy between Taylor and Ritchie, and the attitude of *The Spirit of Seventy-Six,* a paper founded to support Monroe's candidacy in 1808, apparently indicated that the dissensions among the Republicans were not to be easily allayed. [35] At the very time that the embargo had proved itself such a

---

[33] Taylor MSS., Taylor to Ritchie, April 7, 1809.
[34] *Ibid.,* April 7, 11, 14, 1809.
[35] See *Spirit of Seventy-Six,* Nov. 18, 22, 25 and Dec. 13, 1808. It declared that "As to the contest for the presidency, it is carried on by Col. Monroe's friends, and they will not cease to oppose Mr. Madison's elevation to it, until he is formally proclaimed by the voice of the nation expressed by electoral suffrages." (Nov. 18, 1808).

failure that its repeal was inevitable, Monroe expressed to Taylor the confidential opinion that the refusal to accept his treaty was at the bottom of all of our international difficulties. Its acceptance would have placed us on a friendly footing with one of the powers, would have given us a profitable trade, and would have prevented the revival of defunct Federalism. However, he believed that the wise policy for all Republicans was to support the Administration, and aid in relieving it from its embarrassing situation.[36]

Taylor also felt that the support of the Administration was necessary, if Republicanism were to survive. He was ready to extend the olive branch to the Madison supporters, but he made it clear that he was not a slave to party. He did not believe that the bulk of the people were influenced by abstract political principles; they were influenced far more by taxes imposed or taxes removed. His position was this: the good features of our government could and would be best preserved by the Republicans, but not if all Republicans quietly acquiesced in policies, by virtue of the fact that the leaders in power proposed them. Thus he urged Monroe to renew the assault on the Hamiltonian system.[37]

The reader should bear in mind that, during this period of lukewarm support of the Administration, there was no abatement of the policy of the European nations. The Embargo Act had been followed by a non-intercourse Act with France and England, with an additional provision to the effect that if either of these nations removed its restrictions, non-intercourse would be continued with only the one that did not. This policy, being ineffective, was abandoned, and all restrictions on our trade were removed (1810). However, if either nation revoked its policy, we should resume non-intercourse with the nation that did not do so.

---

[36] Writings of Monroe-Hamilton, Vol. V, Jan. 9, 1809, pp. 87–90; Monroe to Taylor.

[37] Taylor MSS., Taylor to Monroe, Nov. 8, 1809 and Feb. 10, 1810. In Branch Historical Papers, Vol. II, pp. 301–304.

Thus Monroe could truthfully say that four years after his contemplated treaty failed, because it had no provision against impressments, sailors were still being impressed, and France still persisted in her policy. But he spoke of the necessity of staying within the party, and of supporting its measures.[38] There had been rumors that Monroe was slated for a position under the Administration. This Taylor advised him to accept, if it were offered. However, he still urged Monroe to stand boldly against any compromise of Republican with Federal principles, a compromise which, in Taylor's opinion, had been going on since before the ending of Jefferson's Administrations.[39] Individuals, he held, should not be linked to a party, when they consider the measures of a government.[40]

In January, 1811, as the result of the resignation of Governor Tyler to take a position on the Federal Bench, there was a vacancy in the executive chair in Virginia. Chapman Johnson, a prominent Republican member of the Assembly, and friend of Monroe, was a strong supporter of the latter for the position, but was apprehensive that he could not win, because some friends of the Administration believed Monroe's election would embarrass the Administration, and hence would not support him. Monroe informed Johnson that he would express his differences, when they existed, within the party ranks, and he hastened to assure Taylor that that position was not different from the one he had consistently manifested.[41]

Taylor's central theme, in his letters to his friend, who had just won the governorship, continued to be political independence. He wished ardently to see Monroe elevated to the presidency, but assured him that the moment he was elected,

---

[38] Writings of Monroe-Hamilton, Vol. V, pp. 121–144. Monroe to Taylor, Sept. 10, 1810.

[39] Taylor MSS., Taylor to Monroe, Oct. 28, 1810. In Branch Historical Papers, Vol. II, p. 309.

[40] *Ibid.*, Nov. 25, 1810, p. 213.

[41] See *Virginia Argus*, Jan. 18 and 25, 1811, for correspondence between Johnson and Monroe. See Writings of Monroe-Hamilton, Vol. V, pp. 161–169 for letter to Taylor, Jan. 23, 1811.

"though by my casting vote, carried an hundred miles in a snowstorm, my confidence in you would be most confoundedly diminished, and I would instantly join again the Republican minority".[42] In the early months of 1811, Monroe was offered the position of Secretary of State by Mr. Madison. By this time Napoleon had at least pretended to revoke the Berlin and Milan Decrees, and our government had revived non-intercourse against England. Taylor advised Monroe to accept the position because the latter would then be in a position to aid the President by advice, to bring harmony out of discord, and to revive credit for the probable peaceable adjustment which Taylor believed would follow with England, when we were convinced that France's policy would aid our commerce but little.[43]

But less than a year later, Taylor had a vision of war, rather than one of peace, so he strongly opposed the impending step. Almost every factor counselled against it, he thought. The masses were opposed to it, for they did not even know what was the nature of the controversy. Voluntary enlistments were precarious if not hopeless, and Congress could not impose a draft. Mercenary armies were dangerous. Agriculture would be ruined. The European world was in a transitory state, and the nations, under normal circumstances, would not pursue policies similar to those then existing. A "permanent interest" was what we should seek out of the transitory situation; therefore a war with England would be "infinitely more calamitous and useless to us than one with France, because we can affect her interest more deeply than we can affect the interest of France; and she ours more deeply than France can. Hence we can weave into a treaty with England a multitude of benefits to ourselves, guaranteed by her interest, the most permanent quality of human nature; whereas there can be no guarantee for the splendid and empty promise of France, but the present

---

[42] Taylor MSS., Taylor to Monroe, Jan. 31, 1811. In Branch Historical Papers, Vol. II, p. 15.
[43] *Ibid.*, Mar. 21 and 24, 1811. Monroe did become Secretary of State.

state of things, which must be overturned before she can be able to fulfill them. If this state shall last, and by its existence, secure the fidelity to her concessions, yet these concessions, however great, cannot be of much benefit to us during the present superiority of the British fleet. If this superiority is lost, then the guarantee of any concessions made by France is also lost, and with their sponsor, the concessions themselves." [44]

Taylor bitterly denounced the policy that tended towards war until the very day that war was officially a fact. By May, 1812, all his hopes of peace, due largely to Monroe's appointment as Secretary of State, had "vanished in the clouds of the war and the embargo". [45] Everyone approved evasion of the latter, and no one whom Taylor conversed with favored the former, except a few Scotch merchants, who had tobacco in England. Fraud in the government, a lessening of respect for the Constitution, a vicious system of paper capital, heavy taxes and standing armies, such would probably be the woeful consequences of war. [46]

There are indications that Mr. Madison's war was simply acquiesced in by most of the people of his native State, but not heartily approved. Taylor felt that everyone should lend his support, once war was declared, but he frankly informed Monroe of the unpopularity of Madison in Taylor's section of the State in the election of 1812. Only twenty in Caroline County voted the Federal ticket, but despite the personal attachment to Madison, and untiring efforts in his behalf by Colonel James Taylor and other popular leaders, only 130 out of a total of 700 voters expressed a preference at the polls for Madison. Taylor did not exercise his right of suffrage, though he indicated a public preference for his friend of boyhood days. [47]

The people of the western section of the State expressed

---

[44] Taylor MSS., Taylor to Monroe, Jan. 2, 1812.

[45] Congress had, in April, 1812, passed a ninety day embargo.

[46] Taylor MSS., Taylor to Monroe, May 10 and June 18, 1812. In Branch Historical Papers, Vol. II, pp. 326 and 339. War was officially declared June 18, 1812.

[47] *Ibid.*, June 18 and Nov. 8, 1812, pp. 339 and 342.

openly their hostility to the war. Representatives from eighteen counties met at Staunton in October, formed an electoral ticket, and placed at its head, as its principles, *"Peace, Union and Commerce, and no Foreign Alliance"*.[48] John Randolph, in letters to his constituents, asked if they were "willing, for the purpose of annexing Canada to the Northern States, to submit to that ever growing system of taxation, which sends the European laborers supperless to bed"? [49]

Taylor urged (it goes without saying, with little avail) upon Monroe the policy of making peace, if we could get from England the slightest concessions. He thought that we should try to get some promise from England, however slight, in regard to impressing our seamen, stipulate that we would not employ hers, and make peace upon this basis, for "no man of sense can expect that the English will place their allegiance principle under the care of our Congress, President, marshals and juries". Taxation, he thought, would soon cure the Nation of whatever war fever it had.[50] It is appropriate to remind the reader at this point that the Federal Government imposed a direct tax in 1813, 1815, and 1816. Slaves, along with other property, were taxed, this time according to their value, and not by head, as in 1798.[51]

In expressing his gratification over the Peace Treaty, which concluded the war, Taylor expressed the conviction that "the general joy on a barren, though an honorable peace, arose from the general, though secret, dislike of the war".[52] The only aspect of the war, of which he spoke in laudatory terms, was the victory of Andrew Jackson, at New Orleans, after peace had been made. "It seems to me, by comparing the periods

---

48 *Richmond Enquirer,* Oct. 6, 1812.
49 See *Virginia Argus,* June 11, 1812 (quoted from *Spirit of Seventy-Six*).
50 Taylor MSS., Taylor to Monroe, March 18, 1813. In Branch Historical Papers, Vol. II, p. 344.
51 See *Manual of Constitution of the United States,* by I. W. Andrews, p. 80.
52 Taylor MSS., Taylor to Monroe, May 26, 1815. Mass. Historical Society Proceedings, Vol. 42, p. 333.

of making the treaty and the attack on Orleans, that the British meant to hold the latter, had they taken it, and to have denied that the treaty extended to its restitution, upon the ground that our mode of acquiring Louisiana did not transfer it to us. If so, the saving of Orleans saved this country from a long war. Indeed, I fear that Spain, and England, if their situation permits it, are not unwilling still to go to war with us upon this ground." [53]

[53] Taylor MSS., Taylor to Monroe, Dec. 3, 1815, p. 347.

CHAPTER VIII

THE CONTROVERSY WITH JOHN ADAMS

As early as 1794 Taylor conceived the idea of writing a book in reply to the ideas of John Adams, as expressed by that distinguished statesman in his *Defense of the American Constitutions.*[1] In a letter written in 1796, Taylor related the substance of a conversation which he had two years before with John Adams and Colonel Langdon, a Congressman from New Hampshire. He quoted Adams as expressing the wish that, before the latter's death, Taylor and William B. Giles would acknowledge that no government could long exist, or no people be happy, without an hereditary First Magistrate, and either an hereditary Senate, or one for life. But since some of Adams's friends claimed that his written sentiments were more democratic than his verbal ones, Taylor suggested that Adams's reference in his book to the *"powers of the one, the few and the many* being balanced", proved the contrary. Our Constitution, he thought, was not based on the idea of balance, or equality, among orders, but on the idea of the supremacy of the power of the many over the one and the few.

This power was preserved in three ways: first, by periodical elections of the one and the few; second, by depriving the one of the right of a negative, when the will of the many is expressed by a prescribed organic majority; and third, by the reservation of a mode, whereby the many may remodel the form of government, without the concurrence of either the one or the few.[2]

Six years later Taylor announced that his purpose in writing

---

[1] C. F. Adams, *Works of John Adams*, Vol. VI, p. 514. Taylor's book was published in 1814, and Adams, in letter to Taylor (no date) refers to fact that latter took twenty years to write it.

[2] Taylor MSS., Taylor to Daniel C. Brent, Oct. 9, 1796. In Branch Historical Papers, Vol. II, p. 260.

a book was to refute the ideas of Adams, to explain the Constitution, and to show the loyalty of Jefferson's measures to its principles, so as to aid in his next election.[3] But Taylor wrote in "such a wild, desultory, careless way",[4] to use his own language, that the book was not to be concluded until many years after the election of 1804.

Six years after the letter to Burr, Taylor humorously used an exclamation mark after the expression, "my book". However, he had written extensively by that time, and stated that the purpose of the work was to reply to Adams's book, and to provide an "antidote against sliding into the English policy upon the skates of legislation". That both the Adamses were monarchists, he never doubted, and "whether monarchists, like pagans, can be converted by benefices", was a problem the solution of which he always feared Mr. Madison would attempt.[5]

The book, consisting of 656 pages, was published in Fredericksburg, Virginia, in 1814, under the title, *An Inquiry into the Principles and Policy of the Government of the United States*. In the preface the author claims that Adams's *Defense of the American Constitutions* pays too much respect to political skeletons, and not enough to moral principles. Here he also contrasts the British and American conceptions of government. "By the British policy, the nation and the government is considered as one, and the passive obedience denied to the king conceded to the government, . . . whereas, by ours, the nation and the government are considered as distinct, and a claim of passive obedience by the latter, would of course be equivalent to the same claim by a British king." [6]

Taylor's work may be divided into five fundamental parts.

---

[3] Taylor MSS., Taylor to W. C. Nicholas, Aug. 26, 1802. Original in Archives of Massachusetts Historical Society.

[4] *Ibid.*, Taylor to Burr, Mar. 25, 1803. In M. L. Davis, *Memoirs of Burr*, Vol. II, p. 235.

[5] *Ibid.*, Taylor to Monroe, Nov. 8, 1809. In Branch Historical Papers, Vol. II, p. 301.

[6] See Preface to Inquiry. The term "Inquiry" will hereafter be used in referring to the work.

First, there is a discussion of Adams and the principle of aristocracy; second, of the nature of our government; third, of the evil qualities or practices of our government; fourth, of funding and banking; and finally, of the good moral principles of our government.

According to Taylor, Adams reared his system upon two assertions: first, "that there are only three generical forms of government, monarchy, aristocracy and democracy, of which all other forms are mixtures; and second, that every society naturally produces an order of men, which it is impossible to confine to an equality of rights". The author interpreted this to mean that Adams thought the President corresponded to a King, the Senate to an hereditary order, and the House of Representatives to a legislative nation.[7]

He quoted Adams to the effect that "there is a natural aristocracy, which is a body of men which contains the greatest collection of virtues and abilities in a free government; the brightest ornament and glory of a nation; and may always be made the greatest blessing of society, if it be judiciously managed in the Constitution". He stated that Adams thought these should be put into one Assembly together, in the Legislature; that over them should be placed a First Magistrate with all executive authority, and with a negative on the Legislature; and that another barrier, a House of Commons, representing the people, should be created to withhold from them and the Crown all supplies.[8]

Taylor claimed that there was no such thing as "a natural aristocracy". Such a doctrine, he thought, was equivalent to the one "that a king is the work of God". Knowledge and commerce had so divided virtues, talents, and wealth among multitudes, as to annihilate that order of men, who in past ages constituted an aristocracy.[9]

---

[7] Inquiry, pp. 3 to 5.
[8] Inquiry, pp. 7-8.
[9] Ibid., pp. 8 to 14.

The aristocracies of all ages had been erected by artificial devices: that of the ancient world, through superstition and ignorance; that of the middle ages, the feudal system, through conquest; that of the modern world, by paper and patronage. "For the sake of perspicuity, I shall call the ancient aristocracy, chiefly created and supported by superstition, 'the aristocracy of the first age'; that produced by conquest, known by the title of the feudal system, 'the aristocracy of the second age'; and that erected by paper and patronage, 'the aristocracy of the third or present age'. . . . To create the aristocracy of the first age, she used Jupiter; of the second, Mars; of the third, Mercury." [10]

He assailed bitterly what he called the third of these aristocracies, claiming that it masqueraded under patriotic terms to cloak its selfish designs. "The aristocracy of superstition defended itself by exclaiming, the Gods! the temples! the sacred oracles! and that of paper and patronage exclaims, national faith! sacred charters! and security of property!" [11] The idea of a perpetual debt, he claimed, was neither strength nor credit, but a diminution of both; and freedom from debt was the only genuine source of national strength depending on revenue. "Taxation to enrich a minority or aristocracy" was robbery! "to endow it gradually with power, treason". [12] The system of paper and patronage had brought incalculable harm to England, but Adams, he felt, had overlooked this aspect of English policy, and had centered nearly all of his attention upon the English system of checks and balances. [13]

As to the nature of our government, Taylor pointed out that the state constitutions denied hereditary power, and proclaimed the equality of men, which he interpreted to mean equality of moral rights and duties, yet that Adams favored the hereditary idea and opposed the doctrine of equality. [14]

---

[10] Inquiry, pp. 20–21.
[11] *Ibid,* p. 31.
[12] *Ibid,* pp. 44 and 48.
[13] *Ibid,* pp. 56-57.
[14] *Ibid.,* pp. 82-85.

Taylor did not consider government a necessary evil. It would be, if we balanced power among orders, as Adams suggested, for such a system inevitably produced bitterness. But ours was a government based on the idea of a division of power, which system made monarchy impossible. Division of power also filtered election of its worst vice, *viz.*, tumult.[15] He charged that Adams, in his second volume, distinctly advocated the balancing of power and property. "And it is explicitly declared, that this allotment must amount to a balance or an equality. Hence, it is obvious that the orders consisting of the one and the few, must each be endowed with a portion of power and property equal to that bestowed on the order consisting of the many. Therefore the system can neither subsist nor be introduced without a vast accumulation of power and property in the individual and the minor order." Division, and not accumulation of power and property, was the policy of the United States.[16]

Ours was not a government based on the idea of privileged orders; it rested upon the sovereignty of the people; the concept of the public good, and a thorough system of responsible representation.[17] The states bestowed on each officer and department of government, only that portion of power necessary to fulfill the annexed functions; and they made these officers and departments all dependent upon the Nation or a section of it.[18]

In this work, as in others, Taylor constantly sensed the idea of abuse of power. Thus he proclaims the doctrine that "an exclusive right to form or alter a government is annexed to society, in every moment of its existence; and therefore a direct or indirect exercise of it by a government, a combination, or

---

[15] Inquiry, pp. 87–88.
[16] *Ibid*, pp. 92–94.
[17] *Ibid.*, p. 110.
[18] *Ibid*, p. 161.

an individual, is a badge of usurpation, and a harbinger of despotism".[19]

Taylor discusses the evil qualities and practices of our government by reference to the three departments. He thought that the executive power was too great and too permanent. Patronage, banks and armies had tended to increase his power, and the only barrier to his continuance in office and the satisfaction of inordinate ambition was election.[20] The President appointed the judges, and thus made it possible to have what law he pleased. He had the power to confer lucrative offices upon members of Congress, and was thus in a position to influence the Legislature too much.[21] Rotation in office for the President he considered a salutary principle, for "the trade being laid open, the wares increase, and are made bitter by competition. Talents, civil and military, are created by the prospect of employment, and smothered by the monoply of experience." Taylor thought that an amendment to the Constitution, reducing the patronage of the President, shortening the time of his service, and making him forever ineligible to the same office, would contribute more to our prosperity and happiness than any other, except one capable of producing a real militia.[22]

Taylor went at some length here into a discussion of the evils that could flow from a judiciary, vague in respect to the definition of its powers, but this phase of thought can be more appropriately discussed in a succeeding chapter.

As regards the legislative department, Taylor thought the six year tenure too long for Senators. Since the legislative department could not bestow offices upon executive and judicial agents, he saw no reason why the Executive should bestow offices and contracts upon members of Congress. The con-

---

[19] Inquiry, pp. 145–146.
[20] *Ibid.*, pp. 167–177.
[21] *Ibid*, pp. 184–186.
[22] *Ibid*, pp. 193 and 199–200.

nection between the Senate and the President in patronage
matters, he regarded as an evil, for the Senators could embarrass
the President, if he refused them patronage; whereas, if he
favored them, they would be tempted to create new offices,
which would result in increased taxation.[23]   Merit, he thought,
should be the guiding principle in respect to appointments.
Any practice that tended to break down our division of power
should be remedied.

Taylor resumed here his assult on the funding and banking
system.   His arguments followed the lines suggested in his
pamphlet published in 1794, though they are given here in
more finished and complete form.   (This portion of this book
is cited in Chapter IV.)

Division of power, Taylor regarded as the outstanding good
principle of our government.   This division would maintain
the sovereignty of the people, but Adams's system of balance
orders, he believed, would destroy it.   There were not three
natural orders in this division, but it was first between the government and the people, with a reservation to the people of
the control of the dividend allotted to the government, then
between the two branches of the government, federal and state,
and finally, between the departments of each government.[24]

The agents given the allotted power were always responsible
to the sovereign power, because "an incapacity of political law
for producing the subordination of its agents to the sovereign
power, would produce the same effects, as an incapacity of
civil law, for producing the subordination of individuals to
the government".[25]   Adams's policy was diametrically opposed
to our system of government, for "our policy divides power,
and unites the nation in one interest; Mr. Adams's divides a
nation into several interests, and unites power".[26]

He strongly upheld the right of a state to instruct its Senators,

---

23 Inquiry, pp. 226–234.
24 *Ibid.*, pp. 400–409.
25 *Ibid.*, p. 417.
26 *Ibid.*, p. 423.

and claimed that the right was a recognition of, and proceeded from, the fact that a state was an entire society.[27]   Congress had such power, and should aid in providing a well regulated militia, for mercenary armies were dangerous to civil power.[28] He paid a glowing tribute to our idea of religious freedom, one of the principles of the Revolution, stating that "it is to this hour unknown, whether established or legal religions have ever carried a single soul into heaven; but there is no doubt of their having carried millions out of this world".[29]

He closed his work with a denunciation of laws which represented a transfer of property, rather than a preservation of it to the individual, and with a warning that party spirit was inimical to a free government.   "In legislation contrary to genuine republican principles, sustained by a dominant party zeal, lies, in my view, the greatest danger to the free form of government of the United States." [30]

Taylor was sending this work to Adams, by sections, before the whole was ready for the public. Adams wrote Jefferson, in 1813, that he had recently received from the post-office a packet "without post-mark, without letter, without name, date or place. Nicely sealed, was a printed copy of eighty or ninety pages, in large, full octavo, entitled,—'Section, first. Aristocracy'.

"I gravely composed my risible muscles, and read it through. It is, from beginning to end, an attack upon me, by name, for the doctrines of aristocracy in my three volumes of *Defense,* etc. The conclusion of the whole is, that an aristocracy of bank-paper is as bad as the nobility of France or England. I most assuredly will not controvert this point, with this man. Who he is, I cannot conjecture. The Honorable John Taylor, of Virginia, of all men living or dead, first occurred to me." [31]

---

[27] Inquiry, pp. 418 and 508.
[28] *Ibid.*, pp. 450–452.
[29] *Ibid.*, pp. 452–462.
[30] *Ibid.*, pp. 544, 576 and 655.
[31] Adams, *Works,* Vol. X, Adams to Jefferson, Sept. 15, 1813.

Soon after this Adams received the *Arator,* Taylor's agricultural treatise. He concluded that "they must spring from the
same brain, as Minerva issued from the head of Jove, or rather,
as Venus rose from the froth of the sea. There is, however a
great deal of good sense in *Arator,* and there is some in his
Aristocracy." [32] By this time Adams had received the entire
work, and soon thereafter a letter from Taylor, saying that it
was sent with his consent. Adams states that he strongly
suspected the author by the time he had read three pages, since
he had heard Taylor in the Senate, and knew his style so well.[33]

Adams first gave his views in regard to a constitution for a
state, when he was engaged in a conversation with George
Wythe. This was six months before the Declaration of Independence. Wythe stated that it would be exceedingly difficult
for the colonies to agree upon a government for future regulation, whereupon Adams suggested that each colony form a
government for itself. He later wrote Wythe a letter suggesting his plan of government, and the latter gave the letter to
Richard Henry Lee, who secured Adams's consent to print it.
This was the germ of Adams's three volume work.[34]

Adams wrote his treatises at a time of great popular agitation in Europe and the United States, and was severely criticized by his enemies, who claimed he wanted to subvert the
republican forms of government already established, and to
introduce the English system of hereditary orders. He paid no
attention to the criticisms until Taylor wrote his *Inquiry.* The
author of Adams's *Life and Works* concedes Taylor sincerity
and ability in respect to his book, but says it is marked by the
characteristics of the Virginia school to which he belonged,
viz., "the tendency to metaphysical niceties of speculation, the
absence of a broad, logical grasp of statesmanship, and the love
for technical distinctions without the corrective of extensive

---

[32] Adams, *Works,* Vol. X, Adams to Jefferson, Nov. 12, 1813.
[33] *Ibid.,* Adams to Jefferson, March 14, 1814.
[34] Adams, *Works,* Vol. X, Adams to John Taylor, April 9, 1814.

generalization".[35]   Some might say that the quoted statement
has a characteristic New England flavor.

Adams wrote Taylor thirty-two letters, which were intended
as a reply to the attack upon him in the *Inquiry*.   They cover
pages 447 to 521 in Volume VI of Adams's works, but only one
has a definite date.   Because of Taylor's "high rank, ample
fortune, learned education, and powerful connections", Adams
thought it proper to offer "a few justifications of a book that
has been misunderstood, misrepresented, and abused, more
than any other, except the Bible, that I have ever read".[36]

Adams claimed that there was a natural aristocracy, which
meant, in general, "those superiorities of influence in society
which grow out of the constitution of human nature. . . . By
aristocracy, I understand all those men who can command,
influence, or procure more than an average of votes; by an
aristocrat, every man who can and will influence one man to
vote besides himself.   Few men will deny that there is a natural
aristocracy of virtues and talents in every nation, and in every
party, in every city and village.   Inequalities are a part of the
natural history of man." [37]

Adams charged that Taylor misrepresented him when the
Virginian stated that Adams asserted "that every society naturally produces an order of men, which it is impossible to confine to an equality of rights".   He wanted to know if Taylor
professed to be "a down-right leveller", and whether he favored
either a community of property, or an equal division of property.[38]   Because Taylor married the daughter of John Penn,
and derived an amiable consort and handsome fortune, it added
greatly to his influence, Adams claimed.   And "would Washington ever have been Commander of the Revolutionary
Army, or President of the United States, if he had not married

[35] Comments of Charles Francis Adams in Vol. VI of Adams' *Works,* pp. 445–446.
[36] Adams, *Works,* Vol. VI, Adams to Taylor, Apr. 15, 1814.
[37] *Ibid.,* Letter II in Taylor Series, pp. 451–452.   Dates not being given, reference
will be to numbers and pages.
[38] *Ibid.,* Letter VI, Taylor Series, pp. 458–459.

the rich widow of Mr. Custis? Would Jefferson ever have been President of the United States, if he had not married the daughter of Mr. Wales?" [39]

The former President claimed that Taylor's references to the *System of America* had no relation to his three volumes, for they were written as a defense of the Constitutions of Massachusetts, New York, and Maryland, against the attacks of Turgot, who claimed they imitated the English customs; and there was no "System of America" except the old Confederation.[40] Taylor, he charged, had misrepresented him from the beginning of the *Defense* to the end. He had not said that democracy was more pernicious than monarchy or aristocracy, but did believe it more bloody while it lasted, though its bloodiest period had not even come when he wrote his work.[41]

Adams saw no objection to the use of the expression, "well born". Good birth, along with superior genius, and superior knowledge, obtained through education and study, constituted natural aristocracy.[42] Property was also a vital element in aristocracy.[43] He discussed this at sufficient length to express the hope that he had convinced Taylor "that property has been, is, and everlastingly will be, a natural and unavoidable cause of aristocracy, and that God Almighty has made it such by the constitution of human nature, and the globe, the land, the sea, the air, the water, and the fire, among which he has placed it".[44] When Adams wrote the thirtieth letter, he reminded Taylor that he had not advanced beyond the twelfth page, but that since twenty years were consumed in writing the *Inquiry*, he reserved that long to answer it.

Five years after the first of this group of letters had been

---

[39] Adams, *Works*, Vol. VI, Adams to Taylor, Letter VII, Taylor Series, pp. 461–462.
[40] *Ibid.*, Letter VIII, p. 463, letter XIX, pp. 486–487.
[41] *Ibid.*, Letter XVII, p. 483 and XVIII, pp. 483–484.
[42] *Ibid.*, four letters, pp. 493–404, are devoted to advantages derived from good birth.
[43] *Ibid*, four letters are devoted to discussion of "property".
[44] *Ibid.*, Letter XXIX, p. 512.

written, Adams stated that he had ceased to pursue his strictures upon the *Inquiry,* because his hand was so shaky that he could not hold a pen. But he agreed with Taylor concerning the evils of banking. "I have never had but one opinion concerning banking, from the institution of the first, by Mr. Robert Morris, and Mr. Gonverneur Morris, and that opinion has uniformly been that the banks have done more injury to the religion, mortality, tranquillity, prosperity, and even wealth of the nation, than they can have done, or ever will do good. . . . Silver and gold are but commodities, as much as wheat and lumber; the merchants who study the necessity, and feel out the wants of the community, can always import enough to supply the necessary circulating currency, as they can broadcloth or sugar, the trinkets of Birmingham or Manchester, or the hemp of Siberia." [45]

Jefferson warmly commended Taylor's first political production in book form. He even put aside his letter writing to complete the section on the good moral principles of our government. He thought the author presented in an unanswerable way the argument for the right of instructing Representatives, and their duty to obey, and he agreed that our system of banking was a "blot" upon our institutions. Funding he considered "as limited, rightfully, to a redemption of the debt within the lives of a majority of the generation contracting it; every generation coming equally, by the laws of the Creator of the world, to the free possession of the earth He made for their subsistence, unincumbered by their predecessors, who, like them, were but tenants for life". He felt that Taylor had "completely pulverized" Adams's system of orders. [46]

---

45 Adams, *Works,* Vol. X, Adams to Taylor, Mar. 12, 1817.
46 Writings of Jefferson, Ford Edition, Vol. X, pp. 27–31. Jefferson to Taylor, May 28, 1816.

CHAPTER IX

THE AGRICULTURAL IDEAL

TAYLOR's wealthy marriage and his large income from his professional practice enabled him to purchase and stock two large farms in Caroline County in the 1780's. He later purchased a third plantation.[1] Hazelwood, Hayfield, and Mill Hill were the plantation names, and during the time he lived, Hazelwood, where Taylor resided, was as closely associated with his name, as Caroline County was then and after his death.[2] His wife inherited from her brother, William Penn, a plantation of 700 acres in Hanover County, Virginia, and this, with the thirty-one slaves on it, was deeded to Taylor's son, Edmund, in 1809.[3]

Taylor's plantation operations expanded rapidly. In 1783 he had six slaves over sixteen years of age, and three under; in 1787 he had twenty-three slaves above sixteen and twenty-four under; in 1798 he had forty slaves above sixteen, and twelve between twelve and sixteen, the others below twelve not being listed.[4] In 1787 he had 1123 acres of land, at an estimated value of 460 pounds, 14 shillings and 11 pence, on which he paid a tax of 6 pounds, 18 shillings and 4 pence. In 1798, he owned 2245 acres of land, valued at $6,701.18 and taxed $25.47.[5]

It was an historic community in which this celebrated planter wrote his pamphlets and his books, and proclaimed by word of mouth the political philosophy which he believed essential to the preservation of the happiness of the American people.

---

[1] Pendleton, Pamphlet, Sketch of Taylor, p. 4.
[2] Wingfield, *History of Caroline County,* pp. 281–282. The names are among the estates listed.
[3] Deed between John Taylor and Lucy, Sept. 12, 1809. In possession of Henry Taylor, Jr., Richmond, Va.
[4] See Personal Property Books of Caroline County for 1783, 1787 and 1798. ·
[5] Caroline County Land Books, 1787 and 1798.

Winding its way in a southeast direction from Fredericksburg
to the Chesapeake Bay, a distance of seventy or eighty miles, is
the Rappahannock River, passing through one of the most
beautiful valleys on the seaboard. As told by one of Taylor's
contemporaries, a noted agricultural leader, "about midway
down this valley, near Port Royal, is the residence of Colonel
Taylor, the Virginia Arator, whose farm is distinguished by
the verdure of its fields, the abundance of its crops, and the
cedar hedges, which for several miles in length, over a level
surface, present a beautiful round top, ever green ridge, absolutely impassable, by hogs or any other kind of stock".[6]

Six miles below Fredericksburg was "New Post", the home
of General Alexander Spottswood, and seven miles below was
"Saint Julian", home of Judge Francis T. Brooke, "situated in
a lovely valley, embowered in fine old shade trees, and sur-
rounded by acres of choice fruits and flowers. The vegetable
garden was closely guarded by a cedar hedge which a cat could
hardly penetrate, while away to the left stretched a meadow
bordered by a clear running brook. . . ."[7]

Fredericksburg was the historic town which was the center
of the life of this Virginia community. Besides Caroline, there
were near Fredericksburg, Spotsylvania County, home of the
Brookes, one, Robert, at one time Governor of Virginia, and
another, Francis, referred to above as a Judge of the Virginia
Supreme Court; King George, the birthplace of Madison; and
Westmoreland, famous for Washington, Monroe and the Lees.
Washington spent a part of his boyhood days in Fredericks-
burg, as did Robert E. Lee; Monroe practiced law there, and
Governor Robert Brooke, about 1795, built his home upon
Federal Hill which looks across a valley a thousand yards to
Marye's Heights, destined to fame about seven decades later.
This town, situated upon the Rappahannock, at the head of

---

6 Description by Skinner, Editor of the *American Farmer*, given during the year
1820. *American Farmer*, Vol. II, p. 198.
7 *Recollections of a Virginian*, by General Dabney Herndon Maury, pp. 9–10.

tidewater Virginia, naturally commanded the trade of the opulent planters of the famous Northern Neck of Virginia and the Piedmont sections as well.[8]

Taylor, like the Pendletons and Fitzhughs, was a member of the Episcopal Church. At these church services in old Virginia, the planters, before services, exchanged business letters, discussed crop prices and fine horses; listened to a short sermon, metaphysical in nature; and strolled around after the sermon, extending mutual invitations to dinner.[9] It was in a gay as well as intellectual atmosphere that Taylor lived. Hospitality was the order of the day, and conversation was scintillating. The following, from the pen of a Virginian, living in the pre-war period, well depicts that atmosphere: "It was once my delightful privilege to pass the Christmas holidays with Judge Butler and a company of bright ladies and gentlemen, old and young, at 'Hazelwood', the old Virginia home of the Taylors of Caroline. We had a dinner party every day and every night had its delightful close in a dance at Gay Mont, or at Port Royal or Hazelwood. The house, big as it was, had no vacant bed, or empty places at the table, and we young people greatly enjoyed the older people. I remember a dinner of twenty or more seats, when we young men and maidens listened with delight to the witty and wise conversation sustained by Judge Butler, William P. Taylor of 'Hayfield', and John H. Bernard of 'Gay Mont'— that cultured trio of gentlemen of the old school." [10]

In Virginia during plantation days, pre-college education was largely through the medium of private academies and private teachers.[11] Woods, in his *History of Albemarle County*, mentions more than a dozen private academies existing there.[12]

---

[8] *Recollections of a Virginian*, by General Dabney Herndon Maury, pp. 1–8.

[9] Journal of Philip Fithian, quoted in Phillips' *American Negro Slavery*, p. 325. Fithian was a northern instructor in 1773, in the section in which Taylor lived.

[10] D. H. Maury's *Recollections of a Virginian*, quoted in Wingfield's *History of Caroline County*, pp. 362–363.

[11] South in *Building of the Nation*, Vol. X, p. 104.

[12] Woods, *History of Albemarle County*, pp. 27–28.

Taylor became president of the board of trustees of the Rappahannock Academy. Church and school were closely connected in the public mind, as shown by the fact that Taylor in advertising for a president for the Academy, indicated that if a minister were employed, the school was so situated as to encourage him in that capacity.[13] The languages were emphasized in the course of study, though pure mathematics and philosophy were also taught. The teachers were paid either on the basis of a stipulated percentage of the tuition fees, which amount was usually between seven and eight hundred dollars a year, or they were given a definite salary of somewhat less than seven hundred dollars.[14] Taylor's approval was sought and secured in regard to the system of instruction given, and the improvements noted on the part of the students, in the Port Royal Female Academy.[15] He, like Jefferson, wished to have the counties divided into wards, each of the latter with a primary school,[16] while his interest in education was further evinced by the fact that he deposited, through Jefferson, and in an anonymous way, $500 in a Fredericksburg bank to help finish the education of the children of Wilson Cary Nicholas, who had, at his death, left his family in very moderate circumstances.[17]

Taylor was generally regarded as the greatest agricultural leader of his day.[18] Not only his practical improvements on his plantations, but his writings as well, gave him that distinction. In 1813 he published the *Arator,* a work consisting of a series of agricultural essays, some of which had received popular notice earlier. By 1818 five editions of that work had

---

13 See advertisement in *Richmond Enquirer,* Oct. 25, 1812.

14 *Ibid.,* Feb. 6, 1816, and January 20, 1818.

15 Advertisement in regard to that school in *Enquirer,* Dec. 9, 1815.

16 Writings of Jefferson, Ford Edition, Jefferson to Taylor, July 21, 1816, Vol. X, pp. 50-55.

17 Taylor MSS., Taylor to Jefferson, Mar. 25 and Feb. 3, 1821. Original in Archives of New York Historical Society.

18 See citations to this effect in "Soil Exhaustion as a Factor in the Agricultural History of Virginia and Maryland, 1606-1860", by Avery O. Craven, pp. 99-100.

been published. John Adams stated that no northern writer who had come to his attention had equalled that agricultural treatise,[19] and Edmund Ruffin warmly commended and throughly familiarized himself with Taylor's writings.[20] Madison warmly praised the "instructive lessons" that "eminent citizen and celebrated agriculturist" had given,[21] and Jefferson, in his "new occupation of a farmer" in 1794, was willing to purchase a much needed drilling machine without examination, because Taylor had recommended it.[22] Later, through Taylor, Martin, the inventor of the machine, sought the aid of Jefferson in securing his patent.[23]

In the *Arator*, Taylor pictured an unhealthy agricultural state in Virginia. He referred to the fact that Strickland, an Englishman who visited this country, stated in a pamphlet in 1801, that Virginia was in an unprofitable condition, as regards the condition of the land. Emigration was further proof that the soil in its natural state was superior to that which had undergone transformation. Small towns had decayed, and tobacco culture had declined, not, as was supposed, because the cultivation of the crop exhausted the soil, but because necessary improvements had not been made.[24] One suggested improvement was to utilize the vegetable matter of the air. This could be done, Taylor suggested, by inclosing, and then raising those crops which absorbed the most vegetable matter, and afforded the greatest supply of offal for conversion into manure. By inclosing he meant to keep cattle away from the land suited for the special crops referred to in the previous sentence. Vege-

---

19 *American Farmer*, Vol. II, p. 93, July 29, 1817. Letter of Adams to Jeffreys, a North Carolina planter.

20 Branch Historical Papers, Vol. III, p. 102, Sketch of Ruffin. Ruffin was Editor of the *Farmer's Register* after 1833.

21 Address before Albemarle Agricultural Society, May 12, 1819. *American Farmer*, Vol. I, p. 171.

22 Writings of Jefferson, Ford Edition, Vol. VI, p. 505, May 1, 1794.

23 Taylor MSS., Taylor to Jefferson, May 6, 1799. In Branch Historical Papers, Vol. II, p. 281.

24 *Arator*, pp. 9 to 14.

table matter was probably the only kind that could enrich the earth, because before mineral substances, such as lime, gypsum and marl, could operate, the atmospheric substance had to be present.[25]

Red clover was an especially valuable vegetable absorber, for its growth was rapid, the quantity was great, and it threw off a great number of lasting stems. Indian corn, because it produced so much offal, was another crop especially desired.[26]   Since gypsum increased the power of vegetation to draw from the air, it should be used frequently.   He believed it to be of the greatest benefit to clover, then to corn, and then to wheat.[27] The three-shift system, corn, wheat and pasture, he considered ruinous, for the land received no fertilizer, no rest, and the hoof did positive harm without giving any recompense.[28]

A special hobby of Taylor's was what he called "live fences", by which he meant cedar hedges and stone fences.   These he had perfected on his plantations.   After the plants which he set out had reached a certain height, he increased their thickness by clipping.   The live fences would shelter his orchards from sunstroke, and would save the woodlands as well.[29]   For sixteen years Taylor tried sheep-raising, during which time he had from one to four hundred.   They required and consumed more food than any other animal, in proportion to size; they were more liable to disease and death, and made the land partially unfit for tillage.   Hogs were mischievous, but in grazing, 100 did less harm than twenty sheep.[30]   Taylor was able to say, in 1817, that one of his sons, with a hilly plantation, had doubled the value of the plantation in seven years, largely as a

---

[25] *Arator*, pp. 79–81.
[26] *Ibid.*, pp. 91–95.
[27] *Ibid.*, pp. 122–124.
[28] *Ibid.*, pp. 117–118.
[29] *Ibid.*, pp. 226–231.   A traveller who had been much in England told Taylor the latter had the prettiest cedar hedges he had seen.   See *American Farmer*, June 16, 1820.
[30] *Ibid.*, 204–214.

result of horizontal plowing, manuring and enclosing. On his own plantation he had, in eighteen years, improved his corn and grass production to an incredible degree.[31]

Another factor which tended to the impoverishment of the soil, and hence demanded improvement, was the overseer system. In 1791 we find a planter signing himself "a citizen of the world", urging through the columns of a newspaper that planters desist from paying an overseer by giving him a share of everything made on the plantation. If paid in this way, the incentive would be on the part of the overseer to rob the soil as rapidly as possible of all its productive strength, and then secure a position on some other plantation.[32] James Barbour spoke of the evils connected with the overseer system, but believed that a money salary, the alternative to crop sharing, would not correct the evils, unless higher than those salaries usually paid at that time (1825).[33] Taylor strongly condemned the practice of crop sharing with the overseer, for the annual crop, and not judicious culture, would advance his interest. "This necessary class of men (overseers) are bribed by agriculturists, not to improve, but to impoverish their land, by a share of the crop for one year; an ingenious contrivance for placing the lands in those states, under an annual rack rent, and a removing tenant. The farm from several gradations to an unlimited extent, is surrendered to the transient overseer, whose salary is increased in proportion as he can impoverish the land."[34]

There were political causes, too, in the opinion of this agrarian philosopher, which contributed to the depressed state of agriculture. Hamilton's policy in every item bore hard upon

---

[31] See letters of Taylor to G. W. Jeffreys in *American Farmer*, Mar. 2 and Oct. 6. 1817, Vol. II, pp. 212 and 348. Jeffreys was a prominent North Carolina agricultural leader. There are nine letters of Taylor to Jeffreys in Vol. II, of the *American Farmer*.

[32] *Virginia Gazette* and *Richmond Advertiser*, June 12, 1791.

[33] See address of Barbour before Agricultural Society of Albemarle, Nov., 1825, in *American Farmer*, Vol. VI, pp. 289–291.

[34] *Arator*, p. 76 also, 77–78.

the landed interests. Armies, navies, loaning, banking, and especially protecting duties were all hostile to the welfare of such interests. Taken together they created a system which derived its sustenance and its special privileges from the government, and at the expense of seven-eighths of the people, the number engaged in agriculture. Especially did he suggest the hardships produced by the import duties necessary to maintain the privileged system. The best market for our agriculture was abroad, but the best for our manufactures was at home. Thus agricultural products had to cross the ocean and encounter competition abroad, while manufacturing interests met competition from abroad here on their own grounds. "The disadvantages of the first competition suffice to excite all the efforts of agriculture to save her life; the advantages of the second suffice gradually to bestow a sound constitution on manufacturing. . . . The American manufactures receive first, a bounty equal to the freight, commission and English taxes, upon their English rivals; and secondly, a bounty equal to our own necessary imposts. . . . To this enormous inequality protecting duties are added, further to enrich the one and impoverish the other." [35]

When Taylor published his second edition of the *Arator* in 1814, he expunged some of his political expressions, lest they be attributed to party motives.[36] In this edition he explained that emphasis upon the militia as a means of defense was more necessary than in 1810, when the first edition was ready for publication. He regarded agriculture and the militia system as mutually interdependent, and their interests as the same, politically. He believed that "by transferring the power of the purse from agriculture to the stockjobbers, or the power of the sword from the militia to a mercenary army, the destruction of a free form of government naturally ensues".[37]

[35] *Arator*, pp. 18–21.
[36] *Arator*, Second Edition, p. 257.
[37] *Ibid.*, pp. 275–278.

In the fifth and last edition, published in Petersburg, Virginia, in 1818, Taylor has a lengthy preface, in which he vigorously advances the idea that agricultural welfare and political knowledge go together, for "if the agriculture is good and the government bad, we may have wealth and slavery; if the government is good and the agriculture bad, liberty and poverty".[38] By the time this edition was published the trend in the direction of the exercise of greater powers by the Federal Government no doubt influenced Taylor to urge the agricultural classes to increased political reflection. He wanted to know "if our health was sound during the presidency of Washington, what must it now be? The pulsation has increased six fold in the link of taxation; in the excrescence of banking, fifty fold; in that of protecting duties enormously; and in the patronage link, its flutterings have become so rapid and indistinct, that Congress have ordered a book to be compiled, to explain what may be called the logarithms of patronage." [39]

Some idea of what Taylor read along agricultural lines may be gathered from a letter written in reply to one from Jeffreys of North Carolina, asking for suggestions in regard to an agricultural library. He regarded Arthur Young as preëminent among agriculturists, as occupying the same place that Bacon does among philosophers. His twenty volumes would be very valuable. Several volumes published by the Agricultural Society of Philadelphia and Tull's works would be desirable, while Professor Humphrey Davy's work containing an analysis of fertilizers, and the proceedings of the board of agriculture of England, would fill a double need.[40]

Taylor was actively connected with the work of agricultural societies. He was a member of the Philadelphia Society for

---

[38] *Arator*, Fifth Edition, preface, p. 2.

[39] *Ibid.*, preface, p. 8.

[40] See letter of Taylor to Jeffreys, written August 16, 1816, but in *American Farmer*, Vol. II, June 16, 1820, p. 93. Jeffreys sent letters also to John Adams and Jefferson on the same subject. The former declared Taylor to be the best agricultural authority in the United States.

Promoting Agriculture, organized in 1787.[41] In 1811 there was formed the Richmond Agricultural Society with John Marshall as president; James Monroe, vice-president; Abraham Venable, treasurer, and George Hay, secretary.[42] This society declined, but was revived in 1817, after which John Taylor became its president.[43] At one time we find Taylor delivering an address to that society on the necessities of agriculture, and at another sending a letter to be read before the society (United Societies of Virginia) on the necessity of defending the rights of agriculture.[44]

A good idea of the purposes of these agricultural societies may be secured by reference to the stated purposes of the Albemarle Society, organized in 1817. They were: the cultivation of the primary staples, wheat, tobacco, etc.; the care and services of useful animals; the rotation of crops and the circumstances which should govern them; the improvement of the implements of husbandry, such as the plow and threshing machine, especially; and the use of the proper soil fertilizers.[45]

But the agricultural ideal involved more than suggesting methods of improving soil and the best instruments of husbandry to use; more than the formation of agricultural societies for definite aims; more than hospitable entertainment; more than the improvement of the labor system. It involved, as far as its leading exponent, Taylor, was concerned, a defense of agriculture from onslaughtes made upon it, for as he saw it, the joys, the pleasures and the moral possibilities of life so close to nature surpassed those anywhere else. Writing to Jefferson in 1799, he deplores politics and says that "hereafter I mean to till a soil which promises to crown my labor with some success.

---

41 Craven, *Soil Exhaustion a Factor in Agricultural History of Virginia and Maryland*, p. 104.

42 Anderson, *Life of Giles*, pp. 214–215.

43 *Richmond Enquirer*, Dec. 16, 1817; *American Farmer*, Vol. I, Nov. 12, 1819.

44 *American Farmer*, Vol. II, Oct. 19, 1818, p. 193; also Vol. III, no date, pp. 131–133.

45 *American Farmer*, Vol. I, p. 262.

Mother earth offers to her children subsistence and repose, of which it seems to be their great business to rob each other. It was foolish to leave the bosom which nourished me for the sake of exposing my own to the unfraternal shafts of all the wicked passions." [46]

He denied that there was or could be a landed aristocracy in America. The great quantity of cheap land, the extent of our country alone would prevent that.[47] Land was the "unde derivatur" of all products for man's use. It comprised the stock for trade and commerce, its true interest was the interest of the whole social and natural life, and it could not be at enmity with the public good. Lest the paper aristocracy might sing too loudly the song of a landed aristocracy, Taylor compared the property created by law to that which existed naturally. "Land cannot be increased by law—paper money may. Land, being incapable of an artificial multiplication, cannot, by increasing its quantity, strengthen its influence—with paper the case is different. Land cannot in interest be at enmity with the public good—paper money is often so. Land cannot be incorporated by law, or by an exclusive interest, into a political junto—paper credit may. Land is permanent—paper, fluctuating. A legislature, by a paper legerdemain, may transfer to themselves the lands of their constituents—a landed interest does not admit of intricate modifications." [48]

As Taylor nears the close of his celebrated work on agriculture, the *Arator*, he pictures the pleasures of agriculture in a

[46] Taylor MSS., Taylor to Jefferson, Feb. 15, 1799. In Branch Historical Papers, Vol. II, p. 278.

[47] Taylor, *Inquiry into the Principles and Policy of the Government of the United States*, pp. 552–556.

[48] Taylor, *Definition of Parties, or the Political Effects of the Paper System Considered*, pp. 8–9. James M. Garnett, a farmer Congressman from Virginia, in delivering an address before the Virginia Agricultural Society of Fredericksburg, of which he was President, spoke of the agricultural life as one "of solace and comfort", and declared that that provision in the Virginia Constitution limiting the right of suffrage to landholders was based on the idea that those who owned its soil should be the legislators of a country. See *American Farmer*, Vol. I, May, 1819, p. 361. Taylor, however, did not favor that clause of the Constitution.

manner that captivates the imagination, and in exalting its virtues, he throws the mantle of divinity around it. The calm and rational thinker reaches to emotional heights not attained or revealed anywhere in his other works. "Benevolence is so closely associated with this interest (agricultural) that its exertion in numberless instances is necessary to foster it. Liberality in supplying its laborers with the comforts of life, is the best sponsor for the prosperity of agriculture, and the practice of almost every moral virtue is amply remunerated in this world, whilst it is also the best security for attaining the blessings of the next.

"At the awful day of judgment, the discrimination of the good from the wicked, is not made by the criterion of sects or of dogmas, but by one which constitutes the daily employment and the great end of agriculture. The judge upon this occasion has by anticipation pronounced, that to feed the hungry, clothe the naked, and give drink to the thirsty, are the passports to future happiness; and the divine intelligence which selected an agricultural state as a paradise for its first favorites, has here again prescribed the agricultural virtues as the means for the admission of their posterity into heaven.

"The capacity of agriculture for affording luxuries to the body, is not less conspicuous than its capacity for affording luxuries to the mind. . . . In short, by the exercise it gives both to the body and to the mind, it secures health and vigor to both; and by combining a thorough knowledge of the real affairs of life, with a necessity for investigating the arena of nature, and the strongest invitations to the practice of morality, it becomes the best architect of a complete man." [49]

---

[49] *Arator*, pp. 278–280.

Chapter X

SLAVERY AND THE MISSOURI QUESTION

No account of the agricultural ideas and ideals of ante-bellum Virginia would be complete without reference to the slave labor system, which, in the case of a large planter like Taylor, was inseparably connected with plantation operations. For the sake of logical presentation, however, this discussion is given here in connection with another aspect of the slavery question, instead of in the preceding chapter.

Jefferson, in writing his *Notes on Virginia* in 1781, bitterly denounced the slaveholding system, both from the theoretical standpoint of injustice to the blacks, and in its effects upon the whites, yet he believed that the ills which would follow emancipation would be so great, that that step would be impracticable without providing for the deportation of the negro.[1] Taylor held that slavery was a "misfortune to agriculture, incapable of removal, and, only within the reach of palliatives",[2] but he did not agree with Jefferson that it was as vicious a system as the latter pictured. He suggested that the "Notes" were written by Jefferson when we were in the heat of a war for liberty, and when the human mind was influenced by revolutionary trends in France, but "despite these circumstances, a stranger would hardly form a more correct idea of the manners of the State, or relationship between master and slaves, by reading what Jefferson has to say, than a stranger to Indians would of their color by seeing one painted coal black". If what Jefferson said were correct, it would be better to emancipate, and run the risk of extermination in fighting the

[1] Jefferson, Notes on Virginia, quoted in Phillips' *American Negro Slavery*, pp. 122–123.
[2] Taylor, *Arator*, p. 62.

blacks, "than to live abhorred of God, and consequently hated of man".[3]

Slavery, he suggested, was carried further among the Greeks and the Romans than among us, yet they produced more great and good patriots and citizens than probably all the rest of the world. Jefferson himself refuted every syllable of the chapter on Virginia manners, and furious passions were "nearly as rare and disgraceful towards slaves as towards horses"; slaves were "more frequently the objects of benevolence than of rage"; and "they open instead of shut the sluices of benevolence in tender minds"; and "fewer good public or private characters have been raised in countries enslaved by some faction or particular interest, than in those where personal slavery existed".[4] But aside from the factor of human sympathy inspiring benevolence, the economy of agriculture counselled kindness rather than brutality to slaves. Even to treat the earth and domestic animals kindly represented the possibility of greater profit, so the planter who starved his slaves, or treated them cruelly, was the greater sufferer, since he lost "the profit produced by health, strength and alacrity"; and suffered "the losses caused by disease, short life, weakness and dejection".[5]

Agricultural economy dictated the working out of a special formula on the part of large planters for feeding, clothing and housing slaves. James Barbour, one of the largest and best known of Virginia planters, had a special clothing formula for them,[6] and was convinced that, among other articles of consumption, "their diet should be bread without limit, a daily allowance of meat, milk in the summer and autumn, and cider, with those who have orchards, in the winter and spring, to supply the absence of milk. Add to this on proper occasions a small quantity of whiskey—six or seven gallons to a laboring

---

[3] Taylor, *Arator*, pp. 68–70.
[4] *Ibid*, pp. 70–71.
[5] *Ibid*, pp. 272–273.
[6] Dabney, *Defense of Virginia*, pp. 314–315.

hand during the year." [7]   Taylor thought their diet should never be bread alone, except as punishment, and at one meal each day they should have salt meat, boiled into soup with peas, beans, potatoes, turnips, cabbages, cymblins or pumpkins. Salt fish, and milk or butter milk would suffice for other meals. There should always be a daily allowance of cider.   Taylor thought cider good not only for slaves, but also a beverage, an abundance of which would lessen the use of hard liquors. His special formula for making it was the mixing of six quarts of rum or brandy with thirty-three gallons of cider.   This planter was precise also in regard to the construction of slave quarters, so that they might afford warmth and ventilation, and be well guarded against fire, while his clothing formula was worked out in regard to every item of wear.   For instance, "a regular supply of a winter's coat, jacket and breeches, with the latter and the sleeves of the former lined, two aznaburg shirts, a good hat and blanket every other year, two pair of stockings annually, a pair of shoes, a pair of summer overalls, and a great coat every third year, will constitute a warm clothing for careful slaves, and the acquisitions they make from their usual permissions, will supply them with finery". [8]

While Taylor held that there were many humanizing factors in the relationship between master and slave, he recognized that slavery was a theoretical evil, yet thought it one that must be faced, because emancipation would bring a greater train of evils. [9]   Santo Domingo, where blacks first became free and then slaughtered or drove out white freemen, was never absent from his mind.   "Were the whites of Santo Domingo morally bound to bring on themselves the massacre produced by the liberation of their slaves?   Is such a sacrifice of freemen to make freemen of slaves, virtuous or wicked? . . . The history of parties in its utmost malignity is but a faint mirror for

---

[7] *American Farmer*, Vol. VII, pp. 289–291.
[8] *Arator*, pp. 136–140; also 230, and 233–235.
[9] *Ibid*, pp. 73 and 131.

reflecting the consequences of a white and black party." A revolutionary enthusiasm "attempted to compound a free nation of black and white people in Santo Domingo. The experiment pronounced that one color must perish." [10]

He strongly condemned that "amiable and peaceful religious sect" (the Quakers) for pursuing a policy which he believed would plunge three-fourths of the Nation into the worst of all civil wars, and he wanted to know if "these hasty, or in the language of exact truth, fanatic philisophers, patriots or Christians, suppose that the negroes could be made free, and yet kept from property and equal civil rights; or that both or either of these avenues of power could be opened to them and yet that some precept or incantation could prevent their entrance; as rivals for rule with the whites, the collision would be immediate, and the catastrophe speedy".[11] Referring to northern newspapers which heaped opprobrium upon the heads of white masters, he suggested that the generation then living had nothing to do with the dilemma in which it was involved, for "how few even of its ancestors were concerned in stealing and transporting negroes from Africa. If some remnants of such monsters exist, they are not to be found in the southern quarters of the Union." With prophetc vision of the future, he suggested that if anti-slavery agitation should reach the point where Southerners were forced to stricter measures of self-defense, they would then be unjustly called tyrants for so doing.[12]

In Taylor's opinion, the only way slavery could be disposed of would be for England and America to foster a settlement for free negroes in some part of Africa, which settlement would soon come to exist by its own energies. He was thus in sym-

---

10 *Arator*, pp. 127–128. The references to Santo Domingo are to the series of movements beginning in the early 1790's and ending in the early years of the nineteenth century, which succession of events culminated in the extermination of the whites, after the blacks had been freed.

11 *Ibid.*, pp. 127 and 129.

12 *Ibid*, p. 131.

pathy with the Colonization Society formed in 1816. The free negro he looked upon as the greatest menace to the safety of the South. He had none of the allowances of slaves, few of the civil rights of masters, and being discontented, was thus admirably situated to forment insurrection among slaves. He made the slaves less happy and the masters more strict. For these reasons, he suggested that the State of Virginia purchase of Congress lands in states where slavery did not exist, and give free negroes the option of removing to them or emigrating where they would.[13]

Previous to the great controversy over the admission of Missouri into the Union, which started in December 1818 and did not end until the summer of 1821, there was no animated slavery controversy. Pursuant to the clause in the Constitution requiring the rendition of fugitive slaves, Congress had passed an act in 1793 to give effect to that clause. Taylor was on the committee that framed the law.[14] Congress had the power to do so after twenty years, and thus legally abolished the foreign slave trade during the session of 1807-8. The New Englanders waxed vehement in their denunciation of the three-fifths ratio, but there was no possibility of removing that clause from the Constitution by amendment, hence Southerners had little to say concerning it. John Quincy Adams declared that that clause decided the fate of the election of 1800, and was responsible for the loss of all of New England's weight and influence in the national councils, and that an even balance between North and South could not be maintained while it was in the Constitution.[15] Timothy Pickering of Massachusetts declared that the three-fifths ratio alone was "adequate ground to demand a separation" of the sections.[16]

---

[13] *Arator*, pp. 62–66.

[14] Annals of Second Congress, Dec. 28, 1792, p. 623.

[15] Writings of Adams, by W. C. Ford, Vol. 3. Paper under heading *"Publius Valerius"*, addressed to Citizens of Massachusetts.

[16] Papers relating to New England Federalism, by Henry Adams. Letter of Pickering to Theodore Lyman, Feb. 11, 1804, pp. 343 *et sequitur*.

When Missouri applied for admission in December 1818, James Tallmadge of New York moved that she be admitted on condition that further introduction of slavery into the State be prohibited, and that the children born of slaves already there be freed at twenty-five years of age. It should be borne in mind that at that time the free state representation in the House of Representatives surpassed that of the slave states, but in the Senate the numbers were equal, since there were eleven free and eleven slave states. Thus if the South lost the principle of equality in the Senate, it could not check, in Congress, hostile legislation of any character.

A brief consideration of the arguments for restriction and of the excited state of public mind in Virginia is necessary to an understanding of Taylor's views on restriction. It was claimed that Indiana, Illinois and Ohio had been required, as a condition of admission, to conform to the Northwest Ordinance prohibiting slavery, and that slavery was an evil and would prevent free laborers from the North from going into Missouri. Slaveholders were pictured as aristocrats who monopolized offices, for "when have we seen a representative on this floor, from that section of our Union, who was not a slaveholder? Who but slaveholders are elected to their State Legislatures? Who but they are appointed to fill their executive and judicial offices?"[17]   It was contended that since Congress guaranteed a republican form of government to the states, "the existence of slavery in any state is so far a departure from republican principles".[18]

The northern Representatives boldly avowed that the three-fifths ratio and the question of preponderance of political power were fundamental considerations in their opposition to admitting Missouri as a slave state. The time might come, said one, when the voice of the slaves, in the councils of the Nation,

---

[17] Speech of J. W. Taylor of New York, in Annals of Fifteenth Congress, Second Session, Feb. 15, 1819.

[18] *Ibid.*, Speech of Timothy Fuller of Massachusetts in House, Feb. 15, 1819.

would be louder than that of the freemen.[19]   Jonathan Roberts,
Senator from Pennsylvania, declared that the restriction guaranteed a republican form of government, and wanted to know,
if the proposition were rejected, to whose benefit would the
consequence inure?   "Clearly to the slaveholding interest,
pecuniarily and politically.   The scale of political power will
preponderate in favor of the slaveholding states.   The effect of
such an event is hardly problematical." [20]   In this debate the
Northerners expressed their hostility to the negro as well as to
slavery.   James Burrill, Senator from Rhode Island, declared
that "the question is no less than this: whether the unexplored
and almost interminable regions beyond the Mississippi are
hereafter to be filled with a race of free white men, or whether
they are to be cultivated by slaves, and blackened with their
continually increasing progency?   I am not only averse to a
slave population, but also to any population composed of blacks,
and of the infinite and motley confusion of colors between the
black and the white." [21]   Sergeant of Pennsylvania reminded
his hearers that the 50,000 slaves of Louisiana might blacken
the country from the Mississippi to the Pacific.[22]

The attempt to place a restriction upon Missouri threw
Virginia into a ferment.   In that State, as will be pointed out
in the next chapter, there had been developing for some years
powerful opposition to the centralizing tendencies embodied in
the decisions of Chief Justice Marshall.   Moreover, the con-
stant clamor for a higher protective tariff, a policy which bore
heavily upon the Southern planter, and for which there was
no express warrant in the Constitution, added zeal to Virginia's
struggle for state rights.

An excellent index to the state of mind in Virginia during
the great fight over admitting Missouri may be found in the

---

19 Annals of Sixteenth Congress. Speech of Sergeant in House, Feb. 9, 1820.
20 *Ibid.*, Feb. 1, 1820.
21 *Ibid*, Jan. 20, 1820.
22 *Ibid.*, Feb. 9, 1820.

letters written to James Barbour, a Senator from Virginia, by members of the Virginia Legislature. Monroe was bitterly criticized for his apparent willingness to admit Maine independently of Missouri. In December 1819, Maine had applied for admission to the Union as a free state, and the Senate had suggested soon thereafter that Missouri be admitted without restriction, as a condition of the admission of Maine. The Northern majorities in the House refused the so-called compromise. Monroe, convinced that there was actually just one majority in the Senate for joining the two admission bills, thought that Maine should be admitted separately. This generosity, he believed, would cement the opposition in the Senate to the restriction on Missouri, and would probably result in bringing that State in without restriction.[23] When the caucus of the members of the Virginia Assembly first met, February 9, 1820, Monroe was sharply criticized, and no presidential electors were named. More than a week later, after a firm protest by the Legislature in regard to his stand, the electors were named.[24]

A fair idea of the attitude of Virginia towards the proposition, that restriction be placed on the Louisiana Purchase territory north of the line of 36° and 30″, as a condition of the admission of Missouri without restriction, may be obtained from the following extracts from letters to Barbour: "A compromise which gives up the fairest and largest part of the Western Territory, and leaves to us a narrow strip intersected with mountains in one direction, destroyed by earthquakes in another, and interspersed in a third with swamps and bayous . . . can never be grateful to us. Still less agreeable is the consideration that prompts the compromise. Is it to secure the admission to Missouri? . . . Is it for fear the President may lose his election? We are unwilling to purchase his service at such a price; still

[23] Barbour Correspondence, Monroe to Barbour, Feb. 3, 1820. In *William and Mary College Quarterly*, Vol. 10.

[24] Introduction to Barbour Correspondence in *William ond Mary College Quarterly*, Vol. 10, pp. 6–7.

less willing to support him if *he* can with a view to his own election thus surrender the valuable rights of the South. I trust in God if the President does sign a bill to that effect, the Southern people will be able to find some man who has not committed himself to our foes; for such are, depend on it, the Northern politicians." [25]

Andrew Stevenson "would never compromise with constitutional principles and rights", yet he appreciated the straits in which Southern Representatives had been placed, and "the motives that permitted them to listen for a moment to anything like compromise".[26] Madison felt that if the principle of settlement were to be partition, that partition, to be equitable, should be in proportion to what the respective sections paid for the common property.[27] W. F. Gordon, destined to a more prominent place in Virginia politics than he then held, did not estimate the compromise in terms of advantage or disadvantage, but he felt that it represented "a spirit of injustice . . . in the Northern politician, which if yielded to, would lead only to farther and more daring vital usurpations". He believed that Rufus King even would pause before he went as far as to produce disunion; for as great as were his and the ambitions of other Northerners, they knew that the interests of that section would suffer by separation.[28]

Linn Banks wrote that practically all the members of the Legislature agreed that Congress had no right to place a restriction on a new state about to be admitted; that the majority agreed that there was no power in that body to restrict slavery in the territories. For the very purpose for which the territories existed was that the citizens of the United States might go there with their property, and enjoy the benefits of those common possessions; and the very purpose in giving Congress the power to make "all needful rules and regulations" for the

---

[25] Barbour Correspondence, Henry St. George Tucker to Barbour, Feb. 11, 1820.
[26] *Ibid.,* Stevenson to Barbour, Feb. 16, 1820.
[27] *Ibid.,* Madison to Barbour, Feb. 14, 1820.
[28] *Ibid.,* Gordon to Barbour, Feb. 18, 1820.

territories was to subserve and promote this common enjoyment, not to defeat it by a policy of prohibition. Moreover, most members of the Legislature agreed that if the compromise were constitutional and expedient, "it would lead directly to a dissolution of the Union, by giving an unjust influence in the national councils, by which the Southern people would become the 'hewers of wood and drawers of water' for those of the North. They will have it in their power to tax the whole agricultural interests of the South for the interest of their manufactures. They will have it in their power to legislate exclusively for our property of every description, and, I have no doubt, from the language ascribed to Mr. King, would sound the tocsin of freedom to every negro of the South, and we may live to see the tragical events of Santo Domingo repeated in our own land." [29]

During the controversy over Missouri, Taylor was writing a book entitled *Construction Construed and Constitutions Vindicated*. This was published in 1820, and the doctrines it contains will be discussed at length in the next chapter. It is concerned in part, however, with the Missouri question. Behind the pretended anti-slavery zeal Taylor discerned the hand of political ambition and avaricious greed. Those who wished to secure special favors from the government were attempting to do so by creating inflamed geographical parties. Through all of our history under the Constitution, this greed had manifested itself. "The great pecuniary favor granted by Congress to certificate-holders, begat banking; banking begat bounties to manufacturing capitalists; bounties to manufacturing capitalists begat an oppressive pension list; these partialities united to begat the Missouri project; that project begat the idea of using slavery as an instrument for effecting a balance of power; when it is put in operation, it will beget new usurpations of internal

---

[29] Barbour Correspondence, Banks to Barbour, Feb. 20, 1820.

powers over persons and property, and these will beget a dissolution of the Union." [30]

The subject of internal slavery, he contended, was left to the states; for thirty years it had given the United States little trouble, but if it were used to excite hostile feelings between two great divisions of states, its mischiefs might "exceed the most apprehensive anticipation". The different parts of the Union could never, by law, be made to think alike upon the subject of slavery, hence "Missouri has no right to compel Maine to admit of slavery, nor Maine any right to compel Missouri to prohibit it, because each state has a right to think for itself. A Southern majority in Congress has no right to compel the Northern States to permit slavery, nor a Northern majority to compel the Southern States to abolish it, because it is a subject of internal state regulation prohibited to Congress, and reserved to the states." [31]   He suggested that the people of the eastern states knew little of conditions in the states on the Mississippi. It was this ignorance of local conditions, but a determination to control them, that led to the Santo Domingo catastrophe, for "the Society of Ami des Noirs in France, zealous for amending the condition of the free people of color, and believing that a conscious philanthropy was local information, invested them with unqualified citizenship, wrote the slaves into rebellion, finally liberated them, and these friends of the blacks turned out to be the real murderers of the whites". Missouri had a relatively large number of slaves, no representation in Congress, and yet that body proposed to regulate the matter for her, and let her suffer the consequences. Even if she had had representation, and Congress had passed the measure proposed, it would still be a law which those who passed it would not feel the effects of at all. [32]

---

[30] *Construction Construed*, pp. 294, 298.
[31] *Ibid.*, pp. 294, 300.
[32] *Ibid.*, pp. 301–302.

In addition to his arguments that political ambition and pecuniary selfishness dictated the Missouri fight, and that Congress could neither in terms of the Constitution nor of justice regulate the internal affairs of a state, Taylor advanced three others, all of a constitutional character.

The Constitution, he pointed out, in its effort to prevent combinations among states, after it had distributed powers between the Federal and state governments, positively prohibited a state from entering "into any agreement or compact with another state". But, he asks, "is not the Missouri *agreement* or *compact* a positive violation of this plain prohibition, and supposing no other argument existed, clearly unconstitutional from this single consideration? It is a compact or agreement by one-half of the states with the other half." [33] This compact, based on the idea of the balance of power, would not only hamper legislation common to the interests of all the states, but each side would, through bargains and contrivances, try to worst the other, until finally the one worsted would be driven by interest or resentment to resort to extreme measures.[34]

Taylor considered the clause in the Constitution, "New states may be admitted by Congress into this Union". He defined a state to mean "a politcal association of people, able to confederate with similar associations". Congress could admit, but it could not make a state. If it could not mould, it could not modify a state. That process inhered in the associated individuals composing a state, and Congress was not a party to that association. *Old* was the relative to *new,* both words were predicates of the same subject; therefore, a new state was considered by the Constitution "as exactly the same moral being, created and moulded by the same right to self-government with the old". The states were to be admitted into "this Union". "If, therefore, 'this Union' does not empower Congress to legislate exclusively in relation to the internal civil government

---

[33] *Construction Construed,* pp. 295–296.
[34] *Ibid.,* pages 291–292.

of each old state, it cannot so legislate as to those admitted. In
fact 'this Union' would never have existed, had such a power
been proposed by the Constitution." [35]

He next proceeded to answer the argument that the restriction on Missouri was necessary in order to fulfill that clause of
the Constitution by which the United States guarantees "to
every state in this Union, a republican form of government".
That argument either failed or it proved too much. "It fails,
if negro slavery does not destroy a republican form of government and it proves too much, supposing that it does, by investing Congress under the powers of a guarantee, with a power to
emancipate all the slaves in the Union." He suggested that all
the states were slaveholding states when they formed their constitutions. But the very essence of the existence of a republican
form of government, was representation, and legislation was
founded upon representation. So the condition upon Missouri
destroyed the very essence of republican government, since
"Congress is not a representation of Missouri, either for legislation or forming a constitution".[36]

Taylor explained that he did not pay a great deal of attention to the subjects of slavery and emancipation, because they
were matters reserved to the states, and had been so considered
by every state in the Union. Emancipation was proceeding as
fast as the circumstances of the slave-holding states would permit, but as if prophetic of the time when rabid abolitionists
would try to settle the problem for the South, he warned that
"there remains a right, anterior to every political power whatsoever, and alone sufficient to put the subject of slavery at rest;
the natural right of self-defence. Under this right, societies
imprison and put to death. By this right, nations are justified
in attacking other nations, which may league with their foes
to do them an injury. And by this right, they are justified, if
they see danger at a distance, to anticipate it by precautions.

---

[35] *Construction Construed*, pp. 304–305.
[36] *Ibid.*, pp. 309–313.

It is allowed on all hands, that danger to the slave-holding states lurks in their existing situation, however it has been produced; and it must be admitted, that the right of self-defence applies to that situation, of the necessity for which the parties exposed to the danger are the natural judges; otherwise this right, the most sacred of all possessed by men, would be no right at all. I leave to the reader the application of these observations." [37]

Thomas Ritchie, editor of the *Richmond Enquirer,* strongly commended to his readers Taylor's profound utterances on the Missouri question. The term "forever", used in regard to the prohibition of slavery from the vast territory north of 36° 30″ would have no binding effect, he suggested, upon future members of Congress nor posterity. He was bitterly critical of the action of Congress in rejecting Missouri, after they had pledged her admission, as a condition of the admission of Maine. She had framed her Constitution, elected her Governor, and her Representatives were ready to enter Congress, but because the Constitution framed had a clause making it the duty of the Legislature to pass laws preventing the emigration there of free negroes, she was refused admission. He claimed that the term 'citizen' as used in the Constitution did not include negroes, and pointed to the action of Ohio in requiring bond for their good behavior as a condition prerequisite to admission, as an illustration of the point for which he contended. Yet, he said, there was no criticism of Ohio. He emphatically declared that "Missouri will never again be a territory. She will never receive another Governor from the Federal Government, unless he is supported by 30,000 bayonets." [38]

The attitude of Taylor and other Virginians in this crisis has been fully enough described not to go into detail in regard to the congressional debates on the part of the anti-restrictionists. James Barbour in the Senate, his brother, P. P. Barbour, and John Tyler in the House, proved themselves able champions of

---

[37] *Construction Construed,* pp. 313–314.
[38] *Richmond Enquirer,* Mar. 3, Nov. 21, Dec. 12, 1820.

their cause.   J. Barbour pictured it as an immeasurable act of injustice that Southerners should be excluded from a vast territory which had been purchased from a common treasury, and which Southerners were exclusively responsible for purchasing, even over the protest of Northerners.[39]   Tyler was convinced that the Constitution conferred no power to impose the restriction, therefore he would not "yield one inch of ground", and should the worst happen, and Congress come to an issue with Missouri, Congress might ponder whether "Southern bayonets will ever be plunged into Southern hearts".[40]

In the final vote on the Missouri Compromise, the two Senators, James Barbour and James Pleasants, voted in the affirmative, while of the twenty-two Representatives in the House, seventeen voted against the compromise, four in favor, and one is not recorded.[41]

---

[39] Annals of Sixteenth Congress, First Session, Feb. 1, 1820.
[40] Tyler, *Letters and Times of the Tylers,* Vol. I, pp. 321–322.
[41] Annals of Sixteenth Congress, First Session, Feb. 17 and Mar. 2, 1820.

CHAPTER XI

THE FOE OF CENTRALIZING TENDENCIES

THE fundamental agency in strengthening the powers of the Federal Government at the expense of the states during the first quarter of the nineteenth century was the Supreme Court, under the leadership of Chief Justice John Marshall. During Jefferson's first Administration an effort had been made to provide an effective check to this possible foe of state rights by making impeachment of judges relatively easy. But the failure to impeach Justice Samuel Chase, charged with a misdemeanor because of his ways and methods of conducting trials under the Sedition Act, demonstrated that impeachment would not be an easy matter. During that Administration also, Marshall had rendered a decision (Marbury vs. Madison) in which he held an act of Congress unconstitutional, while somewhat later he had declared, in his judicial capacity, that an act of the Georgia Legislature was invalid, because it impaired the obligation of a contract. (Fletcher vs. Peck.)

Another decision, given in 1816, brought the state rights and centralizing schools of thought into sharp conflict. The case is entitled "Martin vs. Hunter's Lessee". Hunter brought action against Martin to recover certain lands which the former claimed in Virginia. The case had come before the Virginia Court of Appeals, which had decided in favor of the plaintiff, but since it involved the Treaty of 1783, it was, under the twenty-fifth section of the Judiciary Act of 1789, carried to the United States Supreme Court, and there the decision was reversed.[1] The Virginia court was ordered to execute the decree, but refused. One of the five judges was absent, but each

[1] J. N. Long, *Cases on Constitutional Law*, p. 6. The fundamental question involved was whether there was an appeal from the state courts to the United States Supreme Court.

of the other four gave decisions stating the reasons for his refusal. A brief examination of these decisions will suffice to show the line of argument followed.

The first of the decisions, which are given in full in the *Richmond Enquirer,* to appear was that of Judge Cabell.[2] He held that the Constitution of the United States contemplated the independence of the State and Federal governments, and did not regard the residuary sovereignty of the states as less inviolable than the delegated sovereignty of the United States. The judicial power of the United States was vested in one Supreme Court and such inferior courts as Congress might, from time to time, establish. If he rendered the judgment, he would not be doing it as a Federal judge, and would thus be conceding the appellate jurisdiction of the Supreme Court, and hence its superiority over state courts. "But one court cannot be correctly said to be superior to another, unless both of them belong to the same sovereignty. . . . The courts of the United States, therefore, belonging to one sovereignty, cannot be appellate courts in relation to the state courts, which belong to a different sovereignty." To give to any department of the Federal Government a direct and controlling operation upon the state departments, as such, would change the whole character of our system, and certainly no such power as that claimed was to be found in the Constitution.

Cabell held that in cases where there was a concurrent jurisdiction on the part of the state courts with the Federal, it devolved upon the parties to the action to choose between the jurisdictions; but once the *original* jurisdiction had been decided upon, its decision was *final*. He believed that Congress had

---

2 W. H. Cabell came from a long and distinguished line of ancestry, which goes back to William Cabell, born March 1, 1687, at Warminister, England. The subject of this discussion was born in 1772. He attended both Hampden-Sidney and William and Mary Colleges, supported the Virginia Resolutions in 1798, was a member of the Virginia Assembly 1802 to 1805, Governor of the state three years, Judge of the General Court, and after 1811, Judge of the Court of Appeals. See Hardesty, *Historical and Geographical Encyclopedia.* Special Virginia Edition, p. 355.

the power to create Federal courts to which a defendant might remove his case from the state courts (where there was Federal cognizance of the case), but "if then the plaintiff shall *elect* the state jurisdiction, by bringing his suit in the state court, and the defendant shall also *elect* it by submitting to it, they must, from the nature of the judicial power reserved to the states, be *concluded* by the judgment".[3] (Words underlined in decision.) Like Cabell, Judge Brooke[4] held that section of the Judiciary Act of 1789 which provided for appeals from state courts to be unconstitutional. State courts were not a part of the Federal judicial system, Congress did not organize them, and they were not responsible to the general government for the performance of their duties. He recognized that there were some difficulties arising from the fact that two governments acted upon the same citizens; but those difficulties were inherent in the nature of our governmental system, and could not be completely obliterated unless we changed the system. If cases which might come before either State or Federal courts, came before the former, they decided "in conformity to the law of any government that may come in question". The oath to support the Constitution was the fundamental safeguard against the exercise of power not given by the people.[5]

Judge Fleming, in a somewhat briefer opinion than those rendered by the other judges, held that the appellate jurisdiction of the Supreme Court was in relation only to inferior courts established by Congress, that such regulations as Congress made could apply only to such courts, since that body had no power whatsoever to make regulation for state courts.[6]

---

[3] See decision in *Richmond Enquirer*, Jan. 27, 1816.

[4] Francis T. Brooke was born in 1763, served in the Revolution in Lafayette's campaign against Cornwallis, practiced law in Western Virginia, and later removed to Essex County in Eastern Virginia. He represented that county in the House of Delegates, later became a state Senator from his district, in 1811 was made a judge of the Supreme Court of Appeals, of which he was President soon after. See Hardesty, *Historical and Geographical Encyclopedia*. Special Virginia Edition pp. 352–353.

[5] See decision in *Richmond Enquirer*, Jan. 30. 1816.

[6] See *Richmond Enquirer*, Feb. 3, 1816.

Spencer Roane had long been prominent in Virginia politics. He had become a member of the Virginia Court of Appeals in 1795, when thirty-three years of age, and before had served his State in numerous ways. Had not Oliver Ellsworth resigned as Chief Justice of the United States Supreme Court in time for John Adams to appoint Marshall, Roane would have been appointed to that position by Jefferson. With his cousin, Thomas Ritchie, Roane in 1804 established the *Richmond Enquirer*. He owned extensive plantations in Hanover County, Virginia, but found himself compelled to purchase a residence in Richmond, because of the pressure of his judicial duties.[7]

It was this man, mature in years and in mind and independent in thought, who gave the most elaborate opinion in rejecting the mandate of the Supreme Court. Some idea of his intense antagonism to the action of the Federal court may be gathered from his warning "that there is a Charybdis to be avoided, as well as a Scylla: that a centripetal, as well as a centrifugal principle exists in the government, and that no calamity would be more to be deplored by the American people, than a vortex in the general government, which should engulf and sweep away every vestige of the state constitutions". The power exercised by the Virginia court was that exercised by the courts of every civilized nation, for "on the ground of the contract following the person of the debtor, the laws of the country in which it originated are to be decided on, by foreign tribunals". If the subjects of foreign nations elected to try cases in state courts, then why should such nations complain of the decision rendered? Were not the subjects of foreign nations compelled by the eleventh amendment to sue a state in its own courts, in exclusion of every other; "and that, too, in cases, in which, from the circumstance of the states themselves being parties, it might, perhaps, be plausibly argued, that the judges of the state courts were not free from bias"?

---

[7] Sketch of Roane by D. J. Mays, Pamphlet in Virginia State Library, pp. 5–7; also Branch Historical Papers, Vol. II, pp. 5–15.

If the state courts were courts of the United States, they had become so by implication, for the judges of such courts were not appointed, commissioned, nor paid by the United States, nor impeachable by them. "But what is this implication . . . by which a power is to be taken from the state governments, and vested in that of the Union, and the courts of the former taken into the service of the latter? There is no iota of expression in the Constitution, which either takes it from the states, or gives it to the United States." Referring to the argument of counsel for the appellee that the power then in question resulted to the Supreme Court, from the concurrent power given to state courts over the same subjects, Roane claimed that the idea of a concurrence of power was at war with that of one of the powers possessing a power of reversal and control over the other. The power was common to the courts of the state, as it was to the courts of every other civilized nation, in respect to civil causes, and was not derived from any grant or concession in the Constitution.[8]

After two more decisions, Taylor became the central figure in the Virginia State Rights School. One of these was the case of Cohens *vs.* Virginia. The quarterly session court of Norfolk had prosecuted P. J. and W. J. Cohen under a statute of Virginia, for selling lottery tickets, issued by a lottery established by the city of Washington, under authority of the Act of 1802 incoporating the city. That was the highest Virginia court having jurisdiction of the case, hence the appeal was to the Supreme Court of the United States. The attorney for Virginia moved to dismiss the writ, on the ground that the court did not have jurisdiction in a case involving a state and its own citizens.[9] Whether the Supreme Court had appellate jurisdiction, and whether a state could be made a defendant before the court, were questions involved.

The court, however, took cognizance of the case. The other

---

[8] This decision is in the *Richmond Enquirer*, Feb. 1, 1816.
[9] J. R. Long, *Cases on Constitutional Law*, p. 10.

decision was in the case of M'Culloch *vs.* Maryland. After refusing to recharter the Bank in 1811, the Republicans put aside their constitutional scruples five years later and reversed their position. There were strong objections in some of the states to the establishment therein of branches of the Bank. Maryland registered her objection by placing a tax on the branch there. Marshall declared the State law imposing the tax unconstitutional, and also held, in the decision, that the act establishing the Bank was constitutional. The decision, by its elastic interpretation of the "necessary and proper" clause of the Constitution, charted such a broad course for the Federal Government, as to lead state rights advocates to the conclusion that Marshall had given that government a free pass over any road to any point.

It was soon after this decision that Taylor published (1820) his work entitled *Construction Construed and Constitutions Vindicated,* one of three voluminous works published during the last four years of his life. Thomas Ritchie, editor of the *Richmond Enquirer,* oblivious now of the bitter quarrel of former days with Taylor (see Chapter VII), wrote the preface to this remarkable book. A brief reference to Ritchie's political views after 1815 will aid in explaining the eulogistic spirit embraced in the words of the preface. He had opposed the recharter of the Bank in 1816, the creation of a system of roads and canals by the Federal Government, and had bitterly attacked the *New York Courier,* because the latter charged that Virginia contemplated forcible resistance in 1798–99, and was actuated in her course, at that time, not by a desire to defend the Constitution, but by a desire to defeat Adams for President. He had lauded state rights as "the very cornerstone of the confederacy", and had warned that when such rights were "threatened or invaded", Virginia would "not be the last to sound the tocsin".[10]

The following is, in part, the preface to "Construction Con-

---

[10] *Richmond Enquirer,* Jan. 4, Mar. 11, April 4, 1817, and Mar. 30, 1819.

strued": "The period is, indeed, by no means an agreeable one.
It borrows new gloom from the apathy which seems to reign
over so many of our sister states. The very sound of State
Rights is scarcely ever heard among them; and by many of their
eminent politicians, it is only heard to be mocked at. But a
good citizen will never despair of the republic. Among these
good citizens is John Taylor, of Caroline. Penetrated by the
conviction, that the constitution is in danger; that the balance
has seriously inclined towards the side of consolidation; he
comes forward to commune with his countrymen, and to state
to them frankly his impressions and his fears.

"If there be any book that is capable of rousing the people, it
is the one before us. Bold and original in its conceptions,
without passion, and with an admirable ingenuity to recommend it, it is calculated, we should think, to make a deep
impression. Its author is far removed from the temptations of
ambition. He holds no office. He wishes for none. He writes,
for he has thought much; and the present is a sort of last legacy
to his countrymen. It is unnecessary to dwell upon the particular traits of this work; yet the finger upon the wall is not
to be mistaken. We see here the spirit which breathes in the
pages of 'Arator', and of the 'Political Enquiry'. The first has
made him known throughout America: the last is less generally read; but unless some intelligent men are much mistaken, it is yet to win its way to distinguished reputation. They
have all one trait, without which genius exists not. The man,
who writes them, dares to think for himself." [11]

Almost immediately after the publication of Taylor's new
book, Jefferson praised it, and declared that he and Colonel
Taylor had rarely, if ever, differed on any point. He denounced
the Judiciary of the United States as "the subtle corps of sappers
and miners constantly working under ground to undermine
the foundations of our confederated fabric. . . . An opinion is
huddled up in conclave, perhaps by a majority of one, delivered

---

[11] *Richmond Enquirer*, Nov. 17, 1820; also preface to *Construction Construed.*

as if unanimous, and with the silent acquiescence of lazy or timid associates, by a crafty chief judge, who sophisticates the law to his mind, by the turn of his own reasoning." [12]   Soon after he expressed the view that the states must shield themselves from dangers so palpable as those existing, if Congress would not, and at the same time referred to Taylor's book as "the most effectual retraction of our government to its original principles which has ever yet been sent by Heaven to our aid. Every state in the Union should give a copy to every member they elect, as a standing instruction, and ours should set the example." [13]

At first Jefferson had refused to let his endorsement of the book be made public, because his public utterances were so often misconstrued, but later, and for the second time in his life, he gave public endorsement to a work of this character. This action was due, in part, to the insistent pleading of Spencer Roane.[14] Roane had been responsible for the printing of the work. Ritchie heartily desired public endorsement on the part of Jefferson, and Taylor himself believed such action would affect the western states (Ohio was especially hostile to the Bank) and would produce the necessary circulation of the treatise. He was also desirous that Jefferson write memoirs, which would call the Nation back to true republican principles.   This, in Taylor's opinion, was more important than establishing the University of Virginia.[15]

No one thought "more highly" of Colonel Taylor's book than Nathaniel Macon, long a tower of strength among the North Carolina Republicans, but he was fearful that those thriving on "the public debt, Bank stock, and bank and other

---

[12] Writings of Jefferson, Ford Edition, Vol. X, pp. 169–171.   Jefferson to Ritchie, Dec. 25, 1820.

[13] Ibid., Jefferson to Archibald Thweat, Jan. 19, 1821.

[14] Ibid., Jefferson to Roane, Mar. 9 and June 27, 1821.

[15] Taylor MSS., Taylor to Jefferson, Feb. 25, 1821.   In Archives of Maine Historical Society.

swindling", were too well intrenched to be successfully assailed.[16]

Roane was convinced that "to that work (Taylor's) may already, in a measure, be ascribed the revival which has taken place in the subject of state rights".[17]

Roane himself published numerous letters in the *Richmond Enquirer,* 1819–1821, attacking both the Bank and lottery decisions. (Latter, case of Cohens *vs.* Virginia.)   In these letters he refuted practically every constitutional view held by Marshall.   Suffice it to say here, he held that that part of the Bank decision which dealt with the source from whence the authority of the government was derived, was *obiter,* or extra-judicial, because it had nothing to do with whether the Bank law was constitutional.[18]   As regards the Cohens case, he quoted Marshall as saying in the Virginia Convention of 1788, that the judicial article of the Constitution could not be construed so as to make a sovereign state a defendant in Federal courts.[19] An examination of the debates of that Convention shows that Marshall did use such language.[20]

Taylor's *Construction Construed and Constitutions Vindicated* contains 344 pages.   While touching to some extent such other matters as appeals from state courts to the Supreme Court of the United States and the Missouri Question, it represents, in large part, an attempt to refute the constitutional arguments advanced by Marshall in the Bank case.   Taylor of course denied that there was any constitutional validity for appeals from state courts to the Supreme Court.   The Constitution declares that "the judicial power of the United States shall

---

16 Macon Correspondence, Macon to Jefferson, Oct. 20, 1821.   In Branch Historical Papers, Vol. III, pp. 78–80.

17 Roane Correspondence, Roane to Jefferson, Feb. 25, 1821.   In Branch Historical Papers, Vol. II, pp. 137–138.

18 Roane Correspondence.   All these letters are published in Branch Historical Papers, Vol. II.   This is a reprint from the *Enquirer,* Mar. 30, 1819.

19 *Ibid.,* p. 147.   *Enquirer,* June 5, 1821.

20 "I hope that no gentlemen will think that a state will be called at the bar of the Federal court. . . . It is not rational to suppose that the sovereign power shall be dragged before a court.   Grigsby, Virginia Convention of 1788, Vol. I, p. 299.

be vested in one Supreme Court, and in inferior courts". When the judicial power of the United States is expressly defined and limited it is vested in *the Supreme and such inferior courts as Congress may from time to time establish.* "The word 'supreme' is evidently used in reference to 'inferior'. The supremacy bestowed is over the inferior courts *to be established by Congress,* and not *over the state courts,* either supreme or inferior. This is manifested by the division of jurisdiction between the supreme and inferior courts. In cases 'affecting ambassadors, public ministers, and consuls, and where a state shall be a party, the Supreme Court shall have original jurisdiction. In all other cases *before mentioned* the Supreme Court shall have appellate jurisdiction'. 'Before mentioned.' Thus expressly limiting the jurisdiction of the Supreme Court of the United States, to the subjects defined in the preceding article." He contended that had the word "supreme" bestowed "a supreme jurisdiction", there would have been no occasion for a subsequent delegation of jurisdiction to the Supreme Court; and since the subsequent delegation was in reference to appeals from inferior courts, it thus followed that the word "supreme" did not extend the jurisdiction of the Supreme Court, unless it extended the jurisdiction of inferior Federal courts. And it was not claimed that these had any authority over state courts. The Constitution did not speak of supreme and inferior legislatures, because it considered the state and Federal legislatures independent of each other in their respective spheres; and it would not have used "supreme" in reference to the judiciary, had there been only one Federal court. The Federal Judiciary, he concluded, stands in the same relation to the state judiciary, as the Federal Legislature does to the state legislatures; and "if Congress cannot repeal or injoin state laws, the Supreme Federal Court cannot injoin or abrogate state judgments or decrees".[21]

---

[21] *Construction Construed,* pp. 130–132. All words underlined are italicized by Taylor.

Taylor remarked upon the fact that state legislators, judges, and other officers are required to take an oath to support the Federal Constitution, whereas, Federal legislators and judges are not required to take an oath to support state constitutions. The reason for that distinction, he claimed, was that state legislators and judges had some duties assigned them by the Federal Constitution, and would have others arising from the laws of the United States; but Federal legislators and judges had no duties to discharge under state constitutions or laws, and being confined to the limited spheres defined by the Federal Constitution, no allegiance to state constitutions was necessary on their part. He thought no power more inconsistent with republican principles than that claimed over state laws, and consequently state constitutions, by the Supreme Court; for if it violated its legitimate Federal duties, it violated its oath, and was liable to trial and removal, but if it annulled state laws and advanced the power of Congress, by whom it was paid, it could do so with impunity, since it was not bound by any oath.[22]

Taylor approached the Bank decision from a number of standpoints. He believed that Marshall's language "that the government of the Union is the government of all; its powers are delegated by all, it represents all, and acts for all", was the language of consolidation, and that it embraced the idea of a collective people. Taylor conceived of a union of states, each state with reserved powers, so that there might not be, through the action of the Federal Government, a compulsory uniformity of temporal interests, habits and opinions of the people of many states, with many differing circumstances. Marshall spoke of what "the people have said", but Taylor conceived the term "people" to mean the people of each state. The members of the Convention which made the Constitution were chosen by states, and voted by states, without any regard to the number of people in each state. That instrument was ratified by states. The House of Representatives are chosen by the people of the

---

[22] *Construction Construed,* pp. 134–135.

several states, and the suffrage exercised in choosing them was such as was granted by each state. Had the Constitution been the act of all the people inhabiting the territory of the United States, the right of suffrage would have been made uniform. The Senators are chosen by states, and the Senate is a representation of state sovereignties, not of numbers. The President is elected indirectly by states, and directly by them, in case the electors fail to make a choice, since each state, in such a contingency, has one vote in the House of Representatives.

The states having made the Constitution, they only could amend it. Had the Constitution originated from or been made by the people inhabiting the territory of the whole Union, its amendment would have remained to them, as the amendment of the state constitutions belongs to the people of a state. "A people is a collective being", Taylor contended, "and no people or community has ever been composed in the United States, except by the inhabitants of each state, associating distinctly from every other state, by their own separate consent." There never would have been any union, he thought, had the states thought they were dissolving their own people, and creating one great people, with unrestricted power of legislation, regardless of local circumstances or local habits. The Constitution, he contended, settled "itself the meaning of the word 'people' by the reservation of all powers not delegated, to the states, respectively, or to the people". "Or" is used either to couple synonyms or to denote opposition. The last meaning could hardly apply in this case, *i. e.,* a construction which supposes the people of all the states as opposed to each state, so the term "respectively" clearly indicates that the people of each state is the sense in which the term is used.[23]

Taylor claimed that the Convention which framed the Constitution rejected the proposition to give the Federal Govern-

---

[23] *Construction Construed,* pp. 42–48, 80, 104–108. In referring to the Constitution as the product of the "people", Marshall emphasized the fact that state conventions rather than state legislatures ratified it.

ment power to create banks.[24] There was no power in the Constitution to create corporations, and no power to exempt them from taxation.   Marshall, however, was not trying to justify the creation of corporations, but the Bank as a necessary agency in the financial transactions of the government.   But when Taylor contended that there was no power to exempt corporations from taxation, nor to deny to the states their reserved right of concurrent taxation, his arguments were pertinent to the question at issue.   In exercising their reserved right of taxation, the states could tax either real or personal property.   If Congress could exempt personal property from taxation through the instrumentality of corporations, it could exempt real; for the stock of banks could as easily be composed of land as of money.   Thus not only was the state right of taxation denied, but the possibility of increased taxes upon lands not exempted, existed.[25]

Marshall contended that because the states were forbidden to tax imports and exports, the same authority which restrained them in that respect could in others, where the exercise of state powers was incompatible with the constitutional laws of the Union.[26]   Taylor contended that an unlimited right of taxation was possessed by the states, previous to the Union, and that the solitary exception under the Constitution was the prohibition to tax imports and exports.   He quoted Hamilton to the effect that any attempt on the part of the National Government to abridge the state power of taxation (except in the case of imports and exports) "would be a violent assumption of power", and that a "law abrogating or preventing the collection of a tax laid by the authority of a state (unless upon imports or exports) would not be the supreme law of the land, but an usurpation of power not granted by the Constitution".[27]

---

[24] Taylor, *New Views of the Constitution*, pp. 29-30, 275.
[25] Taylor, *Construction Construed*, pp. 88–91.
[26] *Ibid.*, p. 81.
[27] *Ibid.*, pp. 96–97.   Hamilton's statements are given from the Federalist, pp. 163 and 169.

Marshall's view was that if the end were constitutional, any means could be employed to attain it, provided such means were not prohibited by the Constitution. Since the State of Maryland would defeat the end by taxing the means, it followed that she had no right to tax "the means employed by the government of the Union, for the execution of its powers". Taylor claimed that the power of the state necessarily extended to all the "means" which Congress could employ. That power taxed Federal officers, and their property, personal and real. It taxed the same objects that the Federal Government might tax. "It is necessary to protect the lives, the limbs, and the reputations even of the standing army; and to secure every atom of property, from which the Federal Government can extract resources. Except for the protection of state sovereignty even imports would fail." [28]

As to the principle for which the State of Maryland contended, Taylor summed that up in this manner: "The State of Maryland contends for its original and reserved right to tax property. The court asserts, that Congress by creating corporations may diminish or destroy the state resource for raising revenue, coextensively with its own pleasure. By the first principle, the pecuniary resources for sustaining the Federal Government are untouched; by the second, those of the states become dependent on the Federal Government. By the first, the power of both governments, either original or delegated, as to revenue, remains concurrent; by the second, Congress assumes a power of placing whatever property it pleases beyond the reach of contribution for the support of either. By the first, a sovereignty which created private property, retains its rights; by the second, a right is claimed on behalf of a spurious sovereignty to create private property, or rather to rob the legitimate sovereignty of that which it had previously created." [29]

One of the arguments advanced by Marshall against the State

---

[28] Taylor, *Construction Construed*, pp. 151–153.
[29] *Ibid.*, p. 154.

of Maryland taxing the branch of the National Bank was that the power to tax involved the power to destroy, and that the power to destroy might defeat and render useless the power to create.[30]

Taylor thought this argument both incorrect and irrelevant. What he constantly emphasized was that states had it in their power to hamper the operations of the Federal Government, if they cared to use the power in that way. "Shall not civil government tax, because a power to tax may destroy? Have not both the state and Federal governments a power to tax; can they therefore destroy? . . . May not a power in the Federal Government to destroy state laws, defeat and render useless, the state power to create laws? . . . Has not the Constitution . . . by depending on the states for Senators, and other materials for sustaining the Federal Government, admitted the state powers to destroy and create?"[31]

It was agreed that states could create banks, a right appertaining to sovereignty. When Congress created a bank, it unavoidably created a concurrent power with the states. There was involved a mutual right of concurrent taxation. Congress had placed a slight tax on state banks, and in so doing had recognized the injustice of exempting corporate property from taxation. Yet the Court claimed for Congress the power to defeat the state concurrent right of taxation.[32]

The Court had emphasized the power conferred upon Congress to make all laws "necessary and proper" to carry into execution the powers of the government.[33] Taylor claimed that the powers of the government were simply those that were delegated, those that were "common and general" to the parties which united, and those parties were the states. The words conferred no power to assume undelegated powers, no power

---

[30] Taylor, *Construction Construed*, p. 82.
[31] *Ibid.*, p. 150.
[32] *Ibid.*, pp. 92–93.
[33] *Ibid.*, p. 81.

to make laws for carrying into execution the powers reserved
to the states. The doctrine of inference and necessity under
the "necessary and proper" clause in the Constitution could be
carried to any length; for there was nothing with which war,
taxation and commerce were not either intimately or remotely
connected. This principle (of inference) by giving Congress
power over local objects, would become as detestable as the
English theory of virtual representation, "under which the British Parliament claimed a power of local and internal legislation
over the colonies". The word "proper" used in connection with
"necessary" was meant to confine the meaning of the latter
word, so that there would not be a swerving from the Constitution, and the phrase was not meant to give Congress the
power of amending the Constitution, because that body
imagined it expedient. Wherever there were concurrent and
coördinate powers, there would be clashings, and the framers
of the Constitution must have realized this; but these clashings
were regarded as minor as compared with the evil of an absolute supremacy of Congress over the states. Certainly in the
case of a clashing between an implied Federal power (incor-
porating a bank and exempting its resources from taxation)
and a positive state power (that of taxation not forbidden), the
former could not abrogate the latter under any pretext whatsoever.[34]

The "supremacy" clause of the Constitution[35] was emphasized by the Court in the Bank decision, and was discussed at
length by Taylor in "Construction Construed". The court
declared: *"It is a question of supremacy. It is of the very*

---

[34] Taylor, *Construction Construed*, pp. 164–177. He pointed out that it had been
judicially and practically established that both Congress and the state governments
have a right to tax carriages. If the states imposed a tax amounting to a prohibition
of carriages, he wanted to know if such a state law would be void, because it might
defeat the law of Congress (p. 171).

[35] "The Constitution, and the laws of the United States which shall be made in
pursuance thereof, and all treaties made or which shall be made, under the authority
of the United States, shall be the supreme law of the land, and the judges, in every
state, shall be bound thereby, anything in the Constitution or laws of any state to the
contrary notwithstanding."

essence of supremacy to remove all obstacles to its action within its own sphere, and so to *modify every power vested in subordinate governments, as to exempt its own operations from their influence.*"[36]

But the Court, said Taylor, did not define what this supremacy was, nor how far it extended.[36a] The clause did not mean the supremacy of laws over the Constitution, for the laws passed by Congress had to be in pursuance of the Constitution. It did not bestow the supremacy upon the Federal Government. The clause amounted to no more than that the Constitution was the supreme law of the land. Since this instrument proceeded "from the sovereignty of the people, the highest political authority, the term was proper; because it was paramount and supreme over whatever should proceed from any inferior authority; and as the Constitution embraced our whole system of government, both state and Federal, by delegating and reserving powers, the supremacy bestowed on it was intended equally and coextensively to protect and secure the powers delegated to the Federal Government, and those reserved to the states". The declaration confirmed all the "limitations, divisions, and restrictions of power" embraced in the Constitution.[37]

"Supremacy", in the terminology of the court, had as its very essence the removal of "all obstacles to its action within its own sphere". But then it spoke of a supreme sphere modifying "every power vested in subordinate governments". Taylor thought it useless to concede principles if they could be evaded. Were there not two spheres? "The Court had previously admitted that the Federal and state governments were '*both sovereign* with respect to the objects committed to them, and

---

[36] *Construction Construed*, p. 119. Words underlined italicized by Taylor.

[36a] What Marshall claimed was that the Federal Government was supreme, and that federal implied powers restricted what Taylor regarded as reserved powers. The sphere in which the state was sovereign would thus necessarily be vaguely defined, for it would be determined from time to time by any "means" the Federal Government chose to use in achieving its ends.

[37] *Ibid.*, pp. 122–125.

neither sovereign with respect to the objects committed to the other'; but now it takes it for granted, that the Federal sphere is *supreme,* the state spheres *subordinate,* and that in consequence of this supremacy and subordinacy, the Federal Government has a right 'so to *modify every power* vested in the state governments, as to exempt its own operations from their influence.' " Was not the Federal Government, in its operations, unavoidably influenced by the states in many ways? The state governments, by the Constitution, had the right to appoint Senators and electors of a President, for the very purpose of influencing those operations for their own security. They had the concurrent right of internal taxation with the Federal Government, and the operation of this right could influence that government powerfully. If the position of the Court, in its effort to destroy a positive state power and thus strengthen an assumed Federal power, were correct, that body might appoint Senators, electors, and militia officers, should the states neglect to do it; for these were enumerated influencing state powers, just as was the right of taxation.[38]

Not long after the publication of Taylor's work, the Virginia Assembly, by the overwhelming vote of 138 to 18, protested against the decision of the Court in the case of Cohens *vs.* Virginia, claiming that there was no right of appeal from the courts of one independent government to those of another, and that since the State became the defendant in that case, the action was contrary to the eleventh amendment.[39] Approximately a year before this time, the Legislature had instructed its Senators to work for amendments to the Constitution providing for the creation of a tribunal to decide conflicts between the powers of the state and Federal Government, and prohibiting Congress from establishing any bank or corporation not confined to the District of Columbia. It was declared that the Bank was not authorized by the Constitution.[40]

---

[38] *Construction Construed,* pp. 125–128. Words underlined italicized by Taylor.
[39] Journal of House of Delegates, Feb. 9, 1821.
[40] *Ibid.,* Dec. 22, 1819, Feb. 12, 1820.

Thomas Mann Randolph, Governor of Virginia, in his message of December 1821, devoted half of his message to the humiliation of Virginia in the Cohens Case. He was convinced that the majority of the people thought, when the Constitution was ratified, that it meant a government of limited powers, but if the minority had now become the majority, it was well to know that fact through the medium of a convention for revising the Constitution.[41]

In 1822, Taylor published another book entitled *Tyranny Unmasked*. An able scholar has called this "a powerful and brilliant book", and the man who wrote it "the most brilliant mind in the Republican organization of the Old Dominion".[42] Roane declared that work Taylor's principal one. He felt that "this venerable patriot deserves great praise for his intrepid and unceasing efforts to preserve our beloved Confederacy".[43]

In this work of 349 pages, Taylor makes probably the most powerful and comprehensive attack upon the protective tariff system that can be found in American history. That system he had previously attacked in both *The Arator* and *Construction Construed*. After the close of the War of 1812, there was passed (1816) a bill which was designed to protect from cheap English goods the infant manufacturing industries that had come into existence as a result of the Jefferson-Madison restrictive policy upon American commerce, and as a result of the war itself. Having tasted of the fruits of protection and whetted their appetites, the manufacturing interests longed to appease them. An attempt to pass another tariff bill, raising the scale of duties, failed in 1820 by one vote. In the meantime the opposition to the tariff had been strongly manifested in Taylor's State.[44]

---

[41] Journal of House of Delegates, Dec. 3, 1821.

[42] Beveridge, *Life of John Marshall*, pp. 366 and 335.

[43] Roane Correspondence, Roane to Archibald Thweatt, Dec. 11, 1821. In Branch Historical Papers, Vol. II, pp. 140–141.

[44] See protest of Agricultural Society of Fredericksburg, Dec. 29, 1819, in *American Farmer*, Vol. I, p. 332. See also protests from various organizations in Tyler, *Letters and Times of the Tylers*, Vol. I, pp. 332–333.

Taylor's stated purpose in writing *Tyranny Unmasked* was to check that loss of state internal power and consequent tendency to consolidation, which he believed would end in tyranny, unless checked.[45] Tyranny he defined as a transfer of property by law to feed an oppressive government or to foster exclusive privileges.[46] The attempt to change the natural course of trade by protective duties, a policy designed to enrich capitalists, had been given added emphasis by the favorable report of the Committee of Manufactures on January 15, 1821. Taylor develops his principles by an analysis of this report.[47]

As to all matters of public policy, he applied the test as to whether it was constitutional. The power to impose a protective tariff was claimed under the clause giving Congress the power "to regulate commerce with foreign nations, and among the several states, and with the Indian tribes". Taylor claimed that this conferred no power to regulate internal exchanges between individuals, or to destroy the freedom of exchanges, by conferring monopolies upon some individuals operating upon other individuals. "Foreign nations, states, and Indian tribes, are united in one article, and intended to be affected in one mode. Did this article empower Congress to make one Indian tribe tributary to another; to build factories in one tribe, in order to provide objects for an excise, and to destroy the freedom of exchanges between the individuals composing the tribes? Did it give to Congress the same power as to foreign nations?" Evidently not. It followed that it conferred no such power as regards state internal exchanges, because the power was equivalent as to each, and therefore the construction must be equivalent. If the construction were absurd in the first two cases, it would follow that it was in the third.[48]

For the new school of construction, if an article in the Constitution did not verbally reach the end in view, it was drawn

---

[45] Taylor, *Tyranny Unmasked*, Preface, p. 4.
[46] *Tyranny Unmasked*, p. 41.
[47] *Ibid.*, p. 9.
[48] *Ibid.*, 189–190.

up to it, as if wire, by construction; but if it did verbally reach the end in view, it was considered as if there were no other parts of the Constitution. Why prohibit a tax on the exportation from any state (as the Constitution does), if Congress can impair or destroy the right of exportation to enrich capitalists? Why prohibit preferences, in regulating commerce, to the parts of one state over those of another, if states can be made tributary to other states? What becomes of the equality of states? [49]

Taylor referred to the clause to impose taxation "to provide for the common defense and general welfare of the United States". This he interpreted to mean legislation, in the ways specified in the Constitution, in regard to matters common to the states, since no union existed among the persons composing the states. Legislation for the defense and welfare of private individuals was thus reserved to the states.[50]

The idea of a favorable balance of trade based on the idea of specie coming into the country, Taylor ridiculed. Money was not the regulator of the balance of trade, but had its own value regulated by the price of commodities; and this price was regulated by plenty, scarcity, fashions and follies, climates and soils, and a thousand other things. "This never ceasing fluctuation is the basis of commerce, the invigorator of industry, and the equalizer of comforts. It is also the appraiser of money, and bills of exchange are used to execute its valuations." [51]

Agriculture was the very basis of our prosperity and our commerce, yet by forcing nature out of her course, a protective tariff diminished agricultural operations, and put a stop to the only means we had of drawing money and capital from foreign nations. It restricted the foreign market, yet we had an abundance of uncultivated land. "Have not the laws of nature decided which is the best substratum for commercial rivalry and competition, cheapness or dearness? Shall we build up a

---

[49] *Construction Construed*, p. 221. *Tyranny Unmasked*, pp. 133–134.
[50] *Construction Construed*, pp. 213–214.
[51] *Tyranny Unmasked*, pp. 72 and 78.

competition with foreign nations upon the cheapness of our land, or upon the dearness of our manufactures?" [52]

But it was claimed that the development of manufactures would increase the labor supply and would build up cities, thus creating a "home market" for agricultural products. Taylor thought the idea that home markets could consume all or nearly all of our products absurd. Thus the foreign markets would still consume most of them, but the agriculturists would receive in return money, and this would be paid to the home manufacturer for his articles. The amount paid would be approximately double the value of the article abroad, and the freight upon the exported article would be double, because of lack of return cargoes. The manufacturer, without any protective tariff, would be aided by ocean freights, revenue duties, and cheapness of materials. [53]

Another argument urged by Taylor was that a protective tariff diminished revenue, and hence would force us to resort to unlimited excises and other internal taxes, to supply the deficiency. Yet the collection of duties was less expensive than the collection of excises; duties were collected without invading our homes, and "excises are keys to every lock"; duties fall mostly upon the wealthy, because they purchase foreign commodities, but excises reach chiefly the poor, because they subsist largely on home products. [54]

An argument which will sound very familiar at the time of this writing was that the restrictive policy would produce retaliation on the part of foreign nations. "If we expel foreign commodities, will they not retaliate? If we expel foreign ships, would not foreign nations expel ours? Will these mutual explosions foster commerce?" [55]

Taylor concluded his work with the following references to

---

[52] *Tyranny Unmasked,* pp. 119–122. Taylor meant that we would diminish both the quantity and the value of our exports, easy to produce, and in addition, pay a bounty to the home manufacturer, until manufactures could be exported.

[53] *Ibid.,* pp. 240–242.

[54] *Ibid.,* pp. 168–170.

[55] *Ibid.,* p. 191.

the heterogeneous course of reasoning that had been followed in regard to the relations between Federal and state powers.

"The people of the United States, and not the people of the states, made the Federal Government; and therefore the Federal Government has a right to exercise the powers reserved by the people to the state governments.

"Powers are divided between the Federal and state departments to restrain ambitious men in both. They are accumulated in the hands of ambitious men in one.

"Confederation is union. Consolidation is union.

"Each state has a right to make its own constitution. Congress has a right to make a constitution for each state.

"Each state has a right to make its own local laws. Congress and the court can repeal them, and make local laws for the states.

"The people of the states have a right to make the Federal Constitution, and to prohibit its alteration, except with the concurrence of three-fourths of the legislatures of the several states. Congress and the Supreme Court may make alterations without the concurrence of a single state or a majority of the people of all the states.

"The protection of property is an end of government. Its transfer by fraudulent laws is another end.

"The states have a right to impose local taxes for state use. Congress may make corporations with a right to tax the states, and prohibit the states from taxing them.

"State judges take an oath to be loyal to the state right of internal self-government. Federal judges, who take no such oath, may force them to break it.

"Congress may establish post roads. It may make all roads. It may make war, that is, it may make canals.

"Congress is empowered to govern ten miles square. It may therefore govern all the states internally, with the concurrence of the Supreme Court. This closes the drama by a catastrophe reaching all powers whatsoever." [56]

---

[56] *Tyranny Unmasked*, pp. 342–345.

Chapter XII

A STALWART LEADER TO THE END

In 1823 Taylor published another book entitled *New Views of the Constitution.* It was almost equal in length to the two preceding it by one and three years, respectively, and it was the fifth book published by Taylor. Upon it is the stamp of a disciplined mind, and in it, in the writer's opinion, may be found Taylor's constitutional logic in its most finished form. But the matters treated are in large part those discussed in the preceding works. The tendency to repeat might be suggested as a criticism of the works of this profound thinker.

Madison, whom Taylor sharply criticized in this, his last work, felt that "the distinguished author" may have avoided possible errors by access to "more competent lights as to the proceedings of the Convention" (of 1787) than the ones relied upon, though Madison admitted that he had, at the time his letter was written, read only a few passages in the beginning of Taylor's work.[1] Madison had written Jefferson before he received *New Views,* etc., that he (Madison) held that the judiciary of the United States was the constitutional resort for determining the line between Federal and state jurisdiction, despite "the ingenious reasonings of Colonel Taylor against this construction of the Constitution".[2]

Jefferson was afraid that Taylor's was the voice of one crying in the wilderness, for those who claimed to hold Federal views, but never did, were "marching by the road of construction to consolidation". The Federal Government was our foreign government, he contended, and in purely domestic matters was invested with but one power over the state authorities, that of

---

[1] Writings of Madison, Hunt Edition, Vol. IX. Madison to Robert S. Garnett, Feb. 11, 1824. Garnett was a Virginia Congressman who had sent Taylor's work to Madison.

[2] *Ibid.,* Congressional Edition, Vol. 3. Madison to Jefferson, June 27, 1823.

metallic tenders. He believed that there was danger of disunion, unless three amendments then before Congress were
passed. One of these provided for the limitation of the term
of presidential service, one for keeping the choice of the President effectually in the hands of the people, and one for giving
to Congress the power of internal improvements only on condition that each state's Federal proportion of the monies so expended shall be employed within the state.[3] As we shall see
presently, Taylor sponsored as Senator, the second of these
amendments.

Taylor claimed that all efforts made in the Convention which
made the Constitution to give the Federal Government a negative on state laws were rejected. He referred to the rejection of
Edmund Randolph's suggestion "that a national government
ought to be established, consisting of a supreme legislature,
judiciary and executive", contended that it was never even
suggested to make the judiciary supreme, and that if the Convention refused to give the power to all the Federal departments to construe the articles of union and negative state
laws, it never intended by mere inference to give it to anyone
of those departments. Madison on June 8, 1787, moved to
allow the National Legislature to negative all state laws "which
to them shall seem improper", and only Massachusetts, Pennsylvania and Virginia voted for it. Yet this was the very power
the Court now claimed. Had proposals for such negatives in
the Convention ever been published, Taylor believed every
state would have remonstrated against them.[4]

He strongly attacked Madison, as well as Hamilton, for trying
to lead the people to think it was a Federal Government, when
they were working for ratification of the Constitution, if they
did not believe it was. He then quoted Madison, number 39
of the *Federalist,* as saying that "each state in ratifying the Constitution is considered as a sovereign body, independent of all

---

[3] Writings of Jefferson, Ford Edition, Vol. X, Jefferson to Garnett, Feb. 14, 1824.
[4] Taylor, *New Views of Constitution,* pp. 20–22, 25, 35.

others, and only to be bound by its own voluntary act", and number 45 of the same work, to the effect that "the former (Federal powers) will be exercised principally on external objects, as war, peace, negotiations, and foreign commerce; with which last the power of taxation will for the most part be connected. The power reserved to the several states will extend to all objects, which, in the ordinary course of affairs, concern the lives, liberties, and properties of the people; and the internal order, improvement, and prosperity of the state." [5]

The greatest evils for our future, thought Taylor, were geographical combinations, based on interest. If local interests were left to the states, such combinations could be avoided, but if not left to them, there would come consolidation, which would produce lasting discord and oppression. "If a northern, southern and western interest are not opposed to each other in Congress, by investing it with a supreme power over state rights, they cannot endanger the Union; but if either can acquire local advantages from a national supremacy, it will aggravate the geographical danger apprehended by Mr. Madison (in Convention of 1787), a perpetual warfare of intrigues will ensue, and a dissolution of the Union will result." [6]

If our political system would survive, Taylor felt that three principles must be accepted: first, a supremacy of state and Federal constitutions over the repositories of power created by their articles; second, a limited supremacy in both cases, subject in one to the people of a state, in the other to the supremacy of three-fourths of the states; third, that no power created can violate these supremacies. [7] He wanted to know who were the guardians of the compact, of the guarantee of a republican form of government, of the reservation of undelegated powers? Were they judges who were responsible to another government, or the people of a state? [8] The word supreme was used

---

[5] Taylor, *New Views of Constitution*, pp. 50 and 83.
[6] *Ibid.*, pp. 85–86, 209, 246.
[7] *Ibid*, p. 163.
[8] *Ibid.*, p. 136.

twice in the Constitution, once in reference to the superiority of the high courts over inferior Federal courts, and once in declaring the Constitution, and the laws made according to it, supreme. Did it create two supremacies, and were the judges supreme over the Constitution, or *vice versa?* And were laws made in pursuance of the Constitution, if they violated reserved rights? [9]

As independent political departments, the Federal and state governments acted as mutual checks upon each other, and each possessed a supreme negative power over the other. For of what use was a reserved power, if it could be taken away? Sovereign states created the Union, retained political powers not given away, and instead of saying they may be taken away by the Federal Government, the Constitution says expressly they shall not. This reservation he interpreted to be a positive constitutional veto, a violation of which a state had a moral right to resist.[10]

But if the Federal and state governments should clash, was there no arbiter? Taylor said that there was, and in the Constitution. "Two-thirds of Congress may appeal from an erroneous state construction, and propose an amendment for controlling it, to the tribunal invested with the right of decision. Why was this right of appeal limited to two-thirds of Congress, if a majority was invested with a supreme power of construction, or if the same majority could appeal to the Federal court? Two-thirds were required to prevent hasty and frivolous appeals, and to preserve the rights of the states against party majorities and geographical prepossessions. If two-thirds will not appeal against a state law, it is an admission of its constitutionality, by the constitutional mode established for deciding the question. If this specified mode is defeated by transferring the supremacy of construction from two-thirds of Congress and three-fourths of the states, to a majority of Con-

---

9 Taylor, *New Views of Constitution*, pp. 22–23.
10 *Ibid.*, p. 34; also *Tyranny Unmasked*, pp. 255–257.

gress and a majority of the Court, one of these majorities would be invested with a power of deciding collisions between the state and Federal governments, although neither is invested with a right even to propose an alteration of the powers given to either department by the Constitution. The precision in the mode of amendment, is the remedy provided against any want of precision, in the division of powers, which the licentiousness of construction might lay hold of.... In this provision the Constitution discloses an eminent superiority over every other division of power which has hitherto been invented." [11]

The last words in the last book of this fervent champion of a Federal Union constituted a plea for a faithful adherence to the principle of division of powers between the state and Federal governments, for "if the state and Federal governments may be occasionally scratched by the mutual check resulting from the division of powers, it may still be considered as the only brier which bears the rose called liberty".[12]

Though on two previous occasions Taylor had refused to remain long in the Senate when elected or appointed, he was elected to that position less than two years before his death to succeed James Pleasants, Jr., who became Governor of Virginia.[13] That he served his term until removed by death was probably due to his conviction that consolidation tendencies should be checked, and that he might render service along that line by serving in a public capacity. Extracts from a letter to his lifelong friend, Monroe, indicate that he was firmly convinced that a moneyed aristocracy was thriving upon legislative favors, bestowed at the expense of the true principles of our government. "The assumption of state debts, the creation of a bank, bounties to factory owners, and the pension law, whether they were usurpations or not, united with other causes, have had the effect of transferring from a vast majority, many

---

[11] New Views of the Constitution, p. 256.
[12] Ibid., p. 316.
[13] Journal of House of Delegates, Dec. 18, 1822.

millions annually, to a capitalist and geographical minority, but little interested in the soil. The result, however effected, is neither just nor republican. It is merely a tribute, politically unwise, and personally oppressive, unalleviated by any means of getting the money back. . . . It has established a powerful excitement to political craft and ambitious intrigues. By increasing the profit of pecuniary capital from six to fifteen per antum, whilst that of land remains as low as four or lower, money is made to flee from agricultural investments and improvements, or from loss to gain; and in fact the improvement of agriculture is prohibited by legislation." [14] In this same letter he inquired as to Madison's views, and expressed the opinion that he did not believe Madison could have so far departed from his earlier views as to favor a judicial censorship over the Constitution, and the imposition of an enormous annual tribute (tariff duties) over two-thirds of the states.

Taylor played an active part in the sessions of Congress in 1823 and 1824, though he was in very feeble health before the sessions were concluded. [15] Because there were many aspirants for the presidency to succeed Monroe after 1824, the indications were that the election would go to the House of Representatives. Taylor, who had in a caucus in 1803 been chosen to introduce the twelfth amendment, [16] now suggested another amendment which was designed to keep the election from going to the House. If the Electors failed to make a choice for President at their first meeting, they were to meet a second time, and choose between the two highest candidates, or more, if more than two had an equal number of votes. Then if they failed to make a choice the matter would go to the House. The proposed amendment was later changed, so that if the election was not made by the electoral college, the Senate and House voting jointly and individually would elect. If the majority

[14] Taylor MSS., Taylor to Monroe, April 29, 1823. In Branch Historical Papers, Vol. II, p. 348.
[15] C. F. Adams, Memoirs of John Quincy Adams, Vol. VI, p. 263, Feb. 21, 1824.
[16] Ibid.

present did not render a choice on the first ballot, then a plu-
rality choice would be final.[17] Taylor spoke of the necessity of
constantly repairing the Constitution, so that its powers would
not become merged in legislation and precedent, and of the
possibility of intrigue in a House election.

Mahlon Dickerson, in the same month (January) proposed
an amendment to Taylor's, whereby Electors would be uniformly elected by districts throughout the Union, and would
vote but once before the election went to Congress. Taylor
made an impressive speech against this amendment, claiming
that an election by districts would tend to create an aristocracy
of small states, to throw election into Congress, and to produce
a national rather than a Federal Government. An election by
Congress tended towards an unnatural and illegitimate connection between the legislative and executive departments.
Dickerson stated that he was unable then to reply to Taylor's
speech, and when he did, referred to the Virginian as "a veteran
in constitutional disquisitions, whose opinions on subjects connected with our Constitution, even when unsupported by reasoning or facts, have nearly acquired the weight of conclusive
arguments". He contended that his amendment would produce a needed uniformity in the electoral system, and that Taylor's plan of a second reference to Electors would lead to intrigue
and combinations.[18] At the next session of Congress, after
Benton of Missouri and Hayne of South Carolina had each proposed amendments in regard to electing the President, and
Taylor and Dickerson had staged another debate, the matter
was indefinitely postponed.[19] Jefferson and Thomas Ritchie
both favored Taylor's suggested amendment.[20]

Taylor heartily supported the bill sponsored by R. M. John-

---

[17] Annals of Seventeenth Congress. Second Session, Jan. 10 and 28, 1823.

[18] *Ibid.*, Jan. 30, Feb. 7 and 11, 1823.

[19] Annals of Eighteenth Congress, First Session, Dec. 11, and 15, 1823. March
22, 1824.

[20] See Jefferson above, and Ritchie, *Richmond Enquirer,* Oct. 7, 1823.

son, providing for abolition of imprisonment for debt.[21a] He
was one of a committee, composed of Johnson, Van Buren and
others, which framed a bill designed to reconcile conflicting
opinions in regard to that question. Hayne opposed the bill
on the ground that just debts could not be collected under its
operations.[21b]

Taylor brought in and spoke at length in behalf of a bill providing for the settlement of pecuniary claims against the United
States. All such claims were to be decided, according to the
bill, in district and circuit courts, and not in Congress. Once
decided in courts, they would be settled, and could not be revived again. Such trials diminished the dignity of Congress
and consumed much of its valuable time. Van Buren spoke
against the bill. He believed that it was not wise for Congress
to settle claims, but claimed that some body or commission at
Washington should, since the evidence respecting the claims
was all there.[22]

In the early 1820's, Adams, as Secretary of State, had been
trying to negotiate a convention with England in regard to the
suppression of the African slave trade. The convention finally
agreed upon recognized the slave traffic as piracy under the law
of nations, and provided that traders seized should be tried
under the tribunals of the nations concerned.[23] Adams sought
the aid of Taylor in having the Senate delay action until Monroe had sent his message concerning the Convention. Taylor
approved the Convention, but stated that all the partisans of

---

[21a] The bill was designed to relieve debtors, owing the United States, provided
said debtors could take the proper oath as to their insolvency. Eighteenth Congress,
First Session, Dec. 23, 1823.

[21b] Annals of Seventeenth Congress, Second Session, Jan. 15 and 21, 1823; Annals of Eighteenth Congress, First Session, April 5, 6, 8, 9. The bill passed the
Senate 24 to 19.

[22] Annals of Eighteenth Congress, First Session, April 1, 2, 24. The bill failed
25 to 19.

[23] Du Bois, *Suppression of the African Slave Trade*, pp. 138–140.

Crawford, a candidate for President, were bitterly opposed to it. He specified Holmes of Maine and Van Buren.[24]

A matter of suggested public policy which had provoked much debate since the conclusion of the second war with England, afforded Taylor an excellent opportunity to defend, before the Senate, his strict construction view of the Constitution. That there was a need for internal improvements no one denied, but whether roads and canals should be constructed by the Federal Government or by the states was a question that gave rise to differences of opinion. Madison and Monroe, while favorable to an amendment to the Constitution giving that power, had both vetoed a bill providing for internal improvements by the Federal Government, on the ground that there was no warrant in the Constitution for such action.

Soon after he entered the Senate, Taylor spoke in opposition to a bill making an appropriation for repairing the Cumberland Road from Cumberland to the Ohio River. He claimed that the bill was unconstitutional, that the general government could not make improvements at all in the states, because such would be a departure from the express powers given Congress.[25] The following session he made an extended speech opposing a measure involving an appropriation of $30,000 for surveys for roads and canals. Such measures, he held, would "inflame geographical interests", and would level the "outworks by which the Constitution is defended". He then analyzed three constitutional arguments advanced in behalf of a Federal policy of internal improvements.

"Congress shall have power to establish post roads." Congress, he claimed, could direct the mail to pass from one place to another, but *establish* did not mean to *make*. Moreover, *establish* could not apply in connection with the bill under con-

---

[24] Adams, Memoirs of John Quincy Adams, including his Diary, pp. 344–345, 348–349, May 21, 22, 1824.

[25] Annals of Seventeenth Congress, Second Session, Jan. 7, 1823.

sideration, whatever its meaning, for canals in the bill were united with roads, and "happily the Constitution does not give to Congress a power to establish post canals".

"Congress shall have power to regulate commerce with foreign nations, among the several states, and with Indian tribes." Was the word *commerce* used in a general or restricted sense? If in an unrestricted sense, it would reach the whole intercourse among men, but if in a restricted sense, its meaning would apply in the case of the states, as in the cases of foreign nations and Indian tribes. "Does the word 'commerce' give a power to Congress to make roads and canals for these nations and tribes? If not, as this word is used in the clause as equally applicable to all three of its members, it follows irresistibly, that it does not empower Congress to make roads and canals for the states."

It was contended that since Congress had the power to make war and to tax, it certainly had the inferior power to make roads and canals. Taylor replied that "thus all minor powers are assumed by these two greater powers, and the states possess no reserved powers, unless such as are of greater magnitude than those of war and taxation. . . . Thus a complete subjection is substituted for the sovereignty of the states. The law of power is substituted for the law of compact. . . ." [26]

During this last session of Congress in which he served, Taylor argued with great vigor against the protective tariff system. He contended that it destroyed the equality of states by enriching some at the expense of others, and that it created a special aristocracy by imposing a heavy tax on the community at large. Funding, assumption, banking, the tariff and pensions, all contributed to the building up of this pecuniary aristocracy. What became, he asked, of the uniformity required in the Constitution in respect to taxation, if the word "commerce" were to be construed so as to destroy that uniformity? "The uniformity required in the imposition of imports and other taxes corre-

[26] Annals of Eighteenth Congress, First Session, Apr. 22, 1824.

sponds with a construction of this word (commerce) which leaves unimpaired the local justice and security intended to be established by this uniformity, and visibly interdicts the destruction of one of the plainest principles of our Federal Union, by giving to a single word, used in a particular case, and limited to a special application, a meaning which would obliterate substantially the uniformity required, and expose the members of the Union to the frauds and oppression which this rule was intended to prevent."

He denied that the tariff was national in its nature, and presented figures from official reports, to show that six New England states plus New York, New Jersey and Pennsylvania, rather a small group in them, profited at the expense of the other seventeen states. "The whole amount drawn by the nine from the seventeen states is $28,456,585. Of this sum, $12,628,014 are imposed by legal contrivances, and $15,828,572 gained by tonnage and importations." He claimed that a commercial balance of trade could not be estimated in terms of money nor customs houses. Prices at which different commodities sell, and the difference of labor employed in their production, were factors to be considered. He thought the factor of the balance of trade might be considered in relation to the nine and the seventeen states classified above.

Finally, he warned once more of the dangers and the injustice of consolidation of power in the hands of the Federal Government. "Under our Constitution, neither territories nor representation were intended to be consolidated; or law, geographically partial, to be enacted. It was never intended that the West should be the guardian of the East, nor the North of the South, nor that the specious but false idea of a national representation should be used to abolish a real representation, upon which a republican government must be founded, or finally cease to exist." [27]

Taylor died before the presidential election of 1824, but either

[27] Annals of Eighteenth Congress, First Session, Apr. 29, May 3 and 4, 1824.

Adams or Calhoun was his choice. After Calhoun ceased to be a candidate, Adams was presumably his choice. He hoped that Calhoun was merely for the tariff temporarily, and that Adams would look upon that policy as inimical to commerce. Both had moral rectitude, both were wisely frugal, and neither would be guided by avarice and ambition. Calhoun never believed in monorchy, but regarded the Federal Government as superior to the states, whenever they came into conflict. Adams's monarchical ideas were a thing of the past and his views as to a division of power between the Federal and state governments were not well known.[28]

John Quincy Adams, in his Diary, states that Taylor told him that the Virginia Legislature had been "managed" into the support of Crawford, but that the latter's health was so poor, he thought Virginia would have to support someone else. Taylor was convinced that the members of the House of Representatives from Virginia would support neither Clay nor Jackson, though the Richmond Junta favored Clay. If New York declared for Adams, the Virginia Senator was sure that Virginia would.[29]

One of the last acts of Taylor was to write a letter to his personal friend, but political adversary, of former days, John Adams. That Taylor had a premonition of fast approaching death, extracts from this letter will show. "During a long illness from which I have not yet recovered, the reveries which usually amuse sick people visited me; and among them the idea of writing a farewell letter to you presented itself so often as to leave an impression, which I have not been able to subdue." He referred to the bitter fight for the presidency in 1800, and the party spirit that was manifested, yet reminded Adams that the latter "soared above its prejudices, and saved your country from a ruinous war with France".

---

28 Taylor MSS., Taylor to Monroe, Apr. 29, 1823. In Branch Historical Papers, Vol. II, p. 348.
29 Adams, C. F., Memoirs of John Quincy Adams, comprising Portions of his Diary, 1795–1848. Vol. VI, pp. 356–357. May 25, 1824.

"As the last, at my age it will not be suspected of adulation. For this, no motive exists. My design is to file among your archives some facts, which may meet the eye of a historian, as well as to give some pleasure to a patriot, who, I believe, has served his country faithfully, and has done what man can do to please his God." [30]

Adams replied to Taylor, thanking him for *New Views of the Constitution,* and expressing the hope that he might contribute to the preservation of the Constitution. He felt that Taylor had misunderstood him earlier, so his letter was designed principally to remove misapprehensions Taylor may have had of his views. "I see you have treated me with honor and respect enough, but I think you have not correctly comprehended the intentions of my poor book. That work was written under the old Confederation, and had no relation at all to the general government. It respected only a state government, and particularly the Constitution of Massachusetts, and others that resembled it, as against Turgot who had censured them all. There is but one allusion to the central government in the whole work; in that, I expressly say that Congress is not a representative body, but a diplomatic body, a collection of ambassadors from thirteen sovereign states. A consolidated government was never alluded to, or recommended in any part of the work; nor, indeed, in any moment of my life, did I ever approve of a consolidated government, or would I have given my vote for it. A consolidated government under a monarchy, an aristocracy or a democracy, or a mixture of either, would have flown to pieces like a glass bubble under the first blow of a hammer on an anvil." [31]

Taylor made his will January 7, 1824. This, given in the Appendix, indicates that he had amassed considerable property in both land and slaves since he started plantation operations, and that he was very equitable in providing for his wife, children and grandchildren.

---

[30] C. F. Adams, *Works of John Adams,* Vol. X., Taylor to Adams, Apr. 8, 1824.
[31] *Ibid.,* Adams to Taylor, Apr. 12, 1824.

The distinguished Virginian, who had been in ill health during his last years in the Senate, died on August 21, 1824, at his plantation home, Hazelwood. Thomas Ritchie, in the *Richmond Enquirer,* announced his death in the following language: "The death of John Taylor of Caroline is confirmed. The great lawyer—the profound politician—the friend of the Constitution in its original purity—he who served as a member of the State Legislature in the dark days of '98 and '99—who formerly shone as a member of the United States Senate, and who has been dotted anew with the confidence of Virginia in the same high capacity—he, who both by precept and example has scattered a flood of light over agriculture, the staple occupation of this people, 'the chosen people' of the land, has suddenly descended to the tomb, 'full of years and full of honor'! Let Virginia weep over the ashes of the illustrious patriot." [32]

Equally eloquent was the following tribute paid to Taylor by Thomas H. Benton, a contemporary who was himself destined ere long to great political fame: "All my observations of him, and his whole appearance and deportment, went to confirm the reputation of his individuality of character, and high qualities of the head and heart. I can hardly figure to myself the ideal of a republican statesman more perfect and complete than he was in reality: plain and solid, a wise counsellor, a ready and vigorous debater, acute and comprehensive, ripe in all historical and political knowledge, innately republican— modest, courteous, benevolent, hospitable—a skillful, practical farmer, giving his time to his farm and his books when not called by an emergency to the public service—and returning to his books and his farm when the emergency was over. . . . He belonged to that constellation of great men which shone so brightly in Virginia in his day, and the light of which was not limited to Virginia, or our America, but spread through the bounds of the civilized world." [33]

---

[32] *Richmond Enquirer,* Aug. 27, 1824.
[33] Benton, *Thirty Years' View,* Vol. I, p. 45.

CHAPTER XIII

ESTIMATE OF LIFE AND CHARACTER

MANY times in his quest of material for this study, the author gazed in reflective mood upon the portrait of John Taylor in the Virginia State Library, a portrait which revealed a kind and genial nature, a sterling character, and a profound intellect. In appearance Taylor was tall and slender, and had in common with Jefferson not only political principles, but also red hair. This latter physical trait was said to be a "peculiarity of the Virginians". Two-thirds of the officers who passed through Petersburg on their way to join the army of Greene during the Revolution had red hair.[1]

In both a military and civil sense, Taylor was imbued with the spirit of the American Revolution. After aiding in the winning of independence, he continued to fight for what he regarded as the principles of the Revolution. That movement he interpreted as a protest against centralized control of the colonies by the British Government, and in its place he did not deem it wise to erect a consolidated government, which, in the exercise of its powers, would tend to produce discord among states widely different in their interests. He often lamented the fact that the Revolution did not mean freedom of property, though it did freedom of religion. These were its twin offspring, and he saw no reason to praise the one and to destroy, by legislation, the other.

This Virginia planter, unlike some of the prominent leaders of the same class, was a genuine democrat. In the Virginia Convention of 1829–30, five years after Taylor's death, many of the large slaveholders still clung to the idea that property was an element to be favored in apportioning Representatives for

---

[1] H. B. Grigsby, The Virginia Convention of 1776, p. 202.

the Legislature. Taylor had favored representation according to numbers even before the eighteenth century came to a close. According to Jefferson, he and Taylor both believed the Virginia county court system in need of reform. The justices of the peace in this system often comprised a Cabal, which controlled politics locally, and which frequently selected candidates for State offices. When vacancies occurred in the court, they were filled by the members themselves.[2]

The intellectual power of Taylor is apparent wherever his thoughts are expressed. In his pamphlets, books, correspondence, and speeches, he discusses from almost every conceivable angle the subject with which he is dealing. He fortified the Virginia school of political leaders with logic, such logic that they did not hesitate to praise him as their ablest publicist. His four books on government and the Constitution total 1665 pages. This total does not include his *Arator* of 296 pages, nor his various pamphlets. It may be suggested that one has to read these works carefully to unravel Taylor's thoughts, because he constantly repeats, and frequently does not complete one phase of thought before he passes on to another.

Taylor's marked spirit of independence may account for the fact that he would not participate in public life to a great extent, or the fact that he did not participate to a great extent may account for his independence. It will probably be said that he temporarily sacrificed his fundamental political principles when he supported the Louisiana Purchase. However, at other times he parted company with the Virginia State Rights School, and did not hesitate to criticize them severely, when, in his opinion, they were swerving from the pure principles of the Constitution.

Taylor's thinking embodied the spirit of prophecy. From the beginning of his career to its end he protested against

---

2 Writings of Jefferson, Jefferson to Taylor, July 21, 1816. Vol. X, Ford Edition, pp. 50–55.

special privileges to any class or group through legislative enactments. A public debt, exclusive privileges for corporations, bounties to capitalists, all tended to create a moneyed aristocracy. That governmental favors and extravagance, natural concomitants of the growth of the powers of the Federal Government, have aided in concentrating wealth and in increasing taxation, few will deny. During a period of the rapid growth and expansion of the country, men differed as to the best way to promote its interest. Some claimed that this growth demanded greater energy on the part of the Federal Government; others claimed that it produced an even greater diversity of interests among the states than existed when the Constitution was formed, and that hence due regard for the rights of the states was the only principle that could prevent discord.

Taylor held to the latter view. Matters of common interest to the states were proper subjects for legislation by Congress; but the wielding of broad powers over individuals by that body, or legislation for one group of states at the expense of the other would result in a dissolution of the Union. The exercise of such powers would inflame geographical interests, and would ultimately result in the oppression of a minority by a majority.

One would judge from reading the works of Mr. Phillips and others on slavery that the owners of large plantations were very systematic in the handling of their slaves. Taylor was no exception to this rule. As regards the existence of the institution, his attitude was typical of that of many Southerners. He lamented its existence, had grave apprehensions as to the problems which would follow in the path of emancipation, believed that the slaves were generally happy, and was convinced that those who did not have the problem could not solve it for those who did.

In theory and in practice, in thought and in action, Taylor typified the agricultural ideals of the old South. His practical improvements on his own plantations, his stimulation of improvements on the part of others through his writings, his interest in providing educational facilities for those in agricultural communities, his undying faith in the moral impulses inherent in the rural life, his political philosophy reared upon an agricultural structure, all attest the truth of the preceding statement.

BIBLIOGRAPHY

PRIMARY SOURCES

A. Manuscripts and Correspondence

Works of John Adams, with a Life of the Author, Notes and Illustrations, by his Grandson, Charles Frances Adams, Boston. Charles C. Little and James Brown, 1851. Vols. III, VI and X.

Correspondence of James Barbour. In William and Mary College Quarterly, Volume X.

Writings of Thomas Jefferson. Edited by Paul Leicester Ford. 1892–1899. Putnams Sons. New York. Volumes VI, VII, VIII, and X.

Letters of Joseph Jones, 1777–1787. Washington. Department of State. 1899. Edited by W. C. Ford. Several letters included which throw light on Taylor's policy in the Virginia Legislature in 1783.

Writings of James Madison. Edited by Gaillard Hunt. Putnam's Sons. New York. 1906. Volumes VI, VII, VIII, IX.

Writings of James Monroe. Edited by S. M. Hamilton. Putnam's Sons. New York. 1898 to 1903. Volumes I, III, IV, V and VI.

Correspondence of Leven Powell. In Branch Historical Papers of Randolph-Macon College, Volume I.

Correspondence of Spencer Roane. A number of lengthy letters originally published in the Richmond Enquirer 1819 to 1822, but later in Branch Historical Papers of Randolph-Macon College, Volume II.

Manuscripts or correspondence of John Taylor. Most of the Taylor material of this character used by the writer is in the hands of Mr. David J. Mays, Richmond, Virginia. He has two fair-sized volumes. The largest single collection was from the Branch Historical Papers of Randolph Macon College, Volume II. There are, however, some manuscripts gathered from such places as the New York Historical Society, the New York Public Library, and the Chicago University Library. In addition to these, the writer had access to ten letters in the private Tazewell collection, written by Taylor to Henry Tazewell, approximately the same number in the American Farmer, several in the works of John Adams, and scattering ones from private individuals.

Tyler, Lyon G.—Letters and Times of the Tylers. Richmond. Whittet and Shepperson. 1884. Volume I.

B. WORKS OF JOHN TAYLOR, OTHER THAN MANUSCRIPTS

An Argument Respecting the Constitutionality of the Carriage Tax. 25 pages. 1795. Richmond. Printed by Augustine Davis. In Rare Book Room, Library of Congress, Washington, D. C.

A Definition of Parties, or the Political Effects of the Paper System Considered. 14 pages. Philadelphia. 1794. Original in University of Chicago Library. Photostat copy in Virginia State Library.

An Enquiry into the Principles and Tendency of certain Public Measures. 92 pages. Philadelphia. 1794. By Thomas Dodson.

A Defense of the Measures of the Administration of Thomas Jefferson. By Curtius. Supposed to be John Taylor. 136 pages. Washington. Printed by Samuel H. Smith, 1804.

Memorandum of a Conversation with King and Ellsworth, May 11, 1794. Original in Library of Congress, Published by Gaillard Hunt in 1905 with Explanations.

Speech in the Senate on Twelfth Amendment, December 3, 1803. In Eloquence of the United States. Volume II, by E. B. Williston. Middletown, Connecticut.

The Arator; being a Series of Agricultural Essays, Practical and Political. 296 pages. Printed and published by J. M. and J. B. Carter. Georgetown, Columbia, 1813. Five Editions, the last in 1818.

Construction Construed and Constitutions Vindicated. 344 pages. Richmond. 1820. Printed by Shepherd and Pollard.

Inquiry into the Principles and Policy of the Government of the United States. 656 pages. Fredericksburg. By Green and Cady. 1814.

New Views of the Constitution of the United States. 316 pages. Washington, D. C. Printed by Way and Gideon. 1823.

Tyranny Unmasked. 349 pages. Printed and published by Davis and Force. Washington City.

The Will of John Taylor. In Possession of Henry Taylor, Jr., Richmond, Va.

C. NEWSPAPERS AND PERIODICALS

The American Farmer. Volumes I, II and III. 1819–1822. Library of Congress.

Richmond Examiner, 1799–1803. Virginia State Library, Richmond, Va.

Richmond Enquirer, 1804 to 1824, Virginia State Library, Richmond, Va.

Southern Literary Messenger. Volume IV. Virginia State Library.

The Spirit of Seventy-Six. Scattering copies, 1808. Virginia State Library.

Virginia Argus. Scattering Copies 1800 and 1801. 1807–8, 1811. Virginia State Library.

Virginia Gazette and General Advertiser. Incomplete files 1789 to 1808. Virginia State Library.

D. OFFICIAL

Annals of the Congress of the United States. 2nd Session of 2nd Congress and 1st Session of 3rd Congress, November 5, 1792, to June 9, 1794. 1st Session of 8th Congress, Oct. 17, 1803, to March 27, 1804. 2nd Session of 15th Congress, beginning November 16, 1818, through 1st Session of 16th Congress, ending May 15, 1820. 2nd Session of 17th Congress, beginning December 2, 1822, through 1st Session of 18th Congress, ending May 27, 1824.

Calendar of Virginia State Papers. Volumes II, III, VI, VII, VIII and IX. Virginia State Library.

Hening—Statutes at Large of the State of Virginia, 1779–1780, 1796–1800. Virginia State Library.

Journal of the Virginia House of Delegates, 1779–1808, 1819–1822. Virginia State Library.

Reports of Cases Argued and Adjudged in the Court of Appeals of Virginia. By Daniel Call. 1779–1818. Volumes III and IV.

Reports of the Supreme Court of the United States. Cranch 5 and 7, Wheaton 2, 5, 6, 7 and 9.

E. MISCELLANEOUS

Adams, John Quincy—Memoirs, Comprising Portions of his Diary, from 1795 to 1848. Edited by Charles Francis Adams. Volume VI. Philadelphia. J. B. Lippincott and Company, 1875.

Decisions of Judges of the Virginia Supreme Court of Appeals in respect to United States Supreme Court. Decision in Case of Hunter vs. Fairfax. In Richmond Enquirer, Jan. 27 to Feb. 3, 1816.

Deed between John Taylor and Lucy, and their son, Edmund, Sept. 12, 1809. In possession of Henry Taylor, Jr., Richmond.

Hayden, Rev. Horace E.—Virginia Genealogies. Reprinted Washington, D. C. The Rare Book Shop, 1931.

History of the Virginia Federal Convention of 1788, with some account of the Eminent Virginians of that Era who were members of the Body. By H. B. Grigsby. Edited by R. A. Brock, Corresponding Secretary and Librarian of the Virginia Historical Society. Volumes I and II. Richmond, Va., 1857. This includes the Debates.

Land Books of Caroline County, 1787, 1793 and 1798. Richmond, Virginia.

Military Certificate Book 2. Virginia Land Office, Richmond, Va.

Penn, John—Will. In possession of Henry Taylor, Jr., Richmond, Va.

Personal Property Books of Caroline County, 1783, 1787 and 1798. Richmond, Va.

Resolutions of Virginia and Kentucky, penned by Madison and Jefferson, in relation to the Alien and Sedition Laws: and Debates in the House of Delegates of Virginia, in December, 1798, on the Same. Richmond. Published by Robert I. Smith. Samuel Shepherd and Company, Printers. 1832.

The Virginia Report of 1799–1800, touching the Alien and Sedition Laws, together with the Virginia Resolutions of December 21, 1798, the Debate and Proceedings thereon in the House of Delegates of Virginia, and several other Documents illustrative of the Report and Resolutions. Richmond, J. W. Randolph, 1850.

Wickham, John—Substance of an Argument in the Case of Carriage Duties. 15 pages. Delivered before the Circuit Court of the United States in Virginia. May Term, 1795. In Library of Congress. Washington, D. C.

SECONDARY SOURCES

A. BIOGRAPHIES

Ambler, Chas. A.—Thomas Ritchie: A Study in Virginia Politics. Richmond, 1913.

Anderson, D. R.—Life of William B. Giles. A Study in the Politics of the Nation 1790 to 1830. Menasha, Wisconsin. 1914.

Beveridge, A. J.—Life of John Marshall. 4 Volumes. Houghton, Mifflin and Company. Boston and New York. 1916-1919.

Conway, M. D.—Omitted Chapters of History Disclosed in the Life and Papers of Edmund Randolph. New York and London. G. P. Putnam's Sons. The Knickerbocker Press. 1888.

Garland, H. A.—The Life of John Randolph of Roanoke. New York. Appleton and Company. 1850.

Gilman, D. C.—James Monroe in his relation to the Public Service during Half a Century, 1776-1826. Boston, Houghton, Mifflin and Company. 1883.

Henry, W. W.—Life of Patrick Henry. 3 Volumes. New York. Charles Scribner's Sons. 1891.

Magruder, Allan B.—Life of John Marshall. Boston, Houghton, Mifflin and Company. 1885.

Randall, H. S.—Life of Thomas Jefferson. Three Volumes. New York. Derby and Jackson. 1858.

Rives, W. C.—History of the Life and Times of James Madison. Volumes I and II. Boston, Little, Brown and Company. 1859.

B. MISCELLANEOUS

Andrews, Israel W.—Manual of the Constitution of the United States. New York and Chicago. American Book Company. 1887.

Bassett, J. S.—The Federalist System. Harper and Brothers. New York. 1906.

Chandler, J. A. C.—Address on Life of Taylor before Alumni Society of William and Mary College, 1905. In possession of Henry Taylor Jr., Richmond, Va.

Chandler, J. A. C.—Representation in Virginia. In Johns Hopkins University Studies, Volume XIV.

Craven, Avery O.—Soil Exhaustion as a Factor in the Agricultural

History of Virginia and Maryland, 1606–1860. In University of Illinois Studies in the Social Sciences, Vol. III, 1925.

Dodd, W. E.—Chief Justice Marshall and Virginia, 1813 to 1821. In American Historical Review, Vol. XII. The MacMillan Company. New York, 1907.

Dodd, W. E.—John Taylor, Prophet of Secession. In Branch Historical Papers of Randolph-Macon College. Volume II.

Eckenrode, C. J.—The Revolution in Virginia. Boston and New York. Houghton Mifflin Company. 1916.

Hardesty, H. H.—Historical and Geographical Encyclopedia. Special Virginia Edition. H. H. Hardesty and Company, Publishers. New York. Richmond and Chicago, 1884.

Hill, Frederick T.—Decisive Battles of the Law. New York and London. Harper and Brothers. 1906.

Lingley, Charles R.—Transition in Virginia from Colony to Commonwealth. In Studies in History, Economics and Public Law, Columbia University, Volume 36. Longmans, Green and Company, Agents. 1910.

Long, J. R.—Cases on Constitutional Law. Lawyers Cooperative Publishing Company. Rochester, New York. 1926.

Mays, D. J.—Sketch of Edmund Pendleton, the First President of the Court of Appeals of Virginia. Pamphlet in Virginia State Library. Richmond. 1926.

Mays, D. J.—Sketch of Judge Spencer Roane. Pamphlet in Virginia State Library. Richmond, 1929.

Maury, General Dabney Herndon.—Recollections of a Virginian. New York. Charles Scribner's Sons. 1894.

Pendleton, Edmund.—Sketch of Life of John Taylor. No date. In possession of Henry Taylor Jr.

Randolph, J. W. and English—History of the College of William and Mary from its Foundation, 1660 to 1874. Richmond, 1874.

Sale, Edith T.—Historic Gardens of Virginia. William Byrd Press. Richmond, Va. 1923.

The John P. Branch Historical Papers of Randolph-Macon College. Published annually by the Department of History of Randolph-Macon College from 1901 to 1916. Richmond, Va. 4 Volumes.

The Virginia Convention of 1776. Discourse delivered before the Phi Beta Kappa Society of William and Mary College, July 3, 1855. By H. B. Grigsby, J. M. Randolph, Richmond, Va. 1855.

The Virginia Magazine of History and Biography. Volumes 11, 26, 27, 28, 30, 33 and 34. Richmond, Va.

Tyler, L. G.—A History of Virginia 1763 to 1861. Chicago and New York. 1924.

Tyler, L. G.—Quarterly Historical and Genealogical Magazine. Vol. XII. Richmond, Va.

William and Mary College Quarterly, Volumes 3, 4, 10, 12, 14, 19 and 26.

Wingfield, Marshall.—A History of Caroline County, Virginia. Press of Trevvett, Christian and Company. Richmond, Va. 1924.

Year—Book of Taylor Family Association, 1927—1929. In Possession of Henry Taylor, Jr., Richmond, Va.

APPENDIX

WILL OF JOHN TAYLOR

I, John Taylor, being sick but of sound mind do declare this to be my last will and testament this 7th day of January 1824.

1st. I give to my wife, Lucy Taylor, my estate called Hazelwood including all my lands adjoining to it, bought of sundry persons, and an island in the river, during her widowhood. I also give her Phillis the wife of Norment, and all the descendants of the said Phillis, Angella another house servant and all her descendants, Judy a cook and all her descendants, Charles, Harry, Tom, Matthew, and Eliza husbands and wife of some of these descendants including any born after the date of this will, absolutely. I also give her all the money in the house at the time of my death, the household furniture and liquors, all the stocks, tools, carriages and crops growing or severed on the estate at the time of my death, absolutely, and all the slaves which may be living on it at that time, above those given to her forever, I give to her for and during her widowhood. But I direct that out of the money in the house should a suit or suits in the Court of Appeals against my son John on account of some transactions of his brother in law William Woodford finally go against him, she shall discharge whatever may be recovered.

2nd. I give to my son William my tract of land called Hayfield with all the negroes, stocks, utensils and crops growing or severed thereon at the time of my death, to him and his heirs forever.

3rd. I give to my son Henry all the lands in Westmoreland I bought of Robertson with all the slaves, stocks and utensils thereto belonging and all the crops thereon either growing or severed at the time of my death to him and his heirs.

4th. I give to my son George my two plantations on Pamunky River opposite to each other, with all the slaves, stocks and utensils to them belonging, and all the crops, severed or growing thereon at the time of my death, and also a tract of land on Mattapony usually called Hoomes's, bought of several persons, all to him and his heirs forever.

5th. I give to my Grandson John Taylor the estate called Hazelwood after his grandmother's interest therein shall cease, together with one moiety of the slaves given to her during her widowhood, provided he both attains the age of twenty one years and marries. If both these events should be accomplished these lands and slaves are to go to him and his heirs forever, if either should fail, they are on his death to be equally divided among my heirs. But I make this devise upon condition that my said grandson shall relinquish to any children or child which his father may have besides the three he now has, anything which may fall to him under a settlement relating to the land and negroes of which his father is possessed.

6th. I give to my four sons the other moiety of the slaves given to my wife during her widowhood.

7th. I give to my grand-daughter Lucy P. Taylor ten thousand dollars to be raised out of the debts due to me, a tract of land adjoining Palestine, and a negro girl named Milly, directing my executors to sell the land if they can giving a preference to the Mr. Burks, and to allot the debts of these gentlemen towards the payment of this legacy, whom I wish them to indulge as long as they pay the interest punctually. This legacy is not to become payable unless the said Lucy shall attain to twenty one years of age or marry, and in the mean time I direct my executors to accumulate it by receiving the interest and putting it at interest, for I direct that bonds carrying interest shall be appropriated to the object upon my death. If the said Lucy shall neither attain the age of twenty one nor marry, then everything given to her is to revert to my estate.

8th. I give to my grandson Edmund Taylor all the lands I bought of Spotswood with the slaves, stocks, crops growing or severed and tools, except Humphrey and his family intended to be sold, and Tom given to his grandmother, upon condition that he both arrives to twenty one years of age and marries, upon the accomplishment of both which events he is to have a fee simple, upon the failure of either and his death, the property hereby devised is to revert to my estate and go to my heirs.

9th. I give my books to my four sons reserving to their mother a power to select and retain such as she may choose, for her life.

10th. If the surplus of my debts, after paying my grand-daughter's legacy, should not suffice to pay all demands against me, each of my sons William, Henry and George are to pay one fourth of the deficiency, and the Hazelwood estate the other fourth.

11th. I direct conveyance to be made by my heirs for any lands in Kentucky I have given to my relations there by letter. The gifts were only of my title, and no warranty is to be made against the claims of others.

12th. I give all the rest of my estate, real and personal to be equally divided among my four sons. In this residue is included a large tract of land in Kentucky inherited from my son Edmund 500 acres patented, a 1000 acre entry in the care of a Mr. Waring and some town lots in the care of Genl. Taylor.

13th. I direct that all the lands and slaves devised by this will shall be bound to guarantee the title of each devisee, and that if any eviction or recovery shall take place the same shall contribute in proportion to value to make good the loss.

14th. I direct that the possessor of Hazelwood for the time being shall provide for William Norment during his life as he has hitherto been provided for.

Finally, I appoint my wife Lucy Taylor and my son William P. Taylor executrix and executor of this my will, and direct that neither an inventory, appraisement nor sale be made of any part of my estate, and that neither of them be required to give security. And I subscribe this paper wholly written with my own hand as and for my last will and testament this 7th day of January, 1824.

For removing any doubt which might arise from two clauses of this my will, it is my intention that my two grandsons John and Edmund shall have the possession and use of the property devised to them respectively, the former from the termination of his grandmother's estate, and the latter from my death, each for his life, though the events may never happen, which may make their titles absolute.

JOHN TAYLOR.

Virginia:

At a court holden for Caroline County, at the Court House, on the 13″ day of September 1824.

This writing, purporting to be the last will and testament of John Taylor, Sr. was offered for proof without a subscribing witness thereto, whereupon John Dickinson being first sworn saith, that he is well acquainted with the handwriting of the said deceased, and that he believes the same to be wholly written, and signed by the said John Taylor, Sr. It is ordered that the same be recorded as and for the last will and testament of the said deceased.

Teste:

JOHN S. PENDLETON, CCC

A copy Teste:

JOHN S. PENDLETON

COPY

INDEX

INDEX

229